Shorter Slang Dictionary

The Partridge Collection

A Dictionary of Slang and Unconventional English
Eric Partridge
Edited by Paul Beale
Eight Edition
ISBN 0–415–06568–2 (hb)

A Concise Dictionary of Slang and Unconventional English
Edited by Paul Beale
Based on the work of Eric Partridge
ISBN 0–415–06352–3 (pb)

Origins: An Etymological Dictionary of Modern English
Eric Partridge
Fourth Edition
ISBN 0–415–05077–4 (hb)

A Dictionary of Catch Phrases
Eric Partridge
Edited by Paul Beale
Second Edition
ISBN 0–415–05916–X (pb)

A Dictionary of Clichés
Eric Partridge
Fifth Edition
ISBN 0–415–06555–0 (pb)

Shakespeare's Bawdy
Eric Partridge
Third Edition
ISBN 0–415–05076–6 (pb)

Smaller Slang Dictionary
Eric Partridge
Second Edition
ISBN 0–415–03969–X (pb)

Shorter Dictionary of Catch Phrases
Rosalind Fergusson
From the work of Eric Partridge and Paul Beale
ISBN 0–415–10051–8 (pb)

You Have a Point There
Eric Partridge
ISBN 0–415–05075–8 (pb)

Shorter Slang Dictionary

Compiled by
Rosalind Fergusson

From the work of
Eric Partridge and Paul Beale

London and New York

First published 1994
by Routledge
11 New Fetter Lane, London EC4P 4EE

Simultaneously published in the USA and Canada
by Routledge
29 West 35th Street, New York, NY 10001

© Routledge 1994

Typeset in Baskerville by the EPPP Group at Routledge
Printed and bound in Great Britain by TJ Press (Padstow) Ltd, Cornwall
Printed on acid-free paper

British Library Cataloguing in Publication Data
A catalogue record for this book is available from the British Library

Library of Congress Cataloging in Publication Data
A catalog record for this book is available from the Library of Congress

ISBN 0–415–08866–6

Foreword

This volume has been derived from the magisterial work of Eric Partridge and his collaborator and successor Paul Beale. Most of the entries have been adapted from the eighth edition of the monumental *A Dictionary of Slang and Unconventional English* (1984) and the new material that first appeared in *A Concise Dictionary of Slang and Unconventional English* (1989), although articles have also been specially written for items that came into currency in the 1990s.

The focus throughout is on slang items that are in current daily use, and familiar throughout most parts of the English-speaking world. Items originating in Britain, the United States, Canada, Australia and New Zealand are all to be found within these covers.

The policy of selection differs notably from that of Eric Partridge's own *Smaller Slang Dictionary* (second edition, 1964) in that there has been no policy of 'omitting absolutely all matter that could offend against propriety or even delicacy'. Instead, modern lexicographical practice has been followed in recording the words and phrases current in modern-day English slang without comment on the propriety or delicacy of the expressions or the concepts they describe.

A

a amphetamine. Drug users' slang. Used in the USA since before 1967.

abdabs or **habdabs** in *the screaming abdabs*, a state of enraged frustration, esp. in *to give (sb) the screaming abdabs; to have the screaming abdabs*. Since around 1950. *The screaming abdabs* earlier referred to an attack of delirium tremens.

abo or **Abo** an Australian Aboriginal. Used in Australia from the mid-19th century.

abortion a ludicrous or very ugly thing, as in *that hat's an abortion*. Used mainly in Australia since the late 1940s; also used in the UK.

above, n. the earnings of any gambling enterprise that are listed for tax and other legal purposes. Gamblers' slang. Later 20th century.

above oneself too ambitious, over-confident or conceited, as in *to get above oneself*.

abso-bloody-lutely absolutely, utterly. An intensification of *absolutely* in any of its uses, including *absolutely!*: certainly!; I couldn't agree more! Late 19th–20th centuries.

Abyssinia! goodbye!; a pun on 'I'll be seeing you!'. Since the mid-1930s, but possibly earlier (1920s) schoolboy slang.

ac accumulator. Electricians' slang of the 20th century.

acca an academic rather than an intellectual. Australian.

AC-DC bisexual. Adopted from the USA around 1959. A reference to electrical apparatus that can run on either alternating current (*AC*) or direct current (*DC*).

ace, n. a showy airman. Used ironically since around 1918. From the use of the noun *ace* to denote an excellent fighter-pilot.

ace, adj. excellent, as in *an ace player; his new car is really ace!* From around 1932.

ace in the hole a hidden asset, to be produced when it can be used to the best advantage. Adopted from US poker-players in the mid-20th century.

acid 1 heavy sarcasm; scornful criticism. 2 the psychedelic drug LSD (lysergic acid diethylamide). From around 1967. 3 in *to put the acid on*, to ask (sb) for a loan. Used in Australia from around 1912.

acid-head a habitual user of LSD. Later 20th century.

acid rock modern rock music that is evocative of LSD hallucinations, being highly amplified and often accompanied by bizarre lighting effects. Later 20th century.

ack-ack anti-aircraft guns and gunfire. Used during World War II. From the phonetic alphabet where *ack* = A.

ack emma a.m.; in the morning, as in *nine-thirty ack emma*. Since around 1915. From the army signallers' alphabet, where *ack* = A and *emma* = M. *See also* **pip emma**.

ackers or **akkas** money. Since before 1925. From the Egyptian *akka*, an Egyptian coin.

action 1 activity; great excitement or enjoyment, as in *to go where the action is*. Underground slang, from about 1968. 2 hence *a piece of the action*, an opportunity to participate in what is going on. 3 sexual intercourse, as in *he got all the action he wanted*. Adopted from the USA around 1970.

action man a person who makes a show of being very energetic by taking part in route marches, assault courses and other strenuous activities. From the Action Man doll, which can be dressed in all sorts of uniforms and fighting gear.

actor's Bible, the the periodical *The Stage*. Theatrical slang.

actressy characteristic of an actress; theatrical, melodramatic. Late 19th–20th centuries.

actual, yer *see* **yer actual**.

Adam and Eve, v. to believe, as in *would you Adam 'n' Eve it!* Rhyming slang.

admin, n. administration, as in *Alex is in charge of admin*. Later 20th century.

admin, adj. administrative, as in *admin assistant*. Later 20th century.

adrift off course or wrong, as in *her plans went adrift*. 20th century.

aerated esp. in *don't get (all) aerated!*, don't get excited or angry! Since around 1930. Sometimes mispronounced, intentionally or unintentionally, as *aeriated*.

affair one's current lover. Homosexuals' slang; since the 1970s.

Afro a hairstyle consisting of a bushy tightly-curled mass. Adopted from the USA in 1970.

aft afternoon, as in *this aft*. Since around 1910.

after afternoon, as in *this after*. Used in Australia since around 1906. *See also* **afto**; **arvo**.

afters the second course of a two-course meal; sweet, dessert, pudding, as in *what's for afters?* In general use by 1945.

afto afternoon, as in *this afto*. Used in Australia since around 1920. *See also* **after**; **arvo**.

agen or **agin** against. Late 19th–20th centuries.

agent, v.   to act as literary agent for an author or for an author's work. Authors' slang. Since around 1930.

aggro, n.   trouble-making; aggression, aggressiveness; aggravation or annoyance. Originally hippies' slang. Since around 1965. Short for *aggravation*.

agin   *see* **agen.**

agony aunt   the person who writes replies to readers' problems in an **agony column**. *See also* **sob sister.**

agony column   the letters-and-answers page of a magazine, esp. a women's magazine, where advice is given in response to readers' problems. Since around 1950.

airhead   a stupid empty-headed person. Adopted from the USA in the later 20th century.

airy-fairy   fanciful; unrealistic; vague. Since the mid-1920s.

a.k.a. or **AKA**   also known as. Referring to a false, assumed, former or alternative name. From police jargon.

akkas   *see* **ackers.**

à la . . .   in the style of; in such-and-such a way or manner, as in *surreal comedy à la Monty Python.* Late 19th–20th centuries.

Alan Whickers or **Alans**   knickers, panties. Rhyming slang. Since around 1965. From the TV broadcaster, known esp. for the UK series *Whicker's World.*

albatross   a hole played in three strokes under par. Golfers' slang. Adopted from the USA in 1933. *See also* **birdie; eagle.**

Alec   *see* **smart Alec.**

alibi   an excuse. Since around 1935.

alive-o   lively; sprightly. Late 19th–20th centuries.

alkie or **alky**   an alcoholic. Adopted from the USA around 1943.

all anyhow, adj. and adv.   disordered; chaotic. Probably late 19th century.

all clear   an all-clear signal; permission to proceed, as in *to be given the all clear.* From around 1918. The all-clear signal originally indicated that there was no further danger from hostile aircraft.

all down the line   in every way and thoroughly, as in *they've been cheating us all down the line.* Later 20th century.

alley cat   a promiscuous person, esp. female. Adopted from the USA around 1960.

all for (sth), be   to be entirely in favour of (sth), as in *capital punishment? I'm all for it!* In general use by 1925.

all hot and bothered   very agitated, excited or nervous. From around 1920. A reference to the physical and emotional manifestations of agitation.

all in, adj.   exhausted, as in *I can't go on, I'm all in.*

all of a doodah *see* **doodah 2**.

all of a tiswas *see* **tiswas**.

all over (sb), be to make a great fuss of (sb), often touching and caressing, to an excessive or unwelcome degree, as in *she was all over the president; they were all over each other*.

all over the place utterly disorganized; chaotic. From the 19th century.

all-singing all-dancing particularly versatile, spectacular, impressive or sophisticated. Often used to describe a piece of equipment, as in *the all-singing, all-dancing model*. Since around 1970.

all the best goodbye! A casual but sincere form of leave-taking, elliptical for 'I wish you all the best of everything'. Later 20th century.

all unnecessary esp. in *to go* (or *come over*) *all unnecessary*, to become excited, esp. sexually. Often resulting in weakness or loss of control, as in *when he smiled I came over all unnecessary; my legs went all unnecessary*. Since around 1930.

alphabetical a nickname for a person with a longer than double-barrelled surname, a person whose surname is abbreviated to a string of more than two initials. Since around 1930.

also-ran a nonentity, as in *he's just an also-ran*. Used in Australia since before 1916; in more general use by 1918. From horse-racing.

amateur esp. in *enthusiastic amateur*, a promiscuous girl or woman who copulates for love rather than money (as opposed to a **pro 2**). Since around 1916.

amber gambler *see* **shoot the amber**.

ambidextrous bisexual. Since around 1935.

ambulance chaser a lawyer specializing in accident claims. Adopted from the USA around 1940.

ammo, n. and adj.; military slang since 1915. Ammunition.

amp **1** an ampere. Used by electricians since around 1910; in general used by 1950. **2** an amplifier. Used by pop and rock musicians and hi-fi enthusiasts since the 1960s. **3** an ampoule of a drug. Drug users' slang. Since the early 1950s.

'Ampsteads teeth. Rhyming slang, short for **Hampstead Heath**.

amscray to depart, to make off. Mainly Australian, adopted around 1944 from US servicemen. From the verb *scram*, in Pig Latin.

anchors brakes, as in *to slam on the anchors*. Originally bus-drivers' slang, from around 1930; in general use among motorists since the mid-20th century.

and all that and all such things. Since the 1930s. Probably popularized by Sellar and Yeatman's comic history of England, *1066 and All That*.

and and and and so on. From around 1978.

and that and that sort of thing, as in *they sell computers and that*.

Probably since the mid-19th century.

and the rest! an expression of disbelief, usually relating to the smallness or incompleteness of the amount mentioned, as in *'It only cost about £200.' 'And the rest!'* Since around 1860.

angel an outsider who finances a play. Theatrical slang.

angel dust the hallucinogenic drug PCP, phencyclidine. Drug users' slang. Mainly US, since before 1969.

ankle-biters young children. Since around 1960.

ants in (one's) pants, have to be excited and restless. Adopted from the USA around 1938.

antsy restless; nervous. Adopted from the USA around 1975. From **ants in (one's) pants.**

any amount (or **number**) a large amount or number, a lot, very much or many, as in *there's any number of possible explanations.*

any joy? *see* **joy.**

any old how haphazardly; unsystematically. Probably since the mid-19th century.

A over T *see* **arse over tit.**

ape, go to be reduced to basic animal instincts by the force of sexual attraction, as in *he's the one I go ape for.* Since the late 1950s.

apeshit, go to become very angry. Later 20th century.

apple-polishing toadying. Mainly US and Canadian. Referring to a pupil who polishes an apple before presenting it to the teacher. Hence *apple-polisher,* a toady. *See also* **polish the apple.**

apples 1 in good order, under control, esp. in *she's* (or *she'll be) apples,* everything is (or will be) all right. Australian. Since the mid-20th century. 2 short for **apples and pears.**

apples and pears stairs, as in *up the apples and pears.* Traditional rhyming slang.

archbeak headmaster. Used in some British preparatory schools.

are you fit? are you ready? Since around 1915. Perhaps elliptical for 'are you ready and fit for action?'

Argate a joke place-name; a pun on 'our gate'. Used in response to the question 'Where did you go for your holidays?'

Argies (usu. pl.) Argentinians. Given wide publicity during the Falklands War of 1982.

argue the toss to dispute loudly and long. Since around 1910. From such an argument over the toss of a coin.

argy-bargy or **argie-bargie,** n. an argument. Of Scottish origin; 19th century.

ark, out of the very old, as in *those shoes must have come out of the ark!*

arm influence, power, hold, as in *what sort of arm have you got over them?* Since around 1960.

arrow a dart. Darts-players' slang. Since around 1880. Hence *in good arrow*, in good dart-playing form.

arse buttocks; anus. The term was in Standard English until around 1660, since then it has been considered a vulgarism.

arse about to fool about, to waste time.

arse about face back to front, as in *you've got it arse about face*. Since the late 19th century.

arse bandit a male homosexual, esp. one who is aggressive or predatory.

arsehole, n. 1 anus. Probably 19th–20th centuries, but possibly used in the 18th century. 2 a foolish or objectionable person. The US and Canadian form **asshole** was adopted from the USA in the late 1970s.

arseholed extremely drunk. Since around 1940.

arse over tit or **arse over tip** head over heels. Since around 1910. Sometimes shortened to *A over T*. See also **base over apex**.

arse (sth) up to bungle (sth); to make a mess of (sth).

artic an articulated lorry. Since 1938, but more widespread since around 1960.

artist an expert; a specialist; a person who habitually indulges in the specified activity. Since around 1920. Used in compounds, as in *con artist, rip-off artist*. See also **bull artist; piss artist**.

arvo afternoon, as in *this arvo*, sometimes contracted to *'sarvo*. Used in Australia since around 1940. See also **after; afto**.

ash-cash the fee that is paid for signing the doctor's certificate allowing cremation of a dead body. Medical slang. Probably since before 1967.

ask for (one's) cards *see* **cards**.

as per usual as usual. Since the 19th century.

ass 1 the US and Canadian form of **arse**. 2 a woman considered as a sex object. Originally US and Canadian; also used in the UK from around 1945. See also **piece of ass**.

asshole the US and Canadian form of **arsehole**.

ass in a sling esp. in *to have (one's) ass in a sling*, to be in trouble, to be held responsible. Adopted from the USA in the later 20th century.

astronomical (esp. of sums of money) huge, immense, as in *she was paid an astronomical fee, the bill was astronomical*. Since around 1938.

at it indulging in sexual intercourse, as in *the couple next door have been at it all night*. Late 19th–20th centuries.

attention in *to jump* (or *spring*) *to attention*, to have an erection.

aunt, the the women's lavatory. Since around 1920.

Aunt Edna raditional theatre-goer of conservative tastes. Theatrical slang.

Auntie or **Aunty** the BBC (British Broadcasting Corporation). Since around 1945. The term implies respectability and benevolence. *See also* **Beeb**.

Aussie, n. 1 Australia. From around 1895. *See also* **Oz**. 2 an Australian. From around 1905. The noun Aussie (in both senses) was originally used in Australia.

Aussie, adj. Australian. From 1914.

Aussie rules Australian Rules football. Late 19th–20th centuries. The game resembles rugby football.

awesome wonderful. Mainly US and Canadian. Young people's slang of the late 1970s and early 1980s.

awol (usually pronounced *ay-wol*) absent without leave, esp. in *to go awol*. Originally military, but now used jocularly in general contexts to refer to anybody who has gone missing.

axe 1 in *the axe*, a reduction of expenses, mainly in personnel. Since 1922. Originally in the public services, but later extended to cuts in the private sector. 2 a guitar. Rock musicians' slang. Later 20th century.

Aztec two-step, the travellers' diarrhoea. From the 1970s. *See also* **Montezuma's revenge**.

B

babbling brook 1 a cook. Rhyming slang. Used in Australia and the UK. 2 a crook, a criminal. Rhyming slang. Used in Australia and the UK in the later 20th century.

baby blues the postnatal depression suffered by some new mothers. Since the mid-1970s.

Babylon 1 the Establishment. Used by the media since around 1974. 2 the police. Used by hippies and Afro-Caribbean Londoners since around 1974.

baby's bottom in *like a baby's bottom; as smooth as a baby's bottom*, very smooth and pink. Usually refers to a man's face after shaving. From the mid-20th century.

baby-snatcher a person who marries somebody much younger. Since before 1927. Hence *baby-snatching. See also* **cradle-snatching**.

bach 1 a bachelor. Used in the USA since the 1850s; adopted in the UK around 1900. 2 a holiday cottage. Used in New Zealand since the 1950s. *See also* **batch**.

back 1 in *to get off (sb's) back*, to stop nagging, criticizing or urging (sb), as in the exasperated *get off my back, will you!* Since around 1930. 2 in *to be on (sb's) back about (sth)*, to reprimand or speak sternly to (sb) about (sth), as in *I've been on your back about this before.* Australian. Since around 1910.

back burner esp. in *to put (sth) on the back burner*, to allot a low priority to (sth), as in *we'll put that one on the back burner and deal with this one straight away*. Originally US and Canadian, possibly from the 1920s or 1930s, later adopted in the UK.

back double a back street. Cockney slang of the late 19th–20th centuries.

back number a has-been; a person who is no longer popular or relevant. Adopted from the USA around 1905. Probably from the *back numbers*, previous issues, of periodicals.

back of an envelope, on the a phrase applied to simple and speedy calculations, as in *I worked it out on the back of an envelope*.

back-room boys (usu. pl.) experts, inventors, theorists and technicians who work in secret or out of the limelight. Since the 1940s.

back-seat driver somebody who gives unwanted (and usually irritat-ingly unnecessary) advice to the person in control. Used by motor-ists since the time when cars were first equipped with rear seats; also used in general contexts.

back-to-backs parallel rows of small houses built close together, esp. in industrial towns and inner-city areas.

backward in coming forward, not not shy; the phrase is often used ironically of sb who is offensively forceful. Late 19th–20th centuries.

bad good. The inference is that what is bad in the eyes of the Establishment is good in the eyes of minority cultures. Mainly Black English use; adopted from the USA in the later 20th century.

bad break a stroke of bad luck; a series of misfortunes. Adopted in Canada from the USA around 1910; fairly common in the UK since around 1919. *See also* **break 1**.

baddie or **baddy** **1** a bad or evil person. Mainly used by schoolchild-ren. Since the 1950s. **2** (often pl.) a villain in a film, story, etc, as in *the goodies are beating the baddies. See also* **goodie**.

bad-mouth, v. to malign; to run down; to criticize adversely. Adopted from the USA in the later 1970s.

bad news **1** (of a person) disliked or unlikeable; a bore or a trouble-maker, as in *he's bad news*. **2** dangerous; unpleasant, as in *driving a car with faulty brakes is bad news*. The term (in both senses) was adopted from the USA in the late 1960s.

bad scene unpleasantness; a grave disappointment. Adopted by Brit-ish teenagers around 1970, from the USA.

bad with, get in out of favour with, as in *to get in bad with the police*.

bag, n. **1** an ugly or ill-tempered woman esp. in the phrase *old bag*. **2** an amount of heroin, marijuana, etc., in folded paper. **3** a person's preference or field of interest, as in *he quite likes chamber music but opera's really his bag*.

bag, v. to seek the right to do or have something, as in *he won the toss and bagged the best position*.

baggies loose-fitting boxer shorts, long and wide in the leg, worn as swimming trunks. Australian surfers' slang. Since around 1955.

bag-lady a homeless, often elderly woman who sleeps on the streets and keeps all her possessions in carrier bags. Originally used in New York City, since the early 1970s; adopted in the UK in the 1970s.

bag of tricks a bag of tools; a bag containing anything needed for any purpose. Since around 1910. *See also* **box of tricks**.

bags of plenty of, lots of, much, many, as in *bags of time, bags of mistakes*. Hence *bags*, plenty, a lot, as in *I've got bags to spare*.

baksheesh a tip; a gratuity. Originally Middle Eastern and Anglo-Indian, from the mid-18th century; in fairly general use since the

19th century. From the Persian word for a present. *See also* **buckshee**.

bale out or **bail out**   to help a person, company, etc. out of a predicament.

ball, n.   **1** in *to have a ball,* to have a thoroughly good time. Since around 1945.   **2** in *on the ball,* alert, as in *you need to be on the ball in this job.* Since around 1925.   **3** *see* **balls**.   **4** *see* **play ball**.

ball, v.   to have sexual intercourse (with sb), as in *he balled the boss's wife, they were balling on the sofa.* Adopted from the USA in the late 1960s.

ball and chain   one's wife. Adopted from the USA.

ball-breaker   a person who demands or exacts an extremely difficult task. Adopted from the USA around 1974. The term also refers to the task itself, which may be considered a strain on the testicles.

ball is in (sb's) court, the   it is up to (sb); it is (sb's) turn to act, as in *the ball's in their court now.* Since around 1955.

ballock(s)   *see* **bollock**; **bollock-naked**; **bollocks**.

ball of fire   a notably energetic and effectual person. Often used sarcastically in the negative, as in *he's not exactly a ball of fire, is he?* Adopted from the USA around 1930.

ball-park figures   rough figures; a **gues(s)timate**. Probably adopted from the USA in the mid-1970s. From such phrases as *in the (right) ball-park,* generally in the right place.

balls   **1** testicles.   **2** nonsense. Since before 1890.   **3** courage; masterfulness, as in *he's got balls, all right; she's the one with the balls in that family.*   **4** short for **balls-up**, as in *they've made a right balls of it this time.* Since the mid-20th century.

balls-ache, n.   in *to give (sb) balls-ache,* to annoy or bore (sb). Hence the adjective *balls-aching,* tedious; trying.

balls-ache, v.   to complain; to nag. Hence the noun *balls-aching,* nagging, complaining.

balls chewed off, have (one's)   to be severely reprimanded or taken to task.

balls up, v.   to make a mess of; to bungle or confuse, as in *you've ballsed up our plan; she's ballsed it up again.* The US equivalent is *to ball up.*

balls-up, n.   a mess; bungling, confusion, as in *they've made a right balls-up of it this time; what a balls-up!* Since around 1910. *See also* **balls 4**.

ballsy   tough or aggressive; courageous, as in *Chris became a ballsy, hard-drinking reporter.*

ballyhoo   exaggeration by copy-writers or politicians; advertising or publicity of a sensational or misleading kind. Since around 1910. An abbreviation of *ballyhooly* or *ballyhooly truth,* perhaps from *whole bloody truth.*

baloney   *see* **boloney**.

bananas, go 1 (of a person) to go crazy; to become very excited or angry, as in *he'll go bananas when he finds out*. Adopted from the USA in the 1970s. 2 (of a machine) to go wrong, as in *the photocopier's gone bananas again*. Later 1970s.

bandwagon, jump on the to join a majority, once it's known to be a majority; to favour a person or thing that has proved to be a popular success, as in *all the other manufacturers jumped on the 'environment-friendly' bandwagon*. Adopted from the USA around 1955.

bang, n. 1 an act of sexual intercourse, as in *to have a bang, a quick bang*. 2 a person considered as a sexual partner, as in *she's a good bang*.

bang, v. 1 to have sexual intercourse (with sb), as in *he was banging his girlfriend in the back of his car*. More common in Australia than in the UK. 2 *see* **bang on**.

banged up locked up; imprisoned, as in *we were banged up for 23 hours a day*. Prisoners' slang. Since the 1930s.

banger 1 a sausage, esp. in *bangers and mash*, sausage with mashed potatoes. Since around 1912. From the tendency of unpricked sausages to explode when fried. *See also* **barbie**. 2 (often *old banger*) an old, dilapidated car. Motorists' slang. Since around 1955.

bang on to talk lengthily, loudly, repetitiously or boringly, as in *she's been banging on about her new house all day*. Since around 1960.

bang to rights 1 an expression of satisfaction, as in *now we've got everything bang to rights, we can have a break*. 2 red-handed, as in *to catch (sb) bang to rights*.

barb a barbiturate. Drug users' slang. Adopted from the USA around 1950.

barbie a barbecue. Australian. Later 20th century. Hence *two bangers short of a barbie*, stupid.

bareback riding sexual intercourse without contraception.

barf to vomit; to be seasick or airsick. Used in Canada; probably adopted from the USA around 1950. Imitative of the sound of vomiting.

bar-fly a person who frequents bars. Adopted from the USA around 1930.

barge in to intrude; to interfere, esp. rudely or clumsily.

barge into to collide with; to meet, esp. unexpectedly. 20th century.

barking raving mad. Since around 1965.

barmpot a person who is slightly deranged. Since around 1950. A blend of **barmy** and **potty** (adj.).

barmy insane, mad, crazy. From the noun *barm*, the yeasty froth on fermenting beer. *See* **barmpot**.

barney a quarrel; a fight, esp. in *a bit of a barney*, a scuffle or heated argument. Since the late 19th century.

barrel, v. to move rapidly (and usually dangerously) with the motion of a rolling barrel, as in *these great big lorries come barrelling down the High Street.* Possibly since the mid-20th century.

barrel, n. in *to have (sb) over a barrel*, to have (sb) at a great disadvantage, as in *we've got them over a barrel: they can't refuse.* Adopted from the USA around 1950.

base over apex a refined variant of **arse over tit**. From around 1925.

bash 1 an attempt, a determined try at something, esp. in *to have a bash.* Since around 1935. 2 a party, dance or other social event; a lively time.

basha or **basher** a hut built from bamboo and *attap* (nipa palm). In current usage the term is applied to any self-built shelter made from available materials. Originally Malay; used in other parts of the world since 1955.

bash on to carry on, bravely and doggedly, as in *to bash on regardless.* Since the 1940s.

bash up to beat up, to assault. Schoolboys' slang since around 1940.

basinful, a of trouble, hardship, etc., as in *I've had a basinful,* I've had all I can take. Since the 1930s.

basket a euphemism for **bastard**. From around 1930.

bastard used of an individual, as in *you lucky bastard!; poor bastard!* Probably from the USA. The earlier derogatory sense, a disagreeable or despicable person, is becoming less common.

bat an eyelid, not to show no sign of shock or surprise, as in *he stripped down to his underpants and she didn't bat an eyelid.*

batch a small cottage; a shack. Australian. Since around 1920. *See also* **bach 2**.

bathers a bathing costume, as in *don't forget to bring your bathers.* Originally Australian; also used in the UK.

bat out of hell, like a extremely fast, as in *to go like a bat out of hell.* Since around 1908.

bats in the belfry, have (or **be**) to be mad or very eccentric. Late 19th–20th centuries.

bat the breeze to chatter; to talk. Australian. Since around 1939.

battle-axe esp. in *old battle-axe,* a formidable old or elderly woman who is thoroughly unpleasant, vociferous, argumentative, domineering, etc. Possibly since around 1910.

battle of the bulge, the slimmers' fight against being overweight; often used by, and of, middle-aged people. Since 1945. From the nickname of a World War II battle.

battleship a large, aggressive-looking woman, esp. in the phrase *old battleship.* Since around 1914.

batty mad, crazy. Probably from **bats in the belfry**.

bawl out to upbraid loudly and vigorously, as in *she bawled me out for being late*. Adopted from the USA around 1910. Hence the noun *bawling-out*.

bazookas a woman's breasts. Originally the term was used by male medical students. Later 20th century.

bazooms a woman's breasts. Later 20th century. Probably from the noun *bosom*.

bean the head. Late 19th–20th centuries.

beans money. Teenagers' slang of the early 1980s.

beans, full of *see* **full of beans.**

beans, spill the *see* **spill the beans.**

bear a policeman, as in bear in the air, police helicopter; *wall-to-wall bears*, police everywhere. From US lorry-drivers' slang; used in the UK on Citizens' Band radio. Late 1970s.

beat it to depart, to go away; to run away, as in *beat it!* From the USA; in British use by the mid-20th century.

beat (one's) meat (of a man) to masturbate. Late 19th–20th centuries.

beaut, n. a beautiful or wonderful person or thing, as in *ain't he a beaut?*; *that's a beaut!* Probably of Cockney origin; mainly used in Australia since around 1920 and New Zealand since around 1950.

beaut, adj. beautiful, wonderful, as in *it's a beaut day!* Mainly Australian.

beautiful people, the the wealthy, fashionable people of high society and the arts who set the trend in beauty and elegance. Adopted from the USA in the 1960s. Originally ironic or sardonic.

beaver, n. 1 a woman's pubic hair; the female genitals. Used by pornographic photographers since the early 1970s. Hence *split beaver*, open vulva. 2 *see* **eager beaver.**

beaver, v. esp. in *to beaver away*, to work hard and diligently. Since the late 1960s. *See also* **eager beaver.**

bed and breakfast short-term funds invested at the close of business one day and taken out again first thing the next. London Stock Exchange slang.

beddy-byes sleep; bedtime, as in *time for beddy-byes!* Nursery slang of the 19th–20th centuries.

bed-sit or **bed-sitter** a bed-sitting room: a rented, furnished room containing a bed. Since around 1960.

bed with, get into to merge with, become a partner of, start a venture with. Used in business and finance since the late 1960s.

Beeb, the the BBC (British Broadcasting Corporation). Since the late 1920s. *See also* **Auntie.**

beef, v. 1 to complain, as in *they're beefing about the price of petrol*; *stop beefing!* 2 *see* **beef up.**

beef bayonet penis. Later 20th century. The term was popularized in the UK by the Australian humorist Barry Humphries in the satirical 'Barry McKenzie' comic strip in the magazine *Private Eye*. *See also* **mutton dagger; pork sword.**

beefcake men displayed for their muscular bodies. *See* **cheesecake.**

beef up to strengthen; to enhance.

beer belly a paunch gained from drinking too much beer or lager. Since the 1940s.

bees and honey money. Rhyming slang. Since before 1892.

bee's knees, the the acme of perfection, beauty, skill, desirability, etc., as in *she thinks she's the bee's knees*. From around 1930. *See also* **cat's pyjamas.**

bee-stings a woman's small breasts. Adopted from the USA in the later 20th century.

beetle, n. the original Volkswagen car, and later editions of the same distinctive beetle-like shape. In worldwide usage by 1960. By the 1970s the nickname was featuring in advertisements for the vehicle.

beetle, v. (often followed by *off, along, about*, etc.) to move quickly; to hurry; to scuttle. Since around 1918. The term was much used by **Sloane Rangers** in the early 1980s.

beetle juice Betelgeuse, a star used in astral observation. Since around 1938. From the sound of the star-name.

beezer chap, fellow. Public schoolboys' slang since around 1920. Possibly a blend of **bugger** and **geezer.**

bell, give (sb) a to telephone (sb), as in *I'll give you a bell when I find out*. Later 20th century. Hence the verb *to bell*, to telephone.

belly flop 1 a dive in which one hits the water flat on one's front. Since around 1870. **2** a **belly landing.** Since around 1930.

belly landing the landing of a plane with the undercarriage up, when it is impossible to get the wheels down. Since around 1918.

belly-side up or **belly-up** dying, dead; bankrupt, as in *he was found belly-side up*; *the company went belly-up*. Since around 1960. From the tendency of animals to die on their backs.

belong to be a proper or acceptable member of a club, social class, etc., as in *she didn't belong*.

below (of temperature) below 0°C or 32°F, as in *it was thirty below*.

belt, v. 1 (often followed by *along, through*, etc.) to rush; to move or travel very fast; to do anything very fast, as in *the train was belting along; the vicar belted through evensong tonight*. **2** (also **belt down**) to rain very hard, as in *it's belting down; we went for a drive and it belted all the way*. Late 19th–20th centuries. **3** *see* **belt out; belt up!**

belt-and-braces (with) great care and thoroughness; (taking) extra precautions; (making) a double-check. Since the late 1940s.

belt down *see* **belt 2.**

belter an exciting or wonderful person or thing. Later 20th century.

belt out to sing a song or play music loudly and vigorously. Since around 1940.

belt up! shut up!; be quiet! Since around 1937.

bender a drinking spree, an extended bout of riotous drinking, as in *to go on a bender*. Adopted from the USA in the late 19th century.

bend over backwards to try very hard, as in *you needn't bend over backwards to please the children*. Since the late 1920s.

bends, the decompression sickness; divers' cramp or paralysis.

benny a Benzedrine tablet. Drug users' slang. Adopted from the USA around 1950.

bent 1 (of a person) crooked, criminal; (of a thing) stolen. Since around 1905. 2 sexually deviant, esp. homosexual. Since around 1945. 3 (of a police officer) open to bribery. Since around 1930.

bent as a butcher's hook, as an intensification of **bent 1.**

berk a fool. From around 1930. Possibly from *Berkeley* (or *Berkshire*) *Hunt*, rhyming slang for 'cunt' (*see* **cunt**) or from the Romany *berk*, breast.

bestest best. 19th–20th centuries.

bevvied drunk. From **bevvy,** v.

bevvy, n. 1 a public house. From the mid-19th century. 2 beer; any alcoholic drink, as in *I had a few bevvies with my mates*. Late 19th–20th centuries. Hence *bevvy-merchant*, a heavy drinker.

bevvy, v. to drink alcohol. Late 19th–20th centuries. Hence the adjective **bevvied.**

bezazz or **bezzazz** *see* **pizzazz.**

bf bloody fool. A euphemism of the 20th century.

bible a manual, handbook, guide or rule book; any book that is considered to be an authority on a particular subject, as in *the antique dealer's bible*.

Bible-thumper (or **-basher** or **-puncher**) an aggressively enthusiastic evangelist; a person who tries to thrust his or her religious beliefs on others.

biblio a bibliographical note, usually on the reverse of the title page, in a book. Used in the book world since around 1920.

bicarb bicarbonate of soda. Late 19th–20th centuries.

biccy or **bikky** a biscuit. Nursery slang, also used jocularly among adults. From around 1870.

bicycle a prostitute; a promiscuous woman. Since around 1940.

biddy a woman, as in *an interfering old biddy*. From the 19th century.

big A, the AIDS (Acquired Immune Deficiency Syndrome). Later 20th century.

big bad wolf a threatening or sinister person. Since around 1935. From the popular children's song 'Who's afraid of the big bad wolf'.

big C, the cancer. Late 20th century.

big cheese an important person; the boss. Earlier 20th century.

big E, the in *to give (sb) the big E*, to dismiss, jilt or otherwise get rid of (sb); *to get the big E*, to be dismissed or jilted. Since the 1980s. The *big E* is the **elbow**.

biggie anything big; an important person or thing. Later 20th century.

big-head a conceited person, as in *you big-head!* Since around 1940. Also in the phrase *to have a big head*, to be conceited.

big jobs, do to defecate. Mainly nursery slang. Since the 1940s.

big-mouth a person who tells tales, an informer; a person who talks excessively, loudly, boastfully or indiscreetly. Also in the phrase *to have a big mouth*, to be indiscreet, boastful, etc.

big noise an important person; the boss. Adopted from the USA around 1918.

big O, the an orgasm. Late 20th century.

big on keen on. Australian. Since around 1940.

big shot an important or successful person. 20th century. The term originally referred to a notorious gangster.

big time, the the highest or most successful level of an activity, esp. in show business; a large-scale operation. Adopted from the USA around 1945. Hence the adjective *big-time*, as in *a big-time comedian*; *big-time politics*, and its opposite *small-time*, as in *a small-time crook*.

big way, in a very much, as in *she fell in love with him in a big way*. Since around 1935.

biker a person who rides a bicycle or motorcycle, esp. the latter. Later 20th century.

bikky *see* **biccy**.

bilge nonsense. Used in public schools from around 1906; in general usage by 1919. From *bilge water*, the dirty water that collects at the bottom of a boat.

Bill, the the police. Since the 1970s. Originally *the Old Bill*.

billy-o, like with great vigour or speed, as in *it rained like billy-o all day*. Since the mid-19th century.

bimbo 1 a fellow, a chap; a stupid young man. Adopted from the USA around 1938. From the Italian *bambino*, child. 2 an attractive but empty-headed young woman, esp. one who seeks fame and fortune by having an affair with a public figure. Since the 1980s.

bin, n. (usu. *the bin*) a mental hospital, a lunatic asylum. Since around 1920. Short for **loony bin**.

bin, v. to throw away, to discard or reject, to put (sth) in the rubbish bin, as in *'What should I do with this?' 'Bin it!'* Later 20th century.

binge, n. a bout of excessive eating or drinking; overindulgence in other activities such as shopping, gambling, etc.

binge, v. to have a **binge**. *See* **binge** n.

bingo, like very quickly. From the 1930s.

bins 1 glasses, spectacles. From around 1930. 2 binoculars. Since the 1930s.

bint a girl or young woman; a prostitute. Late 19th–20th centuries. From the Arabic *bint*, daughter.

bio a biography. Mostly journalists' slang.

bird 1 prison; a prison sentence, as in *to do bird*; *in bird*. From *bird-lime*, rhyming slang for 'time'. 2 a young woman; one's girlfriend or sweetheart. Since around 1880. *See also* **dolly-bird**.

birder a bird-watcher, a person who watches birds in their natural surroundings.

birdie a hole played in one stroke under par. Golfers' slang. Since around 1920. *See also* **albatross**; **eagle**.

bird-watching (joc.) the practice of watching young women, esp. in a park. Since the late 1940s. Also *bird-watcher*, a person given to this practice.

birthday suit, in (one's) naked as the day (one) was born. Since the 18th century.

bit 1 a young woman, esp. considered sexually. 19th–20th centuries. *See also* **crackling**; **fluff**; **skirt**; **tail 2**. 2 sexual intercourse, as in *to have a bit*. 19th–20th centuries. 3 *see* **do (one's) bit**.

bitch, n. a thoroughly unpleasant woman, as in *she's a right bitch*. Since the 15th century or earlier.

bitch, v. to complain; to be spiteful, malicious or slanderous. Possibly since around 1925.

bitchy spiteful, malicious, slanderous. Since around 1910.

bite in *to put the bite on*, to ask (sb) for a loan. Used in Canada since around 1910 and in the UK by 1940.

bit much, a excessive; exaggerated; unreasonable, as in *that's a bit much!* From the 1930s. Elliptical for *a bit too much*.

bit of a lad esp. in *he's a bit of a lad*, he's always chasing women, he likes to drink and gamble. Since around 1950.

bit of all right 1 something excellent, esp. an unexpected treat or a stroke of good luck, as in *that's a bit of all right*. Since around 1907. 2 a person who is attractive, esp. sexually attractive, as in *his new girlfriend's a bit of all right*.

bit of spare 1 the illicit lover of a married or engaged person, as in *her husband's found himself a bit of spare*. Since around 1935. *See* **bit on the side**. 2 a person who is available for casual sex, as in *he's always on the look-out for a bit of spare*.

bit of the other   sexual intercourse, as in *we went upstairs for a bit of the other*. Since around 1930.

bit on the side 1 adultery, as in *he's been having a bit on the side*. Later 20th century. **2** *see* **bit of spare 1**.

bits and bobs   bits and pieces, miscellaneous items. Possibly of dialectal origin.

bitser   a mongrel dog; anything made from *bits o' this* and *bits o' that*. Australian. Since around 1910.

bitty   in bits and pieces or imperfectly connected parts; disjointed, as in *the programme was rather bitty*. Since around 1920.

blabbermouth   a person who cannot keep a secret; a person who talks too much. Adopted from the USA around 1944.

black, in the   financially solvent. Since around 1945. *See* **red, in the**.

black and tan   porter (or stout) mixed equally with ale. Since around 1850. From the respective colours of the ingredients.

Black and Tans   the men who were sent to assist the Royal Irish Constabulary in 1921 From their khaki coats and black caps. The nickname was probably also inspired by the famous Black and Tan Hunt near Limerick.

black and white, in   written or printed, and therefore binding, as *don't give them any money until you get the agreement in black and white*. Since the 16th century.

black as the ace of spades, as   very black or dark. Late 19th–20th centuries. The simile is often applied to Black people; *see* also **spade**.

black-out, n.   **1** a temporary loss of consciousness. Since the late 1940s. **2** censorship, suppression of information, as in *a news black-out*. Later 20th century.

black velvet **1** stout and champagne mixed. Public-house slang, mostly Anglo-Irish. From the colour and smoothness of the drink. **2** sexual intercourse with a Black woman, as in *a bit of black velvet*. Late 19th–20th centuries. **3** a Black woman, esp. considered sexually; 20th century.

blad   a sheaf of specimen pages or other illustrative matter. A term used by booksellers and publishers since before 1933.

blag **1** to rob or steal; to snatch something of value, such as money, jewellery, a watch or a handbag. Since around 1920. **2** to wheedle; to scrounge or cadge. Later 20th century.

blah   nonsense, silly or empty talk. Used by publishers and journalists; adopted from the USA around 1927.

blah-blah or **blah-blah-blah**   imitative of worthless or boring talk, as in *and so he went on, blah-blah-blah*.

blank, v.   to ignore a person; to reject a plan or suggestion; not to take part in a crime. Originally used by police officers, it is now used more generally. Since around 1930.

blanket, on the refusing to wear prison uniform. The phrase was applied to self-styled political prisoners in the Maze Prison, Northern Ireland, in the late 1970s.

blast 1 to reprimand, to tell off. 20th century. 2 to take narcotics. Drug users' slang. Since the late 1950s. 3 *see* **blast off**.

blasted intoxicated with drugs. Drug users' slang. Since around 1968.

blast off (of a car, esp. a racing car) to start. Australian. Since around 1960. From the launching of a space rocket.

bleat to complain, to grumble, as in *stop bleating!*

bleeder a person, as in *poor little bleeder!* The term is often used with dislike or contempt, as in *silly bleeder, rotten bleeder.* Mainly Cockney. From around 1880.

bleeding an adverbial or adjectival intensifier, as in *that's bleeding wonderful!; where's my bleeding spanner?* From around 1857.

bleed like a pig to bleed very heavily. 17th–20th centuries.

bleeper a small radio-activated warning device, carried in the pocket by people who may be instantly summoned in an emergency, such as doctors, firefighters, etc. Late 1970s. From the sounds that the device emits when activated.

blighter a person, esp. a man or boy, as in *you lucky blighter!* The term is often used with dislike or contempt, as in *cheeky blighter, rotten blighter.* From around 1896.

Blighty England, the UK; home. Chiefly used by the armed forces serving abroad, esp. in India and during World War I. Since around 1910. From the Hindustani *bilayati,* foreign land, from the Arabic *wilayat,* country.

blimey! an exclamation of surprise. Mostly Cockney at first, but now in general usage. Late 19th–20th centuries. An abbreviation of **gorblimey!**

blimp a small non-rigid dirigible airship. From 1915. Possibly from *B-type* airship plus *limp.*

blind or **blind drunk** very drunk. Since the 17th century.

blind bit of notice, not take a to be oblivious, to ignore or disregard utterly, as in *I warned her, but she didn't take a blind bit of notice.*

blind date an arrangement to meet somebody one has not met before with a view to forming a potential relationship. Adopted from the USA around 1942.

blind (sb) with science to explain something in very technical language, so as to discourage (sb) from asking further questions (or perhaps to conceal the truth). Since around 1940.

blink, on the out of order, as in *the radio's on the blink.* Since World War I. *See also* **fritz, on the.**

blip, n. 1 a spot of light seen on a radar screen or cathode-ray tube. Since around 1930. From the sound made by Asdic or Sonar (equipment for detecting underwater objects using ultrasonic waves). 2 a sharp peak in a line on a radar screen, chart, graph, etc.

blip, v. to switch an aeroplane engine on and off. From 1915.

blistering a euphemism for **bloody 1**.

blitz a brief, thorough, intensive campaign; a concentration of maximum effort, as in *the police have launched a blitz on speeding; I'm having a blitz on the garden*. Since around 1945. From *the Blitz*, the aerial bombardment of World War II, from the German *Blitz*, lightning.

bloated, adj. drunk. USA; since the 1980s.

block the head. Since the 17th century. In the UK the term is now rarely used except in the threat *to knock (sb's) block off*.

blockbuster anything that makes a considerable impact, especially a novel or a movie. From the name of a heavy bomb powerful enough to flatten a city block. Since the late 1940s.

bloke a man; chap, fellow, as in *the bloke next door*. Since before 1839. Perhaps from the Dutch *blok*, a fool, or via Romany from the Hindustani *loke*, a man.

blokery men in general and single men in particular. Used in Australia and New Zealand.

Blondie a nickname for a fair-haired person. Since around 1925.

bloody 1 an adjectival and adverbial intensifier, as in *the bloody car broke down; don't be so bloody awkward!; you can bloody well do it yourself!; not bloody likely!* Since the 17th century. *See also* **abso-bloody-lutely**. 2 elliptical for *bloody well*, as in *I don't bloody care!* Possibly from the mid-19th century.

Bloody Mary tomato juice and vodka. Since around 1944.

bloody-minded obstructive; pig-headed; vindictive. Since 1930. Hence the noun *bloody-mindedness*.

bloomer a mistake. Used in Australia and the UK since before 1889. Perhaps a blend of *blooming error*. *See also* **blooper**.

blooming a euphemism for **bloody,** as in *it's a blooming nuisance, it's blooming impossible*. From around 1882.

blooper a verbal error likely to cause embarrassment. Used in the USA and Canada. *See also* **bloomer**.

blotch blotting-paper. Public-school slang of the late 19th–20th centuries.

blot (one's) copy book to make a mistake; to make a bad impression; to spoil (one's) record.

blotto drunk. From around 1905.

blow, n. marijuana. Drug users' slang of the later 20th century.

blow, v. 1 to depart, quickly and quietly. 2 to smoke marijuana. Drug users' slang. Adopted from the USA in the 1970s. **3** to fail in an enterprise, esp. by one's own bungling ineptitude, as in *this is your last chance, don't blow it!* Used in the USA since around 1920; common in the UK since the early 1980s. **4** *see* **blow up**.

blow! go away! Since before 1935.

blower a telephone, as in *on the blower*. Since before 1935.

blowhard a boastful or blustering person. Used in Australia since around 1880 and in the UK since around 1950.

blow job an act of fellatio, as in *to give (sb) a blow job, to do a blow job*. 20th century.

blow (one's) mind **1** to have a hallucinogenic experience. Drug users' slang. Since around 1962. Also *to blow (sb's) mind*, to give (sb) a hallucinogenic experience, as in *this drug really blows your mind*. **2** to lose one's self-control; to be amazed or astounded. Since around 1963. Also *to blow (sb's) mind*, to amaze or astound. *See also* (for both senses) **mind-blowing**.

blow-out **1** a puncture. Used by cyclists, motorcyclists, and motorists. Adopted from the USA around 1930. **2** a large meal, as in *we had a blow-out at the most expensive restaurant in town*. Since the early 19th century.

blow the lid off (sth) to divulge (sth, such as a plan, conspiracy, scandal or secret) to the public, usually in a spectacular way. Since around 1930.

blow the whistle on to give information, usually to the authorities, about illegal or secret activities. Possibly since around 1960. Hence *whistle-blower*, a person who gives this information.

blow (one's) top to explode with anger. Adopted from US servicemen around 1943.

blow (sth) up to exaggerate the importance of (sth), esp. in the phrase *blown up out of all proportion*. Since around 1960. From photographic enlargement.

BLT abbreviation for a sandwich (or roll) filled with bacon, lettuce and tomato. Used in the USA since the 1950s.

bludge an easy job. Australian. Since around 1920.

bludget a female thief who lures her victims. Used in Australia around 1925–39.

blue balls aching testicles, caused by unfulfilled sexual excitement. Possibly since around 1930. The condition is also known as *lover's nuts*.

bluebottle a policeman. Originally used by Shakespeare and revived around 1840.

blue-eyed boy a favourite, a pet. Since before 1914.

blue in the face, till (one) is with the utmost energy and effort, as in *you can shout till you're blue in the face but they won't take any notice.* Probably from 1850 or earlier.

blue murder esp. in *to cry blue murder, to scream blue murder,* to shout in terror, alarm, pain, etc; to make a great noise or a horrible din. From the late 1850s.

blue-pencil, v. to censor an unprintable word or phrase. 20th century. From editors' use of blue pencil for corrections and deletions.

blue velvet a mixture of paregoric and an antihistamine. Drug users' slang of the 1970s.

Bluey a nickname for a red-haired person. Mainly used in Australia and New Zealand from around 1890.

blurb a publishers' recommendation of a book, usually printed on the jacket. 20th century. The term was coined by the US humorist Frank Gelett Burgess.

blush-making *see* -making.

BO body odour. Originally used by advertisers; in general use since around 1950.

boat race face. Rhyming slang. Since around 1946. Often shortened to *boat.*

bob a shilling. Since the late 18th century. The term was rendered virtually obsolete by the decimalization of British currency in 1971. *See also* **worth a bob or two.**

bobble, v. to handle sth ineptly; to bungle. Of US origin; since the 19th century.

bobby a policeman. Since the early 1840s. From *Robert* Peel, who was mainly responsible for the Metropolitan Police Act of 1828.

bobby-dazzler a dazzling thing or person, as in *she's a real bobby-dazzler,* she's strikingly attractive. Since before 1866.

bobby-soxer an adolescent girl who rigidly adheres to teenage conventions. Adopted from the USA around 1959. From *bobby socks,* cotton ankle-socks; often white.

bob up to appear; to return, as in *he keeps bobbing up.*

bod a person, as in *odd bod.* Since around 1935.

bodge to botch, to make a mess of; to patch up, to repair badly.

bodice ripper a romantic (often historical) novel, containing a judicious and titillating admixture of violent sex. Later 20th century.

boffin an inventor; a scientist. Since before 1939.

boffing sexual intercourse. Since the mid-20th century.

boffo popular; successful. Adopted from the USA around 1970.

bog (usu. *the bog* or *the bogs*) lavatory. Since the early 19th century. An abbreviation of *bog-house,* which dates from around 1670.

bogey or **bogy** a lump of mucus or dirt in the nostril or discharged from the nose. Since 1937.

bog off!   go away! Since around 1937.

bog-rat   *see* **bogtrotter**.

bog-standard   standard, straight from the factory, with no refinement or modification. The term was originally applied mainly to motorcycles, but is now used in general engineering and other contexts. Since the mid-1950s.

bogtrotter   an Irish person. Since the late 17th century. From the numerous bogs of Ireland. Also *bog-rat*.

bog up   to make a mess of; to do incompetently. Since 1939. Hence the noun *bog-up*, a mess.

bogus   sham; spurious. Originally US, since before 1840; adopted in the UK around 1860. From *bogus*, the name of a device used to make counterfeit money.

bogy   *see* **bogey**.

bohunk or **Bohunk**   a labourer from central or eastern Europe. Used in the USA and Canada. 20th century. Probably a modified blend of *Bohemian* and *Hungarian*.

boiler   a middle-aged or old woman, esp. one who is not (or no longer) attractive, as in *an old boiler*. Since around 1925.

boiler-plate   matter already set, on stereotyped plates, for filling up pages of a newspaper. Canadian printers' slang.

bollock, n.   *see* **bollocks, n. 1**.

bollock or **ballock, v.**   to reprimand, reprove or scold. From around 1910. Hence the noun *bollocking*, as in *he got a bollocking from the boss*.

bollock-naked or **ballock-naked**   (of both men and women) stark naked. *See also* **starbolic naked**.

bollocks or **ballocks, n.**   **1** testicles. The term was in Standard English until around 1840, since when it has been considered a vulgarism. **2** nonsense. Late 19th–20th centuries.

bollocks or **ballocks, v.**   to spoil or ruin (a thing, plan, etc). Also *to bollocks up*.

boloney or **baloney**   nonsense. Adopted from the USA around 1930. Possibly from *boloney*, a US name for Bologna sausage, or from the gypsy *peloné*, testicles.

bolshie, adj.   bloody-minded; pig-headed; obstructive. Since around 1930. From the noun *Bolshie*, short for *Bolshevik*, which has been applied to any revolutionary or unconventional person since the mid-1920s.

bomb, v.   **1** to drive fast, and probably dangerously, as in *to bomb down the motorway*. Since around 1950. **2** (esp. of a show, performance, etc) to fail, as in *the musical bombed in Paris*. Adopted from the USA in the early 1970s. **3** *see* **bomb out**.

bombed   extremely drunk or exhilarated by drugs, esp. in the phrase *bombed out of (one's) mind* (or *skull*). Adopted from the USA around 1955.

bomb out to fail to appear as expected, as in *the minister's bombed out.* Chiefly used by the media. Late 1970s.

bomb-proof having an impregnable excuse to avoid an unpleasant duty, as in *they can't touch me: I'm bomb-proof.* Since around 1950, or perhaps earlier.

bombshell a surprise, esp. an unpleasant one, as in *her resignation came as a bombshell; to drop a bombshell,* to deliver a piece of unpleasantly surprising or shocking news. Since around 1960.

Bomfog the Brotherhood of Man, Fatherhood of God. A term used by believers in the later 20th century.

bona, adj. good; pleasant; agreeable. Theatre and circus slang from around 1850. *See also* **bono**.

bona, adv. very. Since around 1860.

boner 1 a bad mistake, as in to make (or *pull*) *a boner.* Possibly from the adjective *bone-headed,* stupid. Since the early 20th century. 2 an erection.

bone up on to study or swot up on (a subject) because the information will soon be needed, as in *you'd better bone up on your Spanish before the holidays.* Adopted from the USA and Canada around 1950.

bone-yard a cemetery. Late 19th–20th centuries.

bonk, v. 1 to hit resoundingly. The term was used in public schools from around 1919 and soon became more widespread. 2 to have sexual intercourse (with sb), as in *he's been bonking the president's daughter.* Since 1975; the term became a vogue word in 1987.

bonk, n. 1 a resounding blow. Since around 1920. The word is also used as an exclamation, *bonk!,* imitative of the sound of such a blow. 2 an act of sexual intercourse. Since 1984.

bonkers eccentric; crazy, mad, as in *you must be bonkers!* Since around 1925. *See also* **stark staring bonkers**.

bono good. From around 1840. *See also* **bona** adj.

bonzer or **bonza** excellent, very good. Australian. Perhaps from the noun *bonanza.*

boob, v. to blunder. Since around 1930.

boob, n. 1 a blunder. Since around 1935. *See also* **booboo**. 2 *see* **boobs**.

boobies a woman's breasts. Since around 1920. From the synonym *bubbies,* which dates from the 17th century. *See also* **boobs**.

booboo a blunder, esp. in *to make a booboo.* Adopted from the USA around 1959. Probably from **boob**, n. 1.

boobs a woman's breasts, as in *a model with big boobs.* Since around 1960. Sometimes used in the singular, as in *he grabbed her left boob.* From the synonym *bubs. See also* **boobies**.

boob tube 1 a woman's strapless sun-top made of stretchy material, such as jersey. From the mid-1970s. 2 television. Chiefly used in the USA and Canada.

booby-hatch a mental hospital; a lunatic asylum. Adopted from the USA.

boogie 1 to dance. Originally used by Black people in the USA. 2 to enjoy oneself, to have a good time. Since the mid-1970s. 3 to make love. Since the late 1970s.

boogie-box a portable radio or cassette player, esp. a personal stereo. Mid-1980s. *See also* **Brixton briefcase**; **ghetto-blaster**.

book, n. in the phrase *in my book,* in my opinion. Since around 1950.

book, v. 1 to catch a person in the act of wrongdoing. Used in public schools from around 1895. 2 (of a police officer) to write down the name and address of a person who has committed a minor offence, as in *to be booked for speeding.* Later 20th century. 3 (of a football referee) to take the name of a player who has infringed the rules.

booked in trouble. *See* **book,** v.

book of words, the any set of printed or typewritten instructions or rules.

boomerang something (esp. a book) that one would like to receive back. Australian. Since around 1930.

boondocks, the the jungle or wilds or outback, esp. in the phrase *out in the boondocks.* Adopted from US servicemen around 1944. From the Tagalog *bundok,* mountain.

boong an Australian Aboriginal. Australian. Since around 1942. The term is sometimes applied to any dark-skinned person.

boot-faced wearing a miserable, downhearted or stony-faced expression. Since around 1930. From the appearance of an old boot with the sole parting from the upper.

Boot Hill a graveyard. Canadian miners' slang. From one of the most famous cemeteries of the US Frontier West.

boot in, put the to kick a prostrate victim. Perhaps of Australian origin; in general use by the mid-20th century. The phrase is also used figuratively, since around 1965, with reference to political or commercial in-fighting and betrayal.

boot is on the other foot, the the case is altered; the situation is reversed. 19th–20th centuries. Originally *the boot is on the other leg:* the *boot* went from the *leg* to the *foot* when knee-boots were replaced by ankle-boots.

bootleg something that is unofficially or illicitly produced and distributed. The term was applied to alcoholic liquor in the 1920s and later (since around 1960) to records. It is also used as an adjective, as in *bootleg liquor, a bootleg record,* and as a verb. *See also* **bootlegger**.

bootlegger 1 a dealer in and distributor of contraband liquor in the USA. Originally US, from before 1919; used in the UK since around 1927. From the days when spirits, in flat bottles, were smuggled or transported in the boots or on the leg. 2 someone who produces and distributes musical recordings illegally. Hence the noun *bootlegging*, used for both senses of the word. *See also* **bootleg**.

boots and all thoroughly; utterly, as in *when you do a thing you go into it boots and all*. Used in Australia and New Zealand from the mid-20th century.

boozer a public house. Since the late 19th century.

bop, n. 1 a blow, a punch. Adopted from the USA around 1945. 2 a dance. Later 20th century.

bop, v. 1 to hit, as in *she bopped him on the head with a rolled-up newspaper*; *do that again and I'll bop you one!* Since the mid-20th century. 2 to dance. Later 20th century.

boracic (often pronounced *brassic*) very short of money. From *boracic lint*, rhyming slang for 'skint'. Since around 1945.

bore the pants off (sb) to bore (sb) to desperation, as in *he was boring the pants off us with his tales of the war*. Since the late 1940s.

bore (sb) to tears to bore (sb) to desperation, as in *she was bored to tears*. A more polite version of **bore the pants off**.

borrow (jocular or euphemistic) to steal. From around 1880. The verb is also used to cadge or scrounge items that are unlikely to be returned, as in *can I borrow a bit of paper?* Hence the phrase *on the borrow*, cadging, on the scrounge.

boss, adj. excellent, very good. Originally used by Black people in the USA.

boss-eyed 1 (of a person, animal) with a squint; with one eye injured. From around 1860. 2 (of a thing) lopsided; crooked. 20th century.

bossy-boots an over-officious or self-willed person, as in *she's a real bossy-boots; shut up, bossy-boots!*

bottle, n. 1 the money taken by an street entertainer. Since the late 19th century. 2 courage, guts, as in *to lose one's bottle; he's got a lot of bottle*. Later 20th century. Originally short for *bottle and glass*, rhyming slang for 'arse'.

bottle, v. to collect money for a street entertainer.

bottle out to lose one's nerve, to be a coward, to back down, as in *he bottled out at the last minute*. Later 20th century.

bottom line, the the crux, the crunch, the crisis, the final result, as in *what's the bottom line?* Adopted from the USA in the late 1970s. From the *bottom line* of a company's annual statement, which shows the net profit.

bottoms up! empty your glass(es)! Usually said when drinking a toast.

The phrase may also be an invitation to finish one's drink so that another may be provided.

bounce   (of a cheque) to be returned by the bank because there are insufficient funds in the account, as in the cheque bounced; *the bank bounced the cheque.* Adopted from the USA around 1938.

bovver boots   heavy, steel-studded boots worn by **bovver boys**, esp. for use as offensive weapons. Since 1969.

bovver boy (often pl.)   a skinhead, yob or lout; a member of a gang given to senseless violence and general hooliganism. From 1968. From *bovver*, a Cockney pronunciation of *bother*, trouble.

box   1 a device worn to protect the male genitals in sport, esp. cricket. 2 in *on the box*, on television. Since the late 1950s. 3 in *out of (one's) box*, crazy, mad. Later 20th century. 4 *see* **boogie-box**.

box clever   to be shrewd or cunning. Since around 1925.

box of birds, like a   fighting-fit and very happy, as in *to feel like a box of birds.* Since around 1945.

box office   (of an actor or a show) successful, having great popular appeal, as in *now, at last, she's box office; it's a good film, but it's not box office.* Used in the theatre and cinema since around 1925.

box of tricks   a tool-box; a box containing anything needed for any purpose. Probably since around 1910. *See also* **bag of tricks**.

bozo   a fellow; a man with more strength than brains. Adopted from the USA in Canada (since around 1918) and Australia (since around 1935); also used in the UK in the later 20th century. Possibly from the Spanish *bozo*, facial down indicative of puberty.

Brahms 'n' Liszt   drunk. Rhyming slang for 'pissed'. Since around 1920.

brainchild   sb's invention; a new idea that sb is very proud of, as in *this project was the brainchild of Henry Ford.* Since around 1945.

brain drain, the   emigration by those with able minds, usually from the UK to the USA, where the rewards and opportunities are thought to be greater. Since the early 1960s.

brains, the   the person who masterminds an operation. Since around 1905.

brain-teaser   a puzzle, a conundrum.

brainwave   a sudden, esp. brilliant, idea, as in *to have a brainwave.* From around 1914.

brass   1 money. The term was in Standard English in the late 16th–17th centuries, but has been considered slang since the 18th century. 2 (usu. *the brass*) military officers and other high-ranking officials. *See also* **top brass**.

brassed off   disgruntled, fed-up. Since around 1927.

brass monkey weather   bitterly cold weather. Since around 1920.

From the phrase *cold enough to freeze the balls off a brass monkey.*

brass neck, n.   **impudence, cheek, as in** *of all the brass neck. See also* **neck.**

brass-neck, adj.   impudent, as in *a brass-neck lie.* The term is also used as a noun, meaning impudence. *See also* **neck.**

brass tacks, get down to   to consider the practical aspects or basic facts, to face realities. Used in the USA since around 1903 and in the UK by 1910.

bread   money. Originally Teddy boys', hippies' and drug users' slang but now in common usage. The term originated in British rhyming slang (short for *bread and honey*), but in modern British use it was adopted from the USA around 1955.

bread and butter letter   a letter thanking one's host or hostess for their recent hospitality. Since around 1905.

break   1 a stroke of good or bad fortune, as in *a lucky break. See also* **bad break.**   2 a chance, an opportunity, as in *to give (sb) a break.* Since the late 1920s.

breakfast, have for   (or **before**)   implying that a thing is easy to do or that a person is easy to beat, as in *I could have six like him for breakfast.*

breathe down (sb's) neck   to be uncomfortably close to (sb), to watch or observe (sb) closely, as in *the cops were breathing down my neck; I can't concentrate on my work with the boss breathing down my neck.* Since around 1930.

breather   a breathing-space; a short rest.

breeze   esp. in *it's a breeze,* it's easy. Since around 1960. Of Australian origin. *See also* **breeze through.**

breeze along   to move or go quickly. From around 1920.

breeze in   to arrive unexpectedly or casually, as in *he breezed in and asked for a pay rise.* From around 1920.

breeze through   to do a task quickly and unfalteringly. Used in Australia since the late 1940s; also used in the UK in the later 20th century. *See also* **breeze.**

breezy   afraid. From around 1918.

brew   (a pot or cup of) tea. Late 19th–20th centuries. *See also* **brew up.**

brewed   drunk, intoxicated. A term used by Hell's Angels and their adherents in the 1980s.

brewer's droop   temporary impotence brought on by drinking beer or other alcoholic liquor. Possibly since the mid-19th century.

brew up   to make tea, as in *whose turn is it to brew up?* Since around 1925. *See also* **brew.**

brick   a loyal, dependable person, as in *she's a real brick.* The term was originally used only of men. Since the early 19th century.

brick it   to be thoroughly frightened, as in *I was bricking it.* A euphemistic abbreviation of **shit bricks.** 1980s.

brief any lawyer, esp. a barrister. Police and underworld slang. Since around 1930.

bright as a button, as highly intelligent; clever and alert, as in *she's as bright as a button, that kid. Doesn't miss a trick!*

bright spark a lively person; a clever person. Often used ironically, as in *some bright spark left the gate open and the dog got out.*

brill excellent, as in *it was a brill party; Michael Jackson is brill!* A teenagers' vogue word. Since the late 1970s. Short for *brilliant.*

bring off to induce an orgasm, as in *my boyfriend never brings me off.* Probably since the 16th century. Also *to bring oneself off,* to masturbate.

brinkmanship the practice of seeing just how far one can go in a situation that is already hazardous. Adopted from the USA around 1961.

Bristols a woman's breasts. From *Bristol Cities* (a reference to Bristol City Football Club), rhyming slang for 'titties' (*see* **tit**).

Brit (often pl.) a Briton, a British person. The term is most frequently used outside the UK.

Brixton briefcase (or **handbag**) a **ghetto-blaster** or **boogie-box**. Since the 1980s.

bro brother, as in *my bro, what's wrong, bro?* Mainly used by boys and men.

broad a girl or woman. The term originally referred to a girl or woman who was readily available for sex. Chiefly used in the USA and Canada.

broad brush in general outline, without details, as in *let me give you the broad-brush picture.* Since the late 1960s.

broke bankrupt; very short of money. Often used in the phrase *stony broke.* From around 1820.

brolly an umbrella. From around 1873.

bromide a commonplace person or saying; a cliché. Used in the USA since 1906 and in the UK by 1909. From the sedative *bromide* (potassium bromide).

broody 1 very thoughtful and taciturn; sullen or moody; lethargic. **2** (of a woman) full of maternal feeling, wanting to have a baby, as in *she's getting broody again.* In both senses the term is derived from *broody hens* that are inclined to sit on their eggs.

brothel-creepers suede shoes; desert boots; any footwear with thick rubber soles. Since around 1939.

brother! a mild exclamation of surprise, disgust, horror, exasperation, etc. Adopted from the USA around 1943.

browned off extremely disgruntled or depressed. Since around 1915.

brownie points marks in one's favour or to one's credit, as in *you* *should get some brownie points for this; he's just trying to get brownie points.* Probably adopted from the USA in the later 20th century. The phrase is generally associated with Brownie Guides, but it may be derived from the Canadian railwaymen's slang term *brownie*, a bad mark.

brown-nose, n. a toady, a sycophant.

brown-nose, v. to be a toady or sycophant.

brush-off, the in *to give (sb) the brush-off*, to dismiss, to snub; *to get the brush-off*, to be dismissed or snubbed. Adopted from the USA around 1943.

brush up to revive one's knowledge of a subject, as in *I went to night-school to brush up my French.* From around 1933.

b.s. bullshit. A euphemism of the 20th century.

bubbly champagne, as in *a bottle of bubbly.* From around 1895.

buck, n. a dollar. Originally US, the term was adopted in Canada and other countries in the late 19th–20th centuries.

bucket about to oscillate. Since before 1923.

bucket down to rain hard, as in *it's bucketing down.*

bucket shop an unauthorized office for the sale of stocks. From around 1887. In 20th century usage the term is chiefly applied to the sale of cheap airline tickets.

buck for, v. to make every effort to gain recognition or honours, as in *to be bucking for promotion.* Since around 1960.

Buck House Buckingham Palace. Since World War II.

buck-passing the act of shifting responsibility away from oneself and on to others (*see* **pass the buck**). Since 1946.

buckshee, adj. and adv. free (of charge). Late 19th–20th centuries. From **baksheesh**.

buddy friend, pal. A US term of address since the mid-19th century; also used in the UK from around 1914. From the noun *brother.*

buddy-buddy very friendly. Often used disparagingly by those outside the relationship, as in *they're very buddy-buddy now, but it won't last.* Adopted from the USA around 1965.

buff an enthusiast, as in *film buff.* Adopted from the USA in the 1940s.

bug, n. **1** an imperfection in a machine, system, computer or computer program. Adopted from the USA before 1960. **2** an enthusiast; a collector, as in *he's a bit of a stamp bug.* Later 20th century. **3** obsession, enthusiasm, as in *she's got the aerobics bug.*

bug, v. **1** to fit a building or room with hidden microphones or other listening and recording devices. Adopted from the USA in 1962. **2** to get on (sb's) nerves, as in *it really bugs me when she does that!*

bugger, n. **1** a person, man, woman, child, etc, as in *poor little bugger!* The term is sometimes (mildly) derogatory, as in *you silly bugger! see* also **play silly buggers**. **2** a difficult or unpleasant thing, as in *this shirt is a bugger to iron; I've had a bugger of a day!*

bugger, v. **1** to spoil, to ruin, as in *that's buggered it!* Since the late 18th century. **2** *see* **bugger about; bugger off.**

bugger! or **bugger it!** a strong expletive. Late 19th–20th centuries.

bugger about to waste time, to act ineffectually; to potter about, to fuss; to play the fool, as in *stop buggering about!; he's been buggering about with that car all day.*

bugger all nothing, as in *it's got bugger all to do with you!*

buggeration factor a natural or artificial hazard that complicates any proposed course of action; the extent to which one's plans or actions can be thwarted by forces beyond one's control.

buggered in *I'm buggered if. . .*, used as an emphatic negative, as in *I'm buggered if I know*, I have no idea; *I'm buggered if I'm going to tell you*, I'm certainly not going to tell you.

bugger me! an exclamation of surprise. Since the 19th century.

bugger off to depart, to go away, as in *they buggered off and left us to clear up the mess; bugger off!* Late 19th–20th centuries.

buggery in *(all) to buggery*, completely; to destruction or ruin, as in *we shelled them to buggery.*

Buggins' turn the granting of a privilege or promotion automatically, perhaps after a certain length of service, rather than on merit. Used in local government and the Civil Service. Also called *the Buggins principle.*

bug off! go away!; stop bothering me! Since around 1965. A euphemistic or jocular variant of **bugger off.**

built for comfort (of a person) stout; a euphemism of the 20th century.

built-in obsolescence (of people) old age. Since the early 1950s. The term is more generally applied to commercial products that are designed to become out of date or deteriorate after a certain length of time.

bull short for **bullshit**, n. Since the early 20th century.

bull artist or **bullshit artist** synonyms of **bullshitter**. Since around 1916. *See also* **artist.**

bulldoze to ride roughshod over; to force; to coerce; to bully. Adopted from the USA around 1959.

bullet, n. dismissal from employment, the sack. Often with *to get the*, as in *after that written warning it's just a matter of time before he gets the bullet.* Since the mid-19th century.

bullshit, n. nonsense, empty talk. Probably adopted from the USA in the early 20th century.

bullshit, v. to indulge in empty or boastful talk or falsehood, in order to impress or deceive, as in *are you bullshitting me?; stop bullshitting!*

Since around 1925.

bullshit artist   *see* **bull artist**.

bullshitter   a person who indulges in empty or boastful talk. Since around 1915. *See also* **bull artist**.

bum, n.   1 buttocks; anus. The term was in Standard English until around 1840, since when it as been considered a vulgarism.   2 a tramp or vagrant; a loafer or idler; a beggar or cadger. From the USA.

bum, v.   1 to beg or cadge, as in *to bum a lift*. From the USA. Hence the noun *bumming*.   2 (often followed by *around*) to loaf about; to wander around, as in *he spent the whole summer just bumming around*. Since around 1920.

bum, adj.   inferior, bad, as in the expressions *bum deal*, a disadvantageous arrangement. Since World War I.

bum-boy   a boy or young man who is available for homosexual sex. Possibly since the mid-19th century.

bumf or **bumph**   1 toilet paper. Since the mid-19th century. An abbreviation of *bum-fodder*, which has been in use since the mid-17th century.   2 any paper or papers, esp. unwanted official documents, forms or memoranda that are of no use or interest to the recipient, as in *another load of bumf from head office*. From around 1870.

bum-freezer   an Eton jacket or any other short jacket. 19th–20th centuries.

bum-hole   anus. Probably since the mid-19th century.

bummer   1 a synonym of **bum trip**. Adopted from the USA in the late 1960s.   2 any bad experience or unpleasant situation. Adopted from the USA around 1969.

bumming   *see* **bum**,v.

bump off   to kill; to murder or assassinate, as in *the hero gets bumped off at the end of the film*. Originally underworld slang, adopted from the USA.

bumper   excellent; abundant, as in *bumper harvest, bumper fun-book*.

bumph   *see* **bumf**.

bum's rush, give (sb) the   to kick (sb) out, to eject (sb) forcibly. The term refers more precisely to the method of forcible ejection that consists of the application of one hand to the seat of the trousers and the other to the scruff of the neck. Probably adopted from the USA in the early 20th century. Also *to get the bum's rush*, to be kicked out.

bum steer   bad advice; wrong or misleading information or directions, esp. in *to give (sb) a bum steer*. Used in the UK since 1944.

bum-tags   deposits of faecal matter in the hair about the anus. Since around 1830.

bum trip   a bad trip (in the drug users' sense of the word). Since around 1965. *See also* **bummer 1**.

bunce   money; profit; commission. Since the 18th century. Possibly from *bonus.*

buncombe   *see* **bunkum.**

bundle, n.   1 a considerable sum of money. Racing slang.   2 in *to go a bundle on,* to think highly of, to approve of. Often negative, as in *I don't go a bundle on her new boyfriend.* Since around 1930.

bundle, v.   to fight with one's fists.

bun-fight   a tea party. Late 19th–early 20th centuries.

bung-full   absolutely full, chock-a-block.

bungie or **bungy**(pronounced *bunjie*) a rubber eraser. Used by typists and schoolchildren since before 1936. *See also* **bunjie.**

bun in the oven, have a   to be pregnant. 19th–20th centuries.

bunjie or **bunjee**   an elastic strap with a hook at either end, used for securing luggage to the pillion of a motorcycle or to the roof-rack of a car. Later 20th century. The term also refers to an elastic line used in the dangerous sport of *bunji(e)-jumping,* in which people jump from bridges and other high places. *See also* **bungie.**

bunk, n.   1 nonsense. An abbreviation of **bunkum.** From the USA. 2 in *to do a bunk,* to run away, to decamp.

bunk, v.   1 to run away, to decamp. From the early 1890s.   2 to absent oneself, to play truant, as in *I'll bunk my class and come with you.* From around 1890. *See also* **bunk off.**

bunk down   to go to bed; to sleep, as in *you can bunk down on the floor if you like.*

bunk off   a variant of **bunk,** v., as in *to bunk off from school.*

bunkum   nonsense, empty talk, claptrap. Used in the USA since before 1827 and in the UK from around 1856. From the US place-name *Buncombe,* which (with a lower case initial) is a rare variant spelling of the noun.

bunk-up, n.   1 in *to give (sb) a bunk-up,* to give (sb) assistance in climbing.   2 in *to have a bunk-up,* to have casual sexual intercourse. Since around 1939.

bunny   a girl or young woman. Since around 1960.

buppie   an ambitious young Black person with a lucrative job; a Black yuppie. An extended acronym of Black Urban (or Upwardly-mobile) Professional. *See also* **yuppie.**

burg   a town, a city. Adopted from the USA by 1932.

burn, n.   a burst of fast driving. Motorists' slang. Since the late 1940s.

burn, v.   to cheat, to swindle. Since the 17th century.

burned, get (or **be**)   to receive bad drugs. Drug users' slang. Used in the USA since before 1966.

burn-up   a race in a car or on a motorcycle, esp. in *to have a burn-up.* Since around 1955.

burp a rainbow to vomit. Australian. Since around 1930. *See also* **lose a meal**; **technicolour yawn**.

bus-boy a person who clears the tables in a restaurant. Adopted in Canada from the USA around 1935. Perhaps from the French slang *omnibus*, a kind of apprentice in the restaurant business.

bushed physically exhausted, as in *I was completely bushed by the time I got home*. Mid-20th century.

bush telegraph unfounded report or rumour; a means of spreading gossip. Of Australian origin.

business anything particularly good, as in *they did the business; it's the business*. Teenagers' slang of the early 1980s.

business girl a prostitute's description of herself. From around 1921.

busker a person who performs in the street for money by playing a musical instrument, singing, dancing, etc. 20th century.

bust, n. 1 a burglary. Since around 1850. 2 a police search, raid or arrest, esp. for illegal drugs. Drug users' and hippies' slang. Adopted from the USA in the late 1950s.

bust, v. 1 to downgrade or demote (sb), as in *he was busted down to corporal.* 2 to arrest (sb), esp. a drug user. Adopted from the USA around 1955.

bust a gut to make an intense effort. Often negative, as in *I'm not going to bust a gut trying to finish it tonight.*

Buster a term used to address a person whose name may or may not be known to the speaker. Often used angrily or threateningly, as in *look here, Buster, this is my property and if you don't clear off I'll call the police!* Adopted from the USA around 1920. Perhaps from the US film comedian Buster Keaton, who made his name in the silent movies of the 1920s.

busty (of a woman) having large breasts. Since the mid-20th century.

busy, n. a detective; a police officer. Since around 1908.

butch, adj. (of a man) aggressively or assertively masculine; (of a woman) having masculine characteristics (esp. physique).

butch, n. 1 a male homosexual who plays an active (rather than a passive) role. Adopted from the USA around 1950. 2 a lesbian. Since around 1945.

butcher's a look, as in *to have a butcher's; to take a butcher's.* Rhyming slang (originally *butcher's hook*). Late 19th–20th centuries.

butt buttocks, as in *to kick (sb's) butt.* The term is also used in more figurative contexts, as in *we've been working our butts off.* Adopted from the USA around 1980, though *butt* was a Standard English synonym for *buttocks* in the 15th–17th centuries.

butterflies (in the stomach) tremors of apprehension, excitement or both; the feelings of nervousness that manifest themselves in the abdominal region, as in *I always get butterflies before an exam.* Since the 1940s.

buttie *see* **butty**.

buttinski an inquisitive person. Since the 1920s or 1930s; of US origin. From the verb *butt in*, interrupt.

button (up) your lip! stop talking (now)!; say nothing (later)! 19th–20th centuries.

butty or **buttie** a slice of buttered bread; a sandwich, as in *a jam butty.* Used in the North, esp. Liverpool, since the late 19th century. The term was popularized by the Liverpool comedian Ken Dodd and became more widespread in the later 20th century.

buy, n. a purchase; an opportunity to purchase. From around 1925.

buy, v. to accept an argument, excuse, etc, as in *I won't buy that!; do you think she'll buy it?* Since around 1930.

buy it to be injured or killed, esp. in war. Since World War I.

buzz 1 a rumour; news, as in *what's the buzz?* From the late 19th century. 2 a thrill, a kick, as in *drugs that give you a buzz; she gets a real buzz from flying.* Originally drug users' slang, since the late 1940s. 3 a telephone call, as in *give me a buzz on Friday.* Since around 1950.

buzzard esp. in *old buzzard,* a contemptuous term used to describe a cantankerous person. Since around 1910. Originally a euphemism for **bastard**.

buzz off! go away! From around 1905. The term is usually addressed to a troublesome person (esp. a child) or animal and may be a euphemism for **bugger off**.

buzz-word a impressive-sounding word that is rendered almost meaningless by misuse or overuse, borrowed from professional or technological jargon to enhance the utterances of the ignorant. Adopted from the USA around 1970.

C

C cocaine. Drug users' slang. Adopted from the USA around 1950. *See also* **H and C.**

cabbage the brain-dead (or severely brain-damaged) victim of a stroke, head injury or other catastrophe.

cabbie or **cabby** a taxicab driver. 20th century.

cabin fever craziness resulting from isolation, esp. in winter in remote locations. Used in Canada, possibly since the late 19th century and the Yukon Gold Rush of 1896.

caboose a kitchen. Tramps' slang of the mid-19th–20th centuries. From *caboose*, a ship's galley.

cack, v. to defecate. Late 19th–20th centuries. From the Latin *cacare*, to defecate.

cack, n. 1 excrement. Late 19th–20th centuries. 2 rubbish, as in *you're talking a load of cack.*

cack-handed awkward, clumsy; left-handed. 20th century.

caddish offensively ill-bred; glaringly deficient in moral and/or aesthetic delicacy. From around 1860.

Caesar a Caesarian section or operation. Since around 1950.

cafe (pronounced *kayf*) a café. Since around 1920. *See also* **caff.**

café au lait, n. and adj. a person whose parents are of mixed race. Since around 1920.

caff a café. Since around 1920. *See also* **cafe.**

cagey unforthcoming, reserved; cautious, wary. Since around 1940.

cahoots, in in collusion, collaboration or co-operation, often with some suggestion of conspiracy or exclusiveness, as in *they are in cahoots; he is in cahoots with the leader.* Also *to go into cahoots (with).* Adopted from the USA around 1945.

cake-hole the mouth, esp. in *shut your cake-hole!*, stop talking! Since 1914 or earlier.

calf-lick or **cow-lick** a quiff of hair hanging over a person's forehead. Hence the adjective *calf-licked.*

call (sb's) bluff to challenge (sb), esp. with the intention of exposing (sb's) weakness. From the USA.

call for (or **cry**) **Hughie** to vomit, usually as a result of drinking too much alcohol. Since the 1960s. Imitative of the sound of violent retching. Other names, imitative of other sounds, such as *Bill, Herb, Ruth* or *Ralph*, may be substituted for *Hughie.*

call-girl a prostitute who is available only by telephone, esp. one who advertises her services as a so-called model, masseuse, etc, in shopwindows and elsewhere. Adopted from the USA. Since around 1945.

call it a day to state one's decision to go no further, do no more, etc; to rest content with one's gain or loss, as in *I'm worn out, let's call it a day.* The word *day* may be replaced by *night,* as in *I'd won over a thousand pounds, so I called it a night.*

cameo part (or **role**) a minor role in a play or film, but usually one in which the actor or actress can make effective use of his or her talents. The term often refers to a small part or brief scene played by a famous actor or actress. Used in the theatre and cinema since the early 20th century.

camp, n. 1 effeminate or affected mannerisms of speech and gesture, esp. the effeminate mannerisms associated with homosexuals. Since around 1945. 2 extravagance of style, form, etc., esp. in the phrases *high camp* (deliberate or sophisticated) and *low camp* (unselfconscious or unsophisticated). Adopted from the USA around 1965 or earlier.

camp, adj. 1 effeminate or affected in manner, style, etc. 2 homosexual; characteristic of homosexuals. Originally theatrical slang. Since around 1920.

camp, v. (often followed by *about*) to behave in an ostentatiously effeminate or affected way; to act in an exaggeratedly homosexual manner. Since the late 1930s. *See also* **camp it up**.

camp it up 1 to render unnecessarily effeminate the part one is playing; to overact, esp. to an outrageous degree. Theatrical slang. Since around 1935. 2 to exaggerate something to the point where it becomes almost too ridiculous. *See* **camp,** v.

can, n. (usually *the can*) the toilet. The term originally referred to an outdoor toilet with a can or other receptacle under the seat. 20th century, of US origin.

can, v. 1 to dismiss or discharge an employee, as in *to get canned.* Used in the USA and Canada since 1910 or earlier. 2 *see* **can it!**

cancer stick a cigarette. Later 20th century.

cane to punish; to damage considerably; to treat badly; to defeat. Since around 1918. Hence the noun *caning,* a beating, a defeat.

can it! be quiet!; stop talking! From the USA. Since around 1918.

canned drunk. Adopted from the USA. Since around 1910.

canned laughter pre-recorded laughter used on TV shows, situation comedies, etc.

canned music recorded music, often bland, background music played in supermarkets or lifts (hence also *lift music*); also called *piped music*. Adopted from the USA around 1925.

cannon fodder soldiers who are destined to be killed in battle in large numbers. The term was used by political agitators during World War II, usually with implied criticism of those who consider human life to be so expendable.

can of worms an unsavoury and/or complicated issue or situation, as in *to open a can of worms*, to uncover such a situation (often inadvertently). Since around 1955.

cans earphones or headphones. Since around 1950.

can't (or **cannot**) **seem to** *see* **seem to**.

Canuck a Canadian. From around 1915. The term was originally used in Canada and the USA to refer to a French Canadian.

caper 1 a dodge; a trick; a performance, as in *you can stop that little caper!* Since before 1851 2 a large-scale crime. Originally US.

caput *see* **kaput**.

carb carburettor. Motorists' slang. Since around 1910. The Australian equivalent is *carby*.

carbon a carbon copy of a typewritten manuscript, document, etc. (or a single sheet thereof). As opposed to the *top (copy)*.

carby *see* **carb**.

cardie or **cardy** a cardigan. Since around 1968.

cards in *to ask for (one's) cards*, to leave a job voluntarily, to resign; in *to get one's cards*, to be dismissed; in *to give (sb) their cards*, to dismiss (sb). The term *cards* refers to documents held by an employer during the employee's period of service, originally an employment card and subsequently a National Insurance card. Since around 1925.

cardy *see* **cardie**.

carpet, n. in *on the carpet*, (about to be) reprimanded by a superior or some other person in authority. From the carpet or rug in the office of the person issuing the reprimand.

carpet, v. to reprimand, as in *he was carpeted for some minor offence*. Since around 1840.

carpet-biter a person who is visibly very angry, who exhibits uncontrollable rage. Since around 1940. From stories of Adolf Hitler, who is alleged to have bitten carpets in his insane rages.

carry a torch for (sb) to be devoted to (sb), often with the implication of unrequited love. Adopted from the USA around 1945.

carrying all before her (of a woman) having a well-developed bust; being obviously pregnant. Since around 1920.

carry the can to be the scapegoat; to take the blame for one's own or another's error; to be landed with the responsibility for an unpleasant task; to do the dirty work while another person takes the credit. Since the late 19th century. Also *to carry the can back*. *See also* **left carrying the can**; **take the can back**.

carsie, carsey or **carsy** *see* **kharsie**.

carve-up, n. **1** a swindle. Since before 1935. **2** the distribution or share-out of booty or the money left by a will. **3** an instance of cutting in sharply after overtaking. *See* **carve (sb) up 3**.

carve (sb) up, v. **1** to spoil (sb's) chances, esp. in business. Since around 1910. **2** to swindle (sb), esp. an accomplice. **3** (of a driver) to cut in sharply after overtaking another vehicle. Since the late 1970s.

carzie, carzey or **carzy** *see* **kharsie**.

case the joint to reconnoitre a building, esp. with a view to subsequent robbery. Since 1930.

cash and carry any large wholesale supermarket. Since the early 1970s.

cash in (often followed by *on*) to profit from, to take advantage of, as in *they tried to cash in on our success*.

cash in (one's) chips (or **checks**) to die. Adopted from the USA, probably in the late 19th century. From *chips* (or *checks*), counters used in gambling games.

casting-couch a divan in a male casting-director's office; an allusion to the alleged practice of assigning female parts on the basis of their apparent appeal. Adopted from the USA around 1955.

casual a young (often working-class) person whose chief interest is fashion, who wears expensive designer clothing. 1980s.

cat 1 a person (usually male); a term of approbation, as in *he's a cool cat*. Used by jazz musicians, Black people, beatniks, hippies and drug users. Adopted from the USA in the late 1950s. **2** a catamaran. Since around 1955.

cat-burglar a burglar who nimbly enters houses from the roof. From around 1919.

catch (sb) flat-footed to catch (sb) at a disadvantage, as in *we were caught flat-footed*. Mid-20th century.

cat-house a brothel. Originally Canadian then via the USA to the UK, around 1925. From the former slang term *cat*, prostitute, which dates from the 15th century.

cat in hell's chance only a very slight chance. Usually negative, as in *they haven't got a cat in hell's chance*, they have no chance at all. Since around 1930.

cat's pyjamas (or **whiskers**)**, the** anything very good, attractive, etc. Since the early 1920s. *See also* **bee's knees**.

caught with (one's) trousers (or **pants**) **down** taken unawares; totally unprepared; caught in an undignified or embarrassing position and without excuse. Since around 1920.

Cav and Pag the late 19th-century operas *Cavalleria Rusticana* (by Mascagni)and *Pagliacci* (by Leoncavallo), which form an almost invariable double bill.

celeb, n. celebrity, as in *you see a lot of celebs on Ken High Street.*

celeb, adj. celebrated, famous, as in *such celeb clients as Princess Margaret.*

certified certified as insane, as in *it's time you were certified,* addressed to a person who is acting the fool or who has been exceptionally stupid.

chain-smoke to smoke incessantly, often lighting the next cigarette from the one before. 20th century.

chair, the 1 the electric chair, used to execute criminals. Adopted from the USA by 1931 2 referring to the person whose turn it is to buy the drinks, as in *are you in the chair?* Later 20th century.

chalk and talk old-fashioned formal teaching methods in which the teacher writes on the blackboard and addresses the whole class at once, as opposed to the use of other visual aids and more child-centred activities.

chalkie a schoolteacher. Since around 1930.

champ a champion. From around 1915.

champers champagne. Since around 1920. The term was originally associated with Oxford undergraduates and the smart young set.

chancer a person who takes chances or foolish risks; an unscrupulous opportunist. Since the 1920s.

chap a man, a fellow. From around 1715. An abbreviation of *chapman,* in the early (or dialectal) sense of 'customer'. The term *chapess* is sometimes used as a jocular feminine form, as in *chaps and chapesses.*

chapel Nonconformist, as opposed to Anglican. Often used disparagingly or snobbishly, as in *she doesn't have much to do with the people next door: they're chapel.* 20th century.

char tea, as in *a cup of char* (or *a cuppa char*), a cup of tea. Since the late 19th century. From the Chinese *ch'a,* tea.

charge 1 a charge nurse, the nurse in charge of a ward or set of wards; the male equivalent of a sister. 2 marijuana. Since around 1943. Referring to the thrill or kick that the drug produces.

charged up under the influence of drugs. Drug users' slang. Used in the USA since before 1922.

chariot a car. Since around 1945.

charlie or **charley** 1 a fool, as in *I felt a right charlie.* Originally Cockney slang; in general use since the late 1940s. Short for *Charlie* (or *Charley*) *Hunt,* rhyming slang for 'cunt'. 2 cocaine. Drug users' slang. Adopted from the USA, probably in the 1970s.

Charlie's dead   your underskirt is showing. Chiefly used by schoolgirls, since the 1950s.

charming!   a stock ironic response to an unpleasant situation or remark. Later 20th century.

chart-buster (or **-topper**)   a very successful song or record; a smash hit. Since around 1955.

chase   1 to keep urging a person to get on with a piece of work. Since around 1920.   2 short for **chase the dragon**.

chaser   a drink taken immediately after another (of a different kind), such as a tot of whisky taken after beer or coffee.

chase the dragon   to burn heroin on a piece of foil and inhale the fumes through a straw or other tube. (The user *chases* the liquefied drug as it runs along the foil.) Probably adopted from the USA in the early 1980s. Sometimes shortened to *chase*.

chat-show   a radio or TV programme in which famous people and/or other guests are informally interviewed by the host of the show. Since around 1960.

chat up   to talk to a person, usually in a flirtatious or seductive manner, with a view to embarking on a romantic or sexual relationship. Since around 1936.

chauff   to act as chauffeur to, as in *I'm chauffing Cynthia*. Since 1925.

cheapie   anything very cheap. Later 20th century.

cheapo   cheap (and nasty), as in *a cheapo watch*. Since the mid-1970s.

cheapskate   a miserly or stingy person. Adopted from the USA around 1944.

cheat-sheet   an instructor's or teacher's *aide-mémoire*. Possibly since around 1960.

check!   OK!; yes! Adopted from the USA in the 1950s. The exclamation has been used in the British armed forces since 1940 to mean 'I've checked, all is well, it's all right.'

chee-chee or **chi-chi**   of mixed European and Indian parentage. Since the mid-18th century.

cheeks   the buttocks. From around 1750.

cheeribye!   goodbye! 1940s. A blend of **cheerio!** and *goodbye*.

cheerio!   1 goodbye! Since 1915.   2 a drinking toast. Since 1915. *See also* **cheers!**

cheers!   1 a drinking toast. Since around 1945. *Cheers!* has virtually replaced **cheerio!** in this sense, and is probably the most common salutation on raising the glass.   2 goodbye! Since around 1960. *Cheers!* is gradually replacing **cheerio!** in this sense.   3 thanks! Since around 1970.

cheesecake   sexually attractive women, usually photographed in a state of undress for magazines, pin-ups, calendars, etc. Adopted from the USA around 1944. The masculine equivalent is **beefcake**.

cheesed off   disgruntled. Since before 1914.

cherry 1 the hymen. Late 19th–20th centuries. *See also* **cherry–popping**. 2 virginity, as in *to lose one's cherry*.

cherry-picker a crane-like vehicle, used to lift or grab or both.

cherry-popping defloration of a virgin. Adopted from the USA in the mid-1960s. Also *to pop the* (or *sb's*) *cherry*, to deflower. *See* **cherry**.

chesty weak in the chest; coughing. Late 19th–20th centuries.

chew (sb's) bollocks off   to rebuke or reprimand (sb) severely. Also *to chew the balls off (sb)*.

chewed up, be to be very nervous and/or off colour. From around 1920.

chew the fat 1 to grumble; to resuscitate an old grievance; to sulk, to be resentful. From around 1880. 2 synonymous with **chew the rag**.

chew the rag to talk, to chat; to argue endlessly or without hope of agreement. 20th century. The phrase was originally synonymous with **chew the fat 1**.

chi-chi 1 affected, particularly in manners. 2 *see* **chee-chee**.

chick a girl or young woman. Adopted from the USA around 1940.

chicken, n. 1 a boy who is homosexual or likely to be preyed upon by homosexuals. 2 a game of daring played by children and young people, esp. one that involves crossing a road or railway in the path of an oncoming vehicle or train, as in *to play chicken*. Adopted from the USA in the early 1950s.

chicken, adj. cowardly, as in *he won't do it: he's chicken*. Adopted from Canada around 1946.

chicken! coward!; a derisive cry hurled at one who shows signs of cowardice. Mainly used by children, but also jocularly by adults. Since around 1955.

chicken-feed a mere pittance, a trifling or derisory sum of money. Since around 1941. The term originally referred to small change.

chicken out to withdraw from a venture, risk, fight, etc, through fear or cowardice, as in *she chickened out at the last minute*. Adopted from the USA around 1943.

chicken-shit, adj. petty, insignificant. Used in the USA and Canada around 1910–30.

chickie 1 a serviceman's girlfriend or sweetheart. Australian soldiers' slang of World War II. 2 any girl. Australian teenagers' slang. Since around 1945.

chief cook and bottle-washer the most important dogsbody in an organization. The term is often used in self-deprecation, as in *I'm the chief cook and bottle-washer around here*.

chiller a thriller that chills the blood. Used in the book world since the late 1950s. Elliptical for *spine-chiller*.

chill out, v. to relax or unwind. Chiefly USA; 1980s.

china a mate, a friend, a pal, as in *me old china*, a jocular term of address. Rhyming slang (originally *china plate*). Since around 1890.

Chinaman a left-hand bowler's leg-break. Cricketers' slang. From around 1905.

Chinese **1** a Chinese restaurant. Since the later 1970s. **2** a Chinese meal; a Chinese take-away.

Chinese burn an act of cruelty perpetrated (esp. by schoolchildren) by gripping a person's arm or wrist with both hands close together and twisting the flesh in opposite directions, as in *to give (sb) a Chinese burn*. Since around 1930.

Chink, Chinkie or **Chinky** a Chinese person. From around 1880. Possibly influenced by *chink*, narrow opening, referring to the shape of the eyes of the Chinese.

chinless wonder a person (esp. male) of the upper classes, whose receding chin suggests gormlessness or lack of resolution. Extended to more general use now. Since the mid-20th century.

chipe (usually of a woman) to talk in a high-pitched voice, often persistently, with a suggestion of complaint, as in *it's that woman chiping on again*. Perhaps a blend of *cheep* and *whine*.

chip on (one's) shoulder, have a to bear a grudge against the world, often for some specific and individual reason. Used in the USA since around 1880; introduced to the UK by US servicemen in 1942. From a method of challenging somebody to a fight, by putting a chip of wood on one's shoulder and daring the other person to knock it off. *See* **chippy**, adj.

chippy, n. a fish-and-chip shop. From the early 20th century.

chippy, adj. resentfully envious, having a **chip on one's shoulder**. 1970s.

chips in *to have had (one's) chips*, to have died, to be dead. Since 1917. *See also* **cash in (one's) chips**.

choc (often pl.) chocolate, as in *a box of chocs*. 20th century.

choccy or **chocky**, n. and adj. chocolate, as in *choccy cake*, *have another choccy!* Nursery slang, also used by adults.

chocker disgruntled, fed up. Since around 1920.

chocky *see* **choccy**.

chocolate-box, adj. (of pictures, scenery, etc.) conventionally or sentimentally pretty, but with little artistic merit or appeal.

chocolate drop a name given by white children to coloured children. 1970s.

choked disgruntled, fed up; disappointed; upset; angry, annoyed, as in *I felt real choked about it, he was too choked to speak*. Since around 1945.

choke-off an admonishment. Military and prison officers' slang. Since around 1914.

choosy fastidious; given to picking and choosing.

chop, get the to be dismissed from one's job. Since the late 1940s.

chop-chop! quickly!; hurry! Since the early 19th century. Pidgin English, from a Cantonese phrase meaning 'hurry up!'

chopper 1 penis. A particularly large one may be referred to as a *whopper chopper*. 2 a helicopter. Probably of US origin. Since around the mid-1950s. From the chopping motion and sound of the rotor blades. 3 a motorcycle that has been extensively modified. Motorcyclists' slang of the 1970s.

choppers teeth, esp. false teeth. Since around 1950.

chow! hello!; goodbye! An anglicized spelling of the Italian *ciao*, meaning the same. Since the mid-19th century. The term fell into disuse in the early 20th century and was revived in the late 1950s. The Italian spelling is preferred in modern English usage.

Chrisake! or **Chrissake!** an oath, esp. in *for Chrisake!*, for Christ's sake! 19th–20th centuries.

Chrissie, n. and adj. Christmas. Used mainly in Australia.

chronic unpleasant; objectionable; very bad; rotten. Late 19th–20th centuries. From an interpretation of the Standard English sense of the adjective (i.e. long-lasting, deep-seated), as in *chronic illness*, understood to mean very bad illness.

chuck, n. a term of endearment. Since the 16th century.

chuck, v. to throw, as in *chuck us an apple will you?* 19th–20th centuries. The term may replace *throw* in other phrases, as in *it's chucking it down*, it's raining heavily; *to chuck up*, to vomit. *See also* **chuck out**.

chuck it! stop it!; drop it!

chuck out, v. 1 to eject forcibly, to cause to leave, as in *he got chucked out of university*. Since before 1880. Hence *chucking-out time*, closing time. 2 to discard, as in *shall I chuck these old photos out?* From around 1910.

chuck-out, n. closing time at a public house. Since around 1920. An abbreviation of *chucking-out time* (*see* **chuck out** 1).

chuff 1 food. From around 1930. 2 bottom, backside, as in *to sit on one's chuff*, to sit back and do nothing; *I had a Porsche up my chuff*, a Porsche was driving very close behind me.

chuffed pleased, delighted, as in *she was dead chuffed*. 20th century.

chuff factor the degree of a person's acceptance, contentment, eagerness, etc.

chug-a-lug! an Australian drinking toast. Since the 1950s.

chummie or **chummy** a prisoner; a suspect. Police slang used in a jocular or euphemistic way. Since around 1925.

chunder, v. and n. (to) vomit. Used in Australia since around 1925. The term was popularized by Barry Humphries in the late 1960s and 1970s. Possibly from the nautical warning *watch under!*, look out below! (referring to seasickness), or from *Chunder Loo* (a cartoon character used in boot-polish advertisements), rhyming slang for 'spew'.

chunter to grumble, to talk at length in a disgruntled or tedious way, as in *he went chuntering on for hours about the government.* Since around 1950.

chute a parachute. Since around 1930.

chutzpah (pronounced *khootspa*) sheer barefaced effrontery or impudence, shameless but impressive audacity or cheek. Of Yiddish origin, adopted from the USA around 1974.

ciao *see* **chow!**

cig or **ciggie, ciggy** a cigarette. Later 20th century.

cinch, be a 1 to be very easy to do, as in *this should be a cinch.* Since around 1930. 2 to be (as good as) a certainty, esp. in *it's a cinch!* 20th century.

circulation, back in a phrase applied to somebody who has been jilted, divorced or widowed and is therefore free from romantic and/or sexual ties. Since around 1945.

city slicker a smart, smooth person from the city. Adopted from the USA around 1944. *See also* **slicker.**

civvies civilian clothes, as opposed to uniform. Since the mid-19th century.

civvy a civilian. In military use since 1895.

civvy street the condition and status of a civilian; civilian life, as in *what did you do in civvy street?* Chiefly used in the armed forces. Since around 1917.

clamp down (usually followed by *on*) to apply the full severity of the law or the regulations, as in *the police have clamped down on speeding and drunk-drivers.* Since the mid-1940s. Hence the noun *clamp-down.*

clang to commit a *faux pas,* as in *I realized I'd clanged as soon as I said it.* Not in common usage before the late 1960s. A back-formation from the phrase *to drop a clanger* (*see* **clanger**). Hence the exclamation *clang!*, usually applied to one's own blunder and accompanied by a gesture such as clapping the hand to the forehead.

clanger a hideously obvious mistake, error, blunder or *faux pas,* esp. in the phrase *to drop a clanger.* Since World War II, perhaps earlier. Possibly from the resounding nature of such a mistake or blunder. *See* **clang.**

clap (usually *the clap*) gonorrhoea. Since the 16th century. The term was in Standard English until around 1840. From the Old French *clapoir*, a venereal sore.

clapped out no longer serviceable, worn out. The term is applied to cars (or their engines), aircraft, bicycles, machinery, and even people. Since around 1922.

clappers, like the very fast or very hard, as in *to run like the clappers*.

claptrap nonsense, idle chatter, pretentious talk. The term originally referred to language deliberately contrived to win applause.

clash a set battle, planned and announced, between two gangs. Used in Glasgow and elsewhere from around 1920. As opposed to a *rammy*, an unplanned fight, often between smaller groups. *See also* **rumble**.

clean 1 cleared by the security vetting services. Since around 1950 or earlier. 2 carrying no drugs. Adopted from the USA around 1955. 3 *see* **come clean**.

Clean, Mr (or **Miss**) a person who maintains an image of virtue in politics, show business, sport, etc, as in *he's football's Mr Clean; I'm fed up with playing little Miss Clean*. Adopted from the USA around 1980.

cleaners, take (sb) to the to cheat or swindle (sb) very badly or thoroughly, esp. in a confidence trick or at gambling, as in *we got taken to the cleaners*. Adopted from the USA around 1945.

clean up, v. 1 to make a considerable profit or gain. Adopted from the USA by 1910. 2 to defeat. Used in Australia since around 1915.

clean-up, n. 1 a considerable profit. 2 a victory; a rout. Used in Australia since around 1920.

clean wheels a motor vehicle to be used in crime that has never previously been stolen or come under police suspicion. Underworld slang of the 1970s.

clear, in the innocent, with no evidence against one, free of suspicion, as in *her ex-husband's in the clear: he was in Paris at the time*.

clever (usu. negative) 1 nice, pleasant, as in *the weather wasn't very clever*. 2 fit, healthy, as in *I don't feel too clever today*.

clever-boots (or **-clogs**) a clever person, as in *well done, clever-boots!* 19th–20th centuries. Sometimes used in the derisive or sarcastic sense of **clever Dick**.

clever Dick a person who is obnoxiously clever or who has an inflated opinion of his or her cleverness, as in *she's a real clever Dick*. Since 1887 or earlier. The term is often used derisively or sarcastically, as in *some clever Dick left the radio on all night and the battery's gone flat*. *See also* **smart Alec, smartarse**.

click, n. a clique; a rather derogatory term for a group or set. Since around 1925.

click, v. 1 to become clear or obvious, all of a sudden, as in *ah, now it's clicked*, now I understand. Since around 1930. Perhaps from the *click* of a mechanical device falling into place, or a light coming on. **2** to be successful; to have a stroke of very good luck. Since 1914. **3** (often followed by *with*) to make a favourable impression on or take an immediate liking to a person, as in *she really clicked with my brother.* The feeling is usually mutual, as in *they clicked from the word go.* Since around 1910. From the interlocking of mechanical devices, as when a key is turned.

clicky cliquey. *See* **click**, n.

cliffhanger the end of an episode of a serialized film or TV programme, in which the hero or heroine is typically left in a precarious predicament. Since before 1914. The term is also applied to the serial itself, and to anything that is similarly exciting, such as a suspense novel.

clinch a prolonged and passionate embrace. Adopted from the USA around 1945.

clip-joint a night-club or restaurant where the prices are extortionately high. Adopted from the USA by 1950. From sheep-shearing: the patrons of such an establishment are swindled.

clippie a female conductor on a bus or train. Since 1939. From the act of clipping the passengers' tickets.

clit clitoris. Since the 1960s.

cloak and dagger secret, undercover, mysterious. The phrase has connotations of intrigue and espionage and was originally applied to the work of the secret service in World War II.

clobber, n. **1** clothes. From around 1850. **2** equipment; any impedimenta; personal belongings. Later 20th century.

clobber, v. **1** to punch or strike; to assault; to batter. Since around 1910. The term is also used metaphorically, as in *the government has been accused of clobbering the poor.* **2** (often followed by *with*) to impose an onerous duty or unwelcome burden on, as in *he got clobbered with cleaning out the oven; to be clobbered with* (or *by*) *higher taxes; she was clobbered by the police for speeding.* Later 20th century.

clock, n. a speedometer or mileometer, as in *a car with 60,000 miles on the clock.* Since around 1920.

clock, v. **1** to punch or strike (with one's fist), as in *I could have clocked him one.* Since around 1930. **2** to catch sight of, to notice. Since around 1935.   **3** to turn back the mileometer or a car or other motor vehicle to make the registered mileage much less than the actual mileage. Second-hand car dealers' slang. Since around 1945. *See also* **clocking**.

clock in (or **on**) to register the time of one's arrival at work, traditionally by inserting a card into a machine. From around 1905. *See also* **clock out**.

clocking   the fraudulent alteration of a vehicle's mileometer. *See* **clock**, v. **3**.

clock out (or **off**)   to register the time of one's departure from work. *See* **clock in**.

clock-watcher   a lazy or bored employee, who frequently looks at the clock to see how time is passing or if it is time to go home.

clockwork orange   a male homosexual, as in *he's as queer as a clockwork orange.*

closet, n.   in *out of the closet*, out of secrecy, into the open, as in *it's time these sponsors brought their motives out of the closet.* Since the later 1970s. The phrase originally referred to people openly declaring their homosexuality (*see* **come out**).

closet, adj.   private, covert, secret, as in *a closet alcoholic, a closet socialist.* Since the later 1970s.

closet queen   a crypto-homosexual, a homosexual who has not come out (of the **closet**). Since the late 1940s and perhaps earlier. See **closet, n.**; **queen**.

clot   a fool, as in *you stupid clot!* Since around 1920.

cloth ears   in *to have cloth ears*, not to hear, listen or respond, as in *have you got cloth ears?* I told you to shut the door! Originally Cockney. Hence *cloth-ears*, a term of abuse addressed to somebody who fails to hear or respond, and the derogatory adjective *cloth-eared*, which is also used in the extended sense of 'insensitive'.

cloud nine, on   in a state of euphoria. Adopted from the USA around 1972.

clout   **1** a heavy blow. The term was in Standard English until around 1850.   **2** power or influence, as in *she has a lot of clout in the industry.* Since around 1960.

club, in the   pregnant, as in *she's in the club, he put his girlfriend in the club,* he made his girlfriend pregnant. Since around 1940. Short for **pudding club**.

clubbability   the possession of qualities fitting a person to be a member of a club. Since around 1875. From the adjective *clubbable,* hence *unclubbable.*

clue, not have a   to be ignorant or incompetent; not to know, as in *he hasn't got a clue what he's doing, 'What time is it?' 'I haven't a clue.'* Since around 1942.

clueless   ignorant or incompetent. Since around 1941.

clue (sb) up   to brief, inform or instruct (sb); to put (sb) in the picture. Since the mid-1940s. Hence the adjective *clued-up,* well-informed, alert.

clumping   large and clumsy, as in *that clumping great thing.* From the verb *to clump,* to walk with heavy boots or wooden clogs. Since the 17th century.

clutz *see* **klutz.**

CMG Call Me God; a pun on the initials of a Commander of the Order of St Michael and St George. From around 1946. The higher ranks of *KCMG* (Knight Commander) and *GCMG* (Grand Cross) are translated as Kindly Call Me God and God Calls Me God.

co or **Co** company. Since the early 19th century. From the written abbreviation . . . *& Co.* Also used in the phrase *and co* (or *Co*), and the rest, and the others, as in *I went to the pub with Mark and co.*

coasting under the influence of drugs. Drug users' slang. Used in the USA since before 1936.

cob 1 in *to have* (or *get*) *a cob on*, to be annoyed. Since before 1935. 2 *see* **sweat cobs.**

cobblers 1 testicles. From *cobbler's awls*, rhyming slang for 'balls'. Since the early 20th century. 2 nonsense, rubbish, esp. in the phrase *a load of (old) cobblers*. The term is also used as an exclamation. Since around 1960.

cock, n. 1 penis. Since 1600 or earlier. 2 nonsense, as in *you're just talking a lot of cock, and you know it!* Since around 1938. Short for **poppycock.** 3 *see* **wotcher!**

cock, v. 1 to copulate. Since the 19th century. 2 *see* **cock up.**

cocked hat, knock into a 1 to damage considerably. From around 1850. An officer's *cocked hat* could be doubled up and carried flat. 2 to defeat, beat or outdo.

cock-eyed 1 askew; distorted, as in *you're looking at it cock-eyed; he's got a cock-eyed view of the world.* 20th century, from the earlier, 19th-century meaning: squinting, cross-eyed. 2 drunk. Since the 1920s.

cock-tease to excite sexually. Hence *cock-teaser*, a woman who does this. *See also* **prick-teaser.**

cock up, v. to make a complete mess of; to bungle, esp. in *to cock it up.*

cock-up, n. a blunder; an utter mismanagement of the task in hand, as in *to make a cock-up; the whole affair was a monumental cock-up from start to finish.* Since around 1925.

cocoa, v. to say so, esp. in *I should cocoa!*, an expression of disbelief, derision or indignation. Rhyming slang for *I should say so.*

coconut a coloured person who is deferential towards White people; a synonym of **Uncle Tom.** Used by coloured people in London. By analogy with a *coconut*, which is brown outside and white inside.

cod 1 burlesque, esp. in *cod acting.* Actors' slang. From around 1890. 2 mock, as in *cod German.* Since around 1965. Both senses are derived from the verb *cod*, to hoax, to play the fool.

codswallop drivel, utter nonsense, as in *a load of (old) codswallop.* Possibly from the noun *cod*, scrotum. Since World War II, perhaps earlier.

co-ed, adj. co-educational, mixed-sex, as in *the school went co-ed five years ago*. From around 1920.

co-ed, n. a female student at a co-educational institution, esp. a college or university. Adopted from the USA around 1950. The noun is never applied to male students.

coffin nail a cigarette. From around 1885. Sometimes shortened to *nail*. Also in the phrase *another nail in (one's) coffin*, said as a person lights a cigarette.

coin it (in) to make a lot of money, esp. quickly, as in *within six months you'll be coining it in; business was bad at first, but they're really coining it now.*

coit backside; behind. Australian slang; 20th century.

coke cocaine. Adopted from the USA around 1920.

cold turkey intense withdrawal symptoms resulting from sudden cessation of drugs, esp. as a method of treating drug addicts. Adopted from the USA in the late 1950s. The term is sometimes jocularly applied to the act or effect of giving up any habit, such as eating sweets or smoking.

collar in *to have (one's) collar felt*, to be arrested by the police. Since before 1950.

combined ops marriage, with particular reference to the sexual aspect. Used in the armed forces since around 1942. From *combined operations*, in which two or more of the armed forces take part in an action.

combo a small jazz or dance band. Adopted from the USA in the late 1950s. From *combination*.

come, v. (sometimes followed by *off*) to reach orgasm. Since the 19th century.

come, n. semen. From **come**, v. *See also* **cum**.

come across to be agreeable or compliant; to yield; to give, as in *come across with it!*, hand it over! Adopted from the USA. Since around 1919. The term is also used in the extended senses of paying money or consenting to sex, esp. reluctantly.

come again? pardon?; what do you mean?; please repeat or explain. Since around 1919.

come apart at the seams to lose one's composure. Since around 1945.

comeback a successful return, after a long break, to the scene of former success, esp. in *to make* (or *stage*) *a comeback*. Chiefly used in sport and show business. Since around 1920.

come clean to tell or confess everything, esp. to the police. Adopted from the USA around 1920.

come down to lose drug-induced exhilaration as it wears off. Drug users' slang. Adopted from the USA in the late 1960s.

come down on (sb) like a ton of bricks   *see* **ton of bricks.**

come good **1** to make money, to be succeeding. Australian. Since around 1930. **2** to turn up trumps, as in *I chatted up the pub-owner's wife, and she came good.* **3** to accede to a request, e.g. for a loan. Australian. Since around 1940.

come it to behave in an aggressive or provocative manner, as in *don't come it with me, young man!*

come-on a look or gesture of sexual invitation, as in *she was giving him the come-on.* Since around 1910.

come out to declare openly that one is homosexual. Used by homosexuals and subsequently by the media. Since around 1970 or earlier. From the phrase *to come out of the closet* (*see* **closet**, n).

come the . . . to act the part of, as in *don't come the (old) innocent,* don't pretend you don't understand. *See also* the following three entries.

come the (old) acid to become sarcastic. Originally Cockney slang.

come the old soldier **1** to wheedle; to impose on, as in *he was coming the old soldier over me.* Since the 18th century. **2** to hector or domineer, as in *don't you come the old soldier with me!* Since the mid-20th century.

come the raw prawn to impose on; to try to deceive. Australian. From around 1942.

come-to-bed eyes a person's eyes or look, considered to be sexually attractive and inviting. 1960s.

come to that! in point of fact; since you mention it, as in *you owe me a tenner, come to that!* Since before 1923.

come unstuck (or **undone**) to experience failure or disaster; to go amiss, as in *the plan came unstuck at this point.* Since around 1914.

come up smelling of violets (or **roses**) to emerge from trouble unscathed, and perhaps with one's situation improved. An allusion to such phrases as *if he fell in the cesspit, he'd come up smelling of violets,* applied to a person who is consistently and remarkably lucky.

come-uppance, get (one's) to receive (one's) just deserts, punishment or retribution. Adopted from the USA around 1944.

commie or **Commie**, n. and adj.   communist. Since around 1943.

commission, out of out of order, not running, as in *the car's out of commission: we'll have to walk.* Since around 1920.

common common sense, as in *use a bit of common!* Since the early 20th century.

comp **1** a competition. Since around 1925. **2** complimentary ticket. Originally theatrical slang, but in wider usage since the late 1960s.

Company, the the CIA, the Central Intelligence Agency of the USA. Adopted from the USA in the mid-1970s.

complex an obsession, as in *inferiority complex; she's got a complex about it.*

From Jung's psychology, in which the term refers to a group of ideas associated with a particular subject.

compo   compensation, as in *on (the) compo*, in receipt of compensation. Australian workers' slang. Since the 1920s.

comprehensively   thoroughly, indisputably, in a very big and often humorous way, as in *he was comprehensively bowled*. Originally cricketers' slang. From around 1960.

con, n.   **1** a convict. Since before 1909.   **2** a confidence trick, a swindle; deception, confidence trickery, as in *it's all a big con*.

con, v.   **1** to subject to a confidence trick; to swindle; to deceive, as in *you've been conned!; they conned us into parting with huge sums of money*.   **2** to persuade, as in *see if you can con her into lending a hand; I think I've conned George out of going so early*. Since the mid-20th century.

conchie, conchy, conshie or **conshy**(pronounced *konshee*) a conscientious objector (to military service). Since World War I.

conflab   a discussion, a familiar conversation or chat, as in *we had a conflab about it*. A 20th-century corruption of the 18th–19th-century colloquialism *confab*, short for *confabulation*, a chat, possibly influenced by the 19th-century slang term *conflabberation*, a confused wrangle.

con-game (or **-trick**) a confidence trick. From the USA.

congratters! or **congrats!**   congratulations! Chiefly British.

conjugals   conjugal rights; marital sex.

conk, v.   (usually followed by *out*) to fail, to break down, as in *the engine conked out*. From 1918. The Australian equivalent is *to go conk*, to fail gradually, to peter out.

conk, n.   nose. Since the early 19th century.

conkey, conkie or **conky**   nose. Diminutives of **conk**, n.

con-man   a confidence trickster. From the USA. *See* **con**, v. **1**.

connect,   to get on very well (with), as in *I really connected with her, they connected from the start*.

connect with   to hit. Used in boxing from around 1920.

conny-onny   condensed milk. Merseyside slang. Since around 1920.

conrod   the connecting rod between a piston and a crankshaft. Engineers' and mechanics' slang.

conshie or **conshy**   *see* **conchie**.

contact   **1** an acquaintance or connection, usually with a view to business or self-interest, as in *she has contacts in the publishing world*. Used in trade and commerce since before 1925; in general usage from around 1930.   **2** a contact lens. Mid-1960s.

contour-chasing, n. and adj.   (of an aircraft) flying very low, following the contours of the ground. Since around 1915.

contours   the curves of a woman's body.

contract a professional killer's engagement to kill a person, as in *to take out a contract on (sb)*. Underworld, espionage and police slang. Adopted from the USA around 1960.

con-trick *see* **con-game**.

cook to falsify, esp. in the phrase *to cook the books*, to falsify accounts. Since the 18th century.

cook up in *to cook up a story*, to produce a plausible but untruthful account of an incident or affair.

cool, n. confidence, self-possession, esp. in the phrases *to keep (one's) cool*; *to lose (one's) cool*. Adopted from the USA around 1955.

cool, adj. 1 very good, pleasing, attractive or satisfactory. Adopted from the USA around 1955. 2 (of a person) self-possessed. Since around 1950. *See also* **play it cool**. In both senses the term originated in jazz and has subsequently been used by beatniks, hippies and teenagers.

cool cat an addict or lover of modern jazz. Since around 1945. *See also* **cat 1**.

cooler a prison; a detention cell, as in *they put him in the cooler*. Since around 1890.

cool it! relax!; calm down!

cool out to relax or unwind, as in *kids sniff glue to cool out from pressures at home or at school*.

coon 1 a Negro. Used in the USA since before 1870 and in the UK from around 1890. From *raccoon*. 2 an Australian Aboriginal. Since around 1920.

co-op a co-operative store or society. From the early 1880s. The local branch shop of the Co-operative Wholesale Society (or, since 1982, Co-operative Retail Services Ltd) has been known as *the Co-op* since the mid-20th century or earlier.

cootie a body-louse. Originally nautical and military slang. 20th century. From the Malay *kutu*, louse.

cop, n. a police officer. Since before 1859. An abbreviation of **copper**.

cop, v. 1 to catch, to capture. From around 1700. Probably from the Latin *capere*, to take. 2 in *to cop it*, to get into trouble; to die. Since the mid-19th century. 3 in *cop a load of that!*, look at that! (said in admiration or, sometimes, derision).

copacetic *see* **copasetic**.

cop a feel to grab or grope a woman's breasts or a man's genitalia; to indulge in heavy petting. Used in the USA and Canada since the 1950s or earlier.

cop a packet 1 (of a person) to be severely wounded. Since World War I. 2 (of a place) to be badly bombed or shelled. Since World War II.

cop a plea   to plead guilty to a lesser charge. Later 20th century.

copasetic, copacetic, copesettic or **copesetic**   all clear; excellent; satisfactory; fine, as in *everything's copasetic.* US and Canadian. Possibly of Chinook or Yiddish origin.

cop out, v.   to evade an issue; to take the easy way out; to compromise; to withdraw. Adopted from the USA around 1960.

cop-out, n.   an evasion; a backing down; a compromise.

copper   a police officer. From the early 1840s. *See* **cop,** n.

cop-shop   police station. Since the mid-20th century.

copter   a helicopter. From 1944. The term has been superseded by **chopper 2.**

copycat   a person given to repeating or imitating others, copying others' work, etc.

cor blimey   *see* **gorblimey!**

corked   very drunk. Earlier 20th century.

corker   a person or thing that is particularly outstanding or attractive, as in *what a corker!; she's a real corker!* Since the early 19th century.

corks!   an exclamation. Since the 1920s. Possibly from an abbreviation of the euphemistic *corkscrew!* (God's truth) or *cock's body!* (God's body).

corny   (of a joke, song, etc.) hackneyed; sentimental; old-fashioned. Adopted from the USA around 1942.

corpse, v.   to burst into uncontrollable laughter, forget one's lines, or otherwise blunder (usually unintentionally) on stage; to cause other actors to do likewise. Theatrical slang. From around 1855.

corral, v.   to obtain or acquire, as in *I'll try and corral a few drinks.* Chiefly Canadian. Since around 1920. From cattle-herding. *See also* **round up; rustle up.**

cosmic   excellent; an expression of high approval. Teenagers' and hippies' slang of the later 1970s.

cossie   (pronounced *cozzie*) a swimming costume. Used in Australia since around 1919; also Merseyside slang.

cost   to be expensive, as in *it'll cost you!* From around 1916. Elliptical for *to cost (sb) a lot of money.*

cost a bomb (or **packet**)   to be very expensive, as in *that car must have cost a bomb!* Since around 1960. *See also* **make a bomb.**

Costa Geriatrica   a coastal area, such as the south coast of England, to which many elderly people retire. Since the early 1970s.

cost an arm and a leg   to be very expensive. Adopted from the USA in the mid-20th century.

cost a packet   *see* **cost a bomb.**

cosy   all very snug and profitable; remarkably convenient. Since around 1940.

cottage 1 a urinal; a lavatory. Since around 1900. 2 hence, a public lavatory used for homosexual encounters. The practice is known as **cottaging**. Since around 1920.

cottaging *see* **cottage 2**.

cotton on to understand. From around 1910.

couch potato a passive, lazy, lethargic person; a compulsive watcher of television. Of US origin; later 1980s. The use of the word *potato* may be an allusion to the vegetable-like existence of such people or to their physical shape (due to lack of exercise and eating too much junk food).

cough to confess. Police slang. Since around 1910.

cough up to produce or hand over, as in *you owe me £20: come on, cough up!* Since the late 19th century.

cover for to substitute for the person who should be on duty, as in *will you cover for me tonight?*; *teachers are refusing to cover for absent colleagues.* Adopted from the USA around 1950.

cow a woman, esp. an objectionable, ugly, or contemptible woman, as in *she's a real cow; fat cow; stupid cow!* Its wider use is ancient; used abusively since the 18th century.

cowabunga! an exclamation of exhilaration; a rallying cry. Used by Australian surfers since around 1961 The term was widely popularized among children in the early 1990s as the battle-cry of the Teenage Mutant Ninja (*or* Hero) Turtles from the film of the same name.

cow and calf or **cow's calf** a half; fifty pence (formerly ten shillings). Rhyming slang.

cowboy any unqualified and irresponsible builder, plumber, electrician, mechanic, etc. Since the later 1970s.

cow-lick *see* **calf-lick**.

cow's calf *see* **cow and calf**.

crack, n. 1 an attempt, esp. in the phrase *to have a crack at (sth).* Since around 1925. 2 a witticism. Since the late 1920s. Short for *wisecrack*. 3 in *the crack*, the latest news, gossip, etc, as in *just thought I'd drop in for the crack.* Anglo-Irish slang. Since around 1976. 4 a form of cocaine which is used for smoking. Drug users' slang. Since the 1980s.

crack, v. to joke or speak in a joking manner. Probably from the phrase *to crack a joke; see* also **crack**, n. **2**.

crack a fat (of a man) to achieve an erection. Australian. Since around 1940. *See also* **fat**.

crack down on to suppress (crime or criminals), as in *the police are cracking down on drunk-drivers.* Since around 1935.

cracker an expression of admiration, as in *she's a right little cracker; it* *was a cracker of a goal.* Later 20th century.

crackers crazy, mad, as in *to go crackers; he must be crackers!*

crack (one's) face to smile broadly; to laugh, as in *don't smile* (or *laugh*), *you might crack your face!*, addressed to a very serious person. Since around 1945.

cracking a term of high approbation, as in *a cracking good book.* 20th century.

crack it to succeed. Since around 1920. The phrase often refers to sexual achievement; in more general usage *it* may refer to a problem or puzzle that is (finally) solved. From the use of the verb *crack* in such phrases as *to crack a code, to crack a safe*, etc.

crackling esp. in the phrase *a bit of crackling*, a young woman, esp. considered sexually. Since around 1890. The term also refers to young women in general, as in *been to the dance, have you? Much crackling there?*

crack on to pretend, as in *he cracked on he'd lost the key.* From the 1880s or earlier.

crackpot (of ideas, schemes, etc) crazy, unworkable.

crack up 1 to praise highly, to boast, esp. in the phrase *it's not all it's cracked up to be.* From around 1840. 2 to break down, physically or mentally. From around 1850.

cradle-snatching marriage to, or romantic/sexual relations with, a person much younger than oneself. Since around 1935. Hence *cradle-snatcher. See also* **baby-snatcher**.

cramp (one's) style to handicap or check; to prevent (one) from doing or being at (one's) best. Since before 1916. From athletics or racing.

crap, n. 1 defecation, esp. in *to have a crap.* From the mid-19th century. 2 rubbish, worthless or inferior goods, as in *this jewellery is crap.* Since around 1910. 3 rubbish, nonsense, as in *you're talking crap.* Adopted from the USA around 1944.

crap, v. to defecate. Since the mid-18th century.

crapper lavatory. Probably from **crap**, v., though the flush toilet is said to have been invented by a certain *Thomas Crapper*.

crash 1 (sometimes followed by *out* or *down*) to go to bed; to sleep; to lie down and fall asleep, as in *I crashed (out) at about three.* 2 (of a computer or computer system) to break down, to fail. Later 20th century. 3 in *to crash a party*, to join a party uninvited, by guile or by force. Since around 1928. Short for the verb *gate-crash*, a back-formation from **gate-crasher**.

crashing bore a very tedious or tiresome person or thing. From around 1915.

crash pad a bed for the night; a temporary shelter. Adopted from the

USA in the late 1960s.

crawl   to behave in a disgustingly sycophantic way, to toady in order to obtain a favour, promotion, etc. Since the 19th century.

crawler   a contemptible toady. From the 19th century.

crawl with   to be filled with, to be overrun by, as in *the place was crawling with tourists.* Since before 1920.

crazy, n.   an insane or extremely eccentric person. Adopted from the USA in the late 1960s.

crazy, adj.   **1** good, very good. Adopted from the USA in 1956.   **2** in the adverbial phrase *like crazy*, to the utmost, as in *we worked like crazy to get it finished in time.* Adopted from the USA in the early 1970s.

crazy mixed-up kid   a young person with psychological problems, esp. one who is unable to distinguish good from bad. Adopted from the USA in the late 1940s.

cream   to become sexually excited, as in *to cream (one's) jeans* (or *knickers*).

cream-crackered   exhausted. Rhyming slang for 'knackered'. Later 20th century.

create   to make a fuss. From around 1910.

creep, n.   an objectionable or unpleasant person; a dull, insignificant, unwanted person. Adopted from the USA around 1944. *See also* **jerk**.

creep, v.   to toady.

creepy-crawly   an insect; a spider. Since the mid-19th century.

creepy weepy   a (type of) popular novel in which gothic horror is combined with romantic melodrama. Publishers' slang of the later 20th century.

crem   a crematorium. Since around 1920 or earlier.

crib, n.   **1** a literal translation illicitly used by students or pupils. From around 1825.   **2** any written aid to cheating in examinations. 20th century.

Crimbo or **Crimble**   Christmas.

cringe!   an expression of acute embarrassment, often accompanied by an action suited to the word. The term is also used in sympathy with another's recounted embarrassment. Since around 1950.

croak   to die; to kill. Since the 19th century. From the death-rattle of a dying person.

cronky   unsound; inferior; unwell. Since around 1920.

crook   **1** inferior; unwell; (of eggs, etc) rotten; (of land) infertile. Australian and New Zealand slang. 20th century.   **2** in *to go crook*, to give way to anger, to express annoyance. Australian and New Zealand slang. From around 1905.

crot   excrement. From around 1935.

crown   to hit (a person) on the head. Since the 18th century.

crucial a term of high approbation. A vogue-word among young people in the late 1980s, popularized by the comedian Lenny Henry.

crud 1 excrement; any dirty or encrusted substance. From the Middle English *crudde*. 2 a worthless or inferior person or thing, as in *what a silly little crud he is!* Since around 1930.

cruise, v. (usu. homosexual) to search the streets (or similar public place) for a sexual partner, as in *young men can be seen cruising in the park most evenings.* From the USA; 20th century.

crumblies grown-ups, esp. one's own (or one's friends') parents. Since the early 1970s.

crumbs! an exclamation of surprise or dismay.

crummy lousy (in the literal or figurative sense of the word); inferior, bad, rotten, as in *a crummy joint.* From around 1840.

crumpet women considered collectively as sex objects. From around 1880.

crush an infatuation, esp. in the phrase *to have a crush on (sb).* Used in the USA since before 1903 and in the UK from the mid-1920s.

cry all the way to the bank *see* **laughing all the way to the bank.**

cry Hughie *see* **call for** (or **cry**) **Hughie.**

crypto a secret communist, a sympathizer with communism. From 1945. Short for *crypto-communist;* the prefix crypto- is derived from the Greek *kruptos,* hidden.

crystal methedrine. Drug user's slang. Used in the USA since before 1967.

cuckoo, n. a fool, an insane person. Since the late 16th century.

cuckoo, adj. mad. Adopted from the USA in the early 1920s.

cuckoo farm a mental hospital. Later 20th century.

cuke a cucumber. Used by greengrocers since around 1910.

cultch culture. A jocular abbreviation. Later 20th century.

culture vulture a person who is avid for culture, esp. one who haunts exhibitions and lectures. Adopted from the USA in the late 1950s.

cum a variant spelling of **come,** n. Late 20th century.

cunt 1 the female genitalia. 2 (offensive) an unpleasant or obnoxious person; a mean or despicable person; a foolish or stupid person.

cupcake a male homosexual. Later 20th century.

cup of tea, be (sb's) to be what (sb) likes, what (sb) would choose or prefer, what suits (sb), as in *that's more my cup of tea.* Often negative, as in *this sort of music isn't everybody's cup of tea.* Since around 1910.

Curly 1 a nickname for a person with curly hair. Since before 1851 2 an ironic nickname for a bald man.

curse, the a woman's menstrual period. A shortening of the euphemistic phrase *the curse of Eve.*

curtains the end, esp. in *it's curtains for (sb),* implying death or dismissal.

Of theatrical origin. Adopted from US servicemen around 1944.

cushy (of a job, task or post) easy, safe, comfortable. Possibly from the Hindi *khush*, pleasant, or the Romany *kushto*, good.

cut to adulterate (drugs). Drug users' slang. Used in the USA since before 1938.

cut! stop!; a command addressed to film cameramen, actors, etc. Used in the cinema since around 1910; sometimes used on other occasions and in other activities.

cut (sb) down to size to reduce the (usually high) opinion that (sb) has of himself or herself; to bring (sb, esp. a conceited person) sharply back to reality. Adopted from the USA around 1960.

cut-glass accent an upper-class or upper-middle-class accent, esp. the clear, piercing accent of the female upper classes. Since around 1950.

cut in (of an automatic switch, such as a thermostat) to make electrical contact. Since the late 1940s.

cutie a smart, appealing or attractive person, as in *she's a little cutie.* Used in the USA since before 1921 and in the UK from around 1930.

cutie-pie a person who is rich in (calculated) sexual attraction. Early 1970s.

cut no ice to fail to impress or influence, as in *his sweet talk cuts no ice with me.*

cut out **1** to cease, to come to an end. Australian. Late 19th–20th centuries. **2** to depart. Canadian; adopted from the USA around 1957. **3** (of an automatic switch, such as a thermostat) to break electrical contact. Since the late 1940s.

cut the mustard to succeed in performing or accomplishing; to be of importance. From 1904 or earlier.

D

d.a. duck's arse; a haircut that was very popular, esp. amongst teddy boys, in the early 1950s. The hair was tapered and curled on the nape of the neck like the feathers of a duck's tail.

dabs (rarely sing.) fingerprints. Since before 1935.

daddy-o esp. one who is older and/or in authority. Used by beatniks in the 1950s.

daddy of them all, the the most notable or important; the largest and/or best. Since around 1970. *See also* **grand-daddy of them all**.

Dad's Army the Home Guard. The term was widely and affectionately used during World War II and became the title of a successful BBC comedy series in the late 1960s.

daft as a brush, as extremely stupid, very silly. Used in the North Country since the mid-19th century and in other parts of the UK since the mid-20th century. Possibly an adaptation of the phrase *as soft as a brush*.

daily a daily cleaner or charwoman. From around 1920. Short for daily help.

daily dozen, (one's) physical exercises, usually performed first thing in the morning. From around 1924.

daisy roots boots. Rhyming slang. Since before 1874. Sometimes shortened to *daisies*. *See also* **roots**.

dame a girl or woman; a sweetheart. The term is of Scottish origin, dating back to the 18th century, but in modern usage it was probably adopted from the USA around 1932.

dammit in *as near* (or *quick, soon*, etc) *as dammit*, very quick, soon, near, etc.

damn all nothing, as in *I learnt damn all at college*.

danger 1 chance or likelihood. The term is used ironically when something desirable is not forthcoming, as in *any danger of you getting a round in?* 2 in *no danger*, certainly, that's a certainty, as in *'Will you be there?' 'Aye, no danger!'*. Since the mid-20th century.

Darby and Joan inseparable companions who live a cosy, unadventurous life. Around 1880–1947.

dark brown voice a voice that is low, well-modulated and sexually attractive. Possibly since around 1950.

darky or **darkie**   1 a Black person. Since the 1840s.   2 a slim, elegant person who dresses in black and frequents cocktail bars in New York. Since 1990.

darling, n.   a term of address for anybody, even a comparative stranger. Since World War I.

darling, adj.   charming; sweet, as in *it was darling of you to offer*. Since around 1900.

dash   the dashboard of a car or other motor vehicle. Used by motorists since around 1910.

date   1 an appointment, often of a romantic nature, as in *she's got a dinner date with him*. Adopted from the USA around 1905.   2 hence, the person with whom one has a date. Adopted from the USA around 1944.

day's dawning   morning. Rhyming slang.

dead, adv.   extremely, utterly, as in *she's dead nice*, *it was dead embarrassing*. Since around 1940. Possibly from such phrases as *dead tired* and *to stop dead*.

dead from the neck up   brainless; very stupid; habitually tongue-tied. Since around 1920.

dead head   a useless person; a person of low intelligence; a bore. Since around 1950.

dead in the water   helpless, as in *I've got him: he can't move, he's dead in the water*. 1980s.

dead loss   a person or thing that is completely useless, inefficient, unserviceable, unprofitable, etc. Since around 1940.

dead-pan, adj. and adv.   without expression; impassive(ly), as in *a dead-pan face*, *she looked at us dead-pan*. Adopted from US servicemen around 1944. From the US slang phrase *dead pan*, an expressionless face; of theatrical origin.

dead ringer for, be a   to be the spitting image of, to resemble very closely, as in *he's a dead ringer for his brother*. See also **ringer**.

dead to the world   1 utterly drunk.   2 very deeply asleep. Later 20th century.

dear John letter   a letter ending a personal relationship. The original recipients of dear John letters were those who were separated from their sweethearts, such as members of the armed forces. Used in the USA since 1942 and in the UK since around 1950.

death seat, the   the front seat of a motor vehicle, next to the driver. Australian motorists' slang. Since around 1945. The occupant of this seat is the most likely to be killed in an accident.

death warmed up, like   very ill, esp. in *to feel* (or *look*) *like death warmed up*.

deb   debutante. From around 1919.

debag   (at Oxford and Cambridge) to remove the trousers of a fellow student. From around 1890. The practice was adopted by other universities and some schools, esp. public schools, in the 20th century. From the slang term *bags*, trousers.

deb's delight an upper-class young man, highly eligible for marriage, with plenty of money and little brain-power. Since the 1930s.

debug to remove faults (*see* **bug**, n. 1) from a machine, system, computer or computer program. Adopted from the USA around 1955.

decider the third or fifth set of a tennis match, when the score is one-all or two-all. From around 1925. The term originated in racing and is also used in other sports and games.

deck the ground; the floor. Late 19th–20th centuries. *See also* **hit the deck**.

deep end in *to go off the deep end*, to get very angry, excited or passionate. Since before 1918. From the act of jumping or diving into the water at the deep end of a swimming-pool.

deep six, the the grave. Since around 1920. From *six feet deep* or *six fathoms deep* (for burial at sea).

def excellent; a term of high approbation. A vogue-word among young people in the late 1980s. Possibly short for *definitive* or *definite(ly)*.

dekko a look, a glance, esp. in *to have* (or *take*) *a dekko*. Since before 1865. Possibly from the Hindi *dekho!*, look!, or from the Romany *dik*, to look.

Delhi belly stomach trouble, esp. diarrhoea, suffered by visitors to India. Since the late 19th century. *See also* **gippy tummy**.

deli a delicatessen. Of US origin; used in the UK since around 1960.

demo a (political) demonstration. From around 1930.

demob, n. demobilization. Also used attributively, as in *demob leave*, *demob suit*. Armed forces' slang. Since 1945.

demob, v. (usu. passive) to demobilize. Since 1918.

demon, n. and adj. applied to a person who is particularly adept, as in *she's a demon at tennis*, *a demon racing-driver*. Since the 19th century.

Denver boot, the the wheel clamp used to trap parking offenders. Since the 1980s. From *Denver*, Colorado, where the wheel clamp was first used.

dero a derelict, a person who is unemployed and destitute. Australian. Since the early 1970s.

derv oil for diesel engines. Used in the UK since 1940. From Diesel Engine Road Vehicle.

Desert Rats, the the Seventh Armoured Division in North Africa. 1941–3. The divisional flash worn on the shoulder and shown on vehicles was the jerboa or desert rat.

Desmond a lower second-class honours degree, also called a *two-two*.

Used jocularly by university students since the mid 1980s. From the South African bishop Desmond *Tutu*.

destiny one's fiancé or fiancée. From around 1910.

dewdrop a drop of mucus on the end of one's nose.

dhobi or **dhobi wallah** a native washerman. Anglo-Indian. Since the 19th century. From the Hindustani *dhob*, washing.

dhobi itch a skin irritation, esp. ringworm. Since the late 19th century.

dhobi wallah *see* **dhobi**.

diabolical an expression of intense disapproval, dislike or outrage, as in *a diabolical liberty; it's diabolical, the way they treat their customers*. Since the late 1960s.

dicey risky, dangerous; chancy, tricky. Since 1940.

dick 1 penis. From around 1880. 2 a detective. 20th century. The term may owe something to the 'Deadwood *Dick*' stories and the '*Dick* Tracy' comic strip. 3 *see* **clever Dick**.

dickey *see* **dicky**.

dickhead an idiot, a stupid fool. Later 20th century.

dicky or **dickey** 1 in bad health or bad condition; ill, inferior; shaky, insecure, as in *he's got a dicky ticker*, he's got a heart condition. From around 1790. 2 risky, tricky, dicey. 20th century.

dicky-bird 1 a word, as in *I never said a dicky-bird*. Rhyming slang. Late 19th–20th centuries. 2 in *not a dicky-bird*, nothing, as in '*Can you see anything?*' '*Not a dicky-bird.*' Since around 1920 or earlier.

di-da, di-da, di-da a mocking burden to a long-drawn-out explanation or complaint.

didakai, diddicoy or **diddikoi** *see* **didicoi**.

diddle 1 to swindle, to cheat, as in *I've been diddled!*; *to diddle the taxman*. Since the early 19th century. 2 to stimulate a girl or woman sexually with the fingers.

diddy small, little. Nursery slang of the 19th–20th centuries. The term became more widespread in the later 20th century, popularized by the comedian Ken Dodd and his 'Diddymen'.

didicoi a gypsy. There are numerous variant spellings, including *didakai, diddicoy, diddikoi*, and *didekei*. From the Romany *didakeis*, half-bred gipsies.

didn't oughter 1 water. Rhyming slang. Around 1890–1920. 2 daughter. Rhyming slang, current in the 1970s.

die the (or **a**) **death** (of a performer, esp. a comedian) to meet with a complete lack of response from the audience. Theatrical slang. Since around 1940. Often shortened to *die*.

different special, unusual, recherché. Since 1912. It is used as a polite escape formula, as in '*Do you like it?*' '*Well, it's – er – different!*'

dig 1 to understand and enjoy, to appreciate, to like and admire. Adopted from the USA around 1945. **2** *see* **dig up**.

digger a common form of address in Australia and New Zealand. Since around 1855. Originally used in the goldfields.

dig up to look for and obtain, usually with effort or difficulty. Used in the USA since the late 19th century and in the UK from around 1910.

dike *see* **dyke**.

dikey *see* **dykey**.

dill a simpleton, a trickster's dupe. Australian; since the 1940s.

dilly a simpleton, a fool. Australian. Earlier 20th century.

dim dull, silly, stupid. Since 1931.

dimwit a stupid person, one who is slow to understand. Since around 1935.

din-din or **din-dins** dinner; any meal; food. Nursery slang, also used jocularly among adults. Late 19th–20th centuries.

dingaling an eccentric or oddball. US and Canadian.

dingbat 1 a thingummy; an unnamed thing. Used in Canada since around 1920. **2** an eccentric or crank. Used in Australia since around 1930.

dingbats eccentric, mad. Australian. In general use since around 1925. Probably from *the dingbats*, delirium tremens, hence madness.

ding-dong a quarrel; a fight, as in *they were having a right old ding-dong*. Probably from the noise or violence of bells being struck.

dinkum, adj. and adv. honest(ly), genuine(ly), esp. in the phrase *fair dinkum*, fair and square, above board. Australian. Since the late 19th century.

dinky-die 1 honest, genuine, real, right. A variant or intensive form of **dinkum**. **2** fine, as in *everything's dinky-die*.

diplobrat a child with a parent in the diplomatic service whose cosmopolitan upbringing has led to precociousness and excessive self-assurance. Since 1990.

dippy extremely eccentric or foolish; mad. Since around 1910. Possibly from the Romany *divio*, mad, or from **dipso**.

dipso a dipsomaniac, a confirmed drunkard.

dip squad, the detectives operating against pickpockets. Since the late 1940s. From the 19th-century slang term *dip*, pickpocket.

dipstick a fool, a stupid person. Often used as a term of abuse, as in *you dipstick!* The term was used in Canada in the late 1960s and early 1970s, and in the UK (esp. by teenagers) from the early 1980s.

dip (one's) wick (of a man) to copulate. Since around 1880. From *wick*, penis (*see* **Hampton Wick**).

dire objectionable; very unpleasant. From around 1920.

dirt scandal. Adopted from the USA around 1930. From the phrase *to fling* (or *throw*) *dirt* (or *mud*), to be vituperative or malicious, which dates from around 1640.

dirty 1 an intensifier, chiefly used with *great* and *big*, as in *you dirty great bastard!*; *a dirty big truck.* Since around 1910 or earlier. **2** *see* **do the dirty on (sb)**.

dirty daughter water. Rhyming slang. Perhaps from the words of a popular song: '. . . water,/In which you wash (ed) your dirty daughter'.

dirty end, get the to come off worse or worst in a deal or encounter.

dirty mac brigade, the men who enjoy pornographic magazines and films, frequent strip clubs and sex shops, etc. Since the early 1970s. From the grubby old grey mackintosh that is regarded as the 'uniform' of voyeurs and exhibitionists.

dirty pool dirty tricks; unfair tactics. Used in the USA and Canada. From the game of *pool.*

dirty weekend a weekend spent with one's lover, often in a hotel, as in *they had a dirty weekend in Paris.* The term is also used jocularly of a weekend spent with one's partner but without the children. Since around 1930.

disgusting unpleasant; silly; rude, as in *don't be disgusting!* From around 1920.

dish an attractive person. Since around 1955.

dish it out to be physically or verbally severe towards others, as in *he can dish it out, but he can't take it.* Since around 1925.

dish out to distribute food equally; to distribute military decorations indiscriminately. Since 1914.

dishy attractive, as in *her new boyfriend is really dishy.* Since around 1960.

distance in *to go* (or *last*) *the (full) distance,* to finish a race; to last the scheduled number of rounds in a boxing match; to be able to continue to the end; to succeed in completing a task. From around 1910.

ditch to discard or abandon (a person or thing). Since around 1942.

div a dim-witted fool, as in *what a div!* The term is used of people who are looked down on by their peers for being weak or odd. *See also* **divvy**, adj.

divine very pleasant; splendid or perfect. From around 1920.

divvy, v. (sometimes followed by *up*) to divide or share. From around 1880. Hence the noun *divvy-out.*

divvy, adj. daft, stupid, eccentric, odd. Possibly from the Romany *divio*, mad.

DIY do-it-yourself, as in *a DIY store; a DIY enthusiast; a book about DIY; he's not very good at DIY.* Since the late 1960s.

dizzy scatterbrained; wild; foolish. Since around 1930.

dizzy blonde   a blonde who is foolish, flighty, or highly conspicuous in appearance and behaviour. Of US origin; used in the UK by 1956. *See also* **dumb blonde**.

dizzy limit, the   a variant of **giddy limit**. Mostly Australian.

d.j.   1 disc jockey. Since around 1970.   2 dinner jacket. Later 20th century.

DMs   abbreviation for Doctor Martens, a brand of sturdy lace-up boots with thick, hard-wearing soles, favoured by skinheads, punks and devotees of **grunge**. Since the 1980s.

do, n.   1 a social function, as in *a formal do; the firm's Christmas do; we're having a bit of a do on Saturday*. Since 1820. *See also* **proper do**.   2 *see* **fair do's**.   3 *see* **do-do; doggy-do**.

do, v.   1 to arrest; to prosecute. *See also* **done 1**.   2 to have sexual intercourse. *See also* **do it**.

do a runner   *see* **runner 4**.

doat   a person or thing that is (fit to be) doted on. Anglo-Irish.

do (one's) bit   1 to do one's share, to help a general cause. Late 19th–20th centuries.   2 hence to serve in the armed forces. World War I and World War II.

doc   doctor. Often used as a term of address.

doddle   anything that is very easily accomplished or obtained, esp. in the phrase *it's a doddle!* Since around 1945.

dodgy   1 difficult, complicated or tricky; risky, likely to become dangerous; dubious, unreliable. Since around 1943.   2 stolen; illicit, as in *dodgy gear*, stolen property. Since around 1955.

do-do (pronounced *doo-doo*) excrement. Schoolchildren's slang of the late 19th–20th centuries.

do for   to kill; to ruin, as in *I'm done for*, I'm ruined. Since the earlier 18th century.

dog   1 something worthless. US and Canadian.   2 an ugly or unpleasant girl or woman. Adopted from the USA in the 1980s.   3 *see* **dogs**.   4 *see* **put on dog**.

dog and bone   telephone. Rhyming slang. Since around 1945.

dog-end   a cigarette-end. Originally Cockney slang. Since the late 1920s.

dog-fashion or **doggy-fashion**   in *to have* (or *do*) *it dog-fashion*, to have sexual intercourse in which the man enters the woman from the rear.

dog-fight   a battle between fighter aircraft manoeuvring at close quarters. Since 1915.

dogged-up   in one's smartest clothes; in a stylish or showy manner, esp. in the phrase *all dogged-up*. Since around 1925.

doggy-do   dog faeces. A euphemism of the later 20th century.

doggy-fashion   *see* **dog-fashion**.

dog-house, in the   in disgrace, as in *I'm in the dog-house for being late.* Probably of US origin. Since around 1954. From the act of banishing a dog from the house to its kennel.

do-gooder   a person who does social work or voluntary work; a person's whose attempts to do good are well-intentioned but sometimes misguided. The term dates from the late 19th century but did not become widespread until around 1957.

dogs   feet. The term often refers to sore feet, as in *dogs that bite, my dogs are barking,* my feet are sore. Adopted from the USA around 1935.

dogsbody   a person who does all the menial tasks in an office or other place of work, a person who is given all the unwelcome jobs that nobody else wants do, as in *the office dogsbody, a general dogsbody.* Late 19th–20th centuries.

dog's bollocks   the typographical mark that comprises a colon followed by a dash (:–). *See also* **dog's prick**.

dog's breakfast   a mess; confusion, as in *to make a dog's breakfast of (sth),* to bungle (sth). Since the early 1930s. *See also* **dog's dinner**.

dog's dinner   1 a synonym of **dog's breakfast**. Since around 1945. 2 *see* **dressed up like a dog's dinner**.

dog's prick (or **cock**)   an exclamation mark. Authors' and journalists' slang.

do-hickey   a variant of **hickey 1**.

do in   to kill. Late 19th–20th centuries.

doings, the   an unnamed thing, as in *I've lost the doings that goes on the front of the lawn-mower.* The term often refers to something that is needed or relevant at the present moment, the name of which is unknown or temporarily forgotten. From around 1912.

do it   1 to have sexual intercourse, as in *have you (ever) done it?* 18th–20th centuries. 2 to be generally ready to indulge in sexual intercourse, as in *does she do it?* 19th–20th centuries.

dole, the   unemployment benefit, esp. in the phrase *on the dole,* unemployed. Since around 1925. From the earlier meaning of the distribution of food or money given in charity (since the 14th century or earlier).

doll   1 an attractive girl or woman. Mainly US and Canadian. In modern usage the term is sometimes applied to a good-looking man. 2 any drug in the form of a pill or pills. Drug users' slang. Since around 1972.

doll up   to dress very smartly, as in *to doll oneself up.* Hence the adjective *dolled-up.*

dolly-bird   a sexually attractive girl or young woman. Since the early 1960s.

done 1 arrested; caught and penalized, as in *he was done for speeding*. *See also* **do**, v. **1**. **2** socially acceptable or correct, according to etiquette, good form or fashion, as in *it's the done thing, it isn't done to wipe your nose on your sleeve*.

dong penis. Since the mid-20th century.

donkey's years a long time. Perhaps from *donkey's ears*, with reference to their length.

donnybrook a fracas. Used in Australia since around 1920. From *Donnybrook* Fair, famous for its free-for-alls.

do (one's) nut to explode with anger. Since around 1945.

doobri 1 an unnamed thing; a thingummy. **2** an unnamed person; whatsisname. Since the 1950s.

doodah 1 an unnamed thing; a thingummy. Since around 1910. **2** in *all of a doodah*, very nervous or excited. From 1914.

doodlebug the V-1, a German flying bomb. Since mid-June 1944.

doofah or **doofer** an unnamed or unspecified thing; a gadget; something that will *do for* the time being. Since around 1936.

doohickey a variant of **hickey 1**.

doolally off one's head; mad, as in *to go doolally*. Originally military slang. Since the late 19th century. Probably from *Deolali*, a military sanatorium in Bombay. The original full form of the term was *doolally tap*, from the Hindustani *tap*, fever. *See also* **tapped**.

doomy very depressed and discouraged; dismal. Since around 1960. A blend of *doom-laden* and *gloomy*.

doorstep, v. to intercept or accost people as they enter or leave their home, for a story, interview, etc. Journalists' slang of the later 20th century.

doorstepping hanging around a person's home or waiting around before a newsworthy event, e.g. a royal wedding. Journalists' slang of the later 20th century.

do (sb) over 1 to search (sb) thoroughly. **2** to beat (sb) up. Both meanings 18th–19th centuries.

do (one's) own thing or **do (one's) thing** to express oneself in one's life; to do what one most wants to do. Originally hippies' slang. Of US origin; used in the UK from around 1969.

dope 1 a drug or drugs, esp. cannabis. Since the late 19th century. **2** information. From around 1910.

dopey or **dopy** dull, stupid; lethargic, half-asleep. Since the late 19th century.

dork a harmless fool. Later 1970s. From the US slang term *dork*, penis.

dose of salts, like a very quickly and effectively, esp. in the phrase *to go through (sth) like a dose of salts*.

dosh money, esp. cash. Since around 1944. The term enjoyed a revival in the UK in the late 1970s and 1980s. Perhaps a blend of *do*llars and ca*sh*.

doss, n.   (a) sleep; a cheap and/or rough lodging, a bed for the night. Originally vagrants' slang. Since the mid-19th century. The earlier (18th–19th century) form of the noun (and verb) was *dorse*.

doss, v.   **1** (often followed by *down*) to sleep, to lodge, esp. cheaply and/or roughly, as in *can I doss down at your place tonight?* Since the mid-19th century. **2** (often followed by *around* or *about*) to idle around, to loaf about, to waste time. Later 20th century.

dosser   a person who frequents doss-houses or sleeps rough; a tramp, vagrant or homeless person. From around 1865.

doss-house   a cheap and/or rough lodging-house or hostel, esp. one used by homeless people or **dossers**. Since the late 19th century.

dot, on the   at exactly the right time, as in *at nine on the dot*; *on the dot of six, she arrived on the dot*. Since around 1920.

do the dirty on (sb)   to play a mean or unkind trick on (sb). From around 1912.

do the honours   *see* **honours, do the**.

do (one's) thing   *see* **do (one's) own thing**.

do things to (sb)   to excite or arouse, esp. sexually, as in *that girl does things to me*. Since around 1930.

double-take, do a   to take a second look, usually as a delayed reaction to what one saw the first time; to be shocked or amazed by what one sees. Since around 1948.

double talk   ambiguous or deliberately misleading speech or writing. Adopted from the USA around 1959.

double top   a good shot. RAF slang of World War II. From *double top*, the score of 40 (double 20, in the outer ring at the top of the board) in darts.

doughboy   a punch in the face, as in *to give (sb) a doughboy*. From around 1919.

down, n.   esp. in *to have a down on (sb)*, to be prejudiced against or hostile towards (sb), as in *she's got a down on me*. Used in Australia from around 1850 and in the UK in the later 20th century.

down, v.   to drink, esp. quickly, as in *he downed his beer and left*. Since around 1910.

downer   **1** a barbiturate, tranquillizer or sedative. Drug users' slang. Since around 1962. *See also* **upper**. **2** a depressing situation or experience.

down on (sb) like a ton of bricks   *see* **ton of bricks**.

dozy   lazy; inefficient; dull; stupid.

draft-dodger   (in the UK) a serviceman who avoids being sent overseas; (in the USA) a person who avoids conscription.

drag 1 female clothing as worn by men, esp. by transvestites or by an entertainer or actor playing a female role. Often in the phrase *in drag.* Originally theatrical slang. Since before 1887. **2** a quick draw at a cigarette. Since around 1920. **3** a person or thing that is boring or tedious, as in *what a drag!* Adopted from the USA around 1950.

draggy (of people or things) boring, tedious. Since around 1955. From **drag 3**.

drag (one's) heels to be reluctant or intentionally slow to co-operate or do one's duty, as in *the council have been dragging their heels over this issue.* Since around 1940.

dragon heroin. Drug users' slang. *See also* **chase the dragon**.

drag queen a male homosexual transvestite. Since the 1930s.

drag race a contest between drivers of specially built vehicles to achieve the fastest acceleration over a very short distance. Hence the noun drag-*racing*.

drag strip a short stretch of road on which young people try out or race their motorcycles or cars. Used by Australian teenagers since the late 1950s.

Drain, the the Waterloo and City underground railway under the Thames. Railwaymen's slang. Since around 1920.

drainpipes short for *drainpipe trousers,* particularly narrow-cut and tight-fitting trousers, worn esp. by teddy-boys. Since around 1950.

drapes a man's suit of clothes. Originally beatniks' slang. Since around 1958.

draw an inhalation from a cigarette, as in *to have a quick draw.*

dread a Rastafarian. Since the early 1970s. *See* **dreadlocks**.

dreaded lurgi, the any illness or minor ailment. From the BBC radio comedy series 'The Goon Show', first broadcast in 1951.

dreadlocks the long (plaited, matted or tightly curled) strands of the traditional Rastafarian hairstyle, worn by some Afro-Caribbeans (mainly men) in the UK, often beneath a multicoloured woolly hat. *See* **dread**.

dream-boat a very attractive person, as in *he's quite a dream-boat.* Since the 1940s.

dreamy (of a person) very attractive. Since around 1965.

drecky of inferior quality. From Yiddish.

dressed up like a dog's dinner wearing one's best clothes. Since around 1925. *See also* **dog's dinner**.

drill, the the correct way to do anything; the appropriate course of action. Since around 1910.

drink, the the sea, as in *to land in the drink.* Originally RAF slang, referring specifically to the English Channel. From around 1925.

drinkies a drinking party. Middle-class slang of the early 1980s.

drip a person who is inane, boring, insipid or wet. Since around 1920.

dripping for it inflamed with sexual desire (said generally of a woman). Since around 1910.

drive (sb) up the wall to send (sb) mad. Since the mid-1940s. *See also* **wall 2**.

drongo an undesirable human being; a lazy or slow-witted person. A term of contempt used in Australia, esp. Sydney, since around 1925. Perhaps from *Drongo*, the name of a second-rate racehorse.

droog a hooligan imitating those of the film *A Clockwork Orange*, esp. in dress and violence. The term was popular in the early 1970s, during the period when the film (based on a novel by Anthony Burgess) was being shown. From the Russian-based argot of the book.

droop-snoot a nickname for the Anglo-French supersonic airliner *Concorde*, which can lower its nose (*see* **snoot**). The term was originally applied to an experimental supersonic aircraft of the 1950s.

drop, n. an address or place where secret messages, illicit goods or money can be left for another person to pick up. Possibly since around 1950.

drop, v. to take a drug, esp. by swallowing, as in *I dropped my first acid in Paris*. Adopted from the USA in the late 1960s.

drop a clanger *see* **clanger**.

drop-dead very impressive or stunning, as in *she looked drop-dead gorgeous in that green dress*. Of US origin.

drop (one's) guts *see* **drop one**.

drop (sth) like a hot potato *see* **hot potato**.

drop like flies *see* **go down** (or **drop**) **like flies**.

drop of the hard (stuff) a drink of spirits. Since around 1930. *See also* **hard stuff**.

drop one to break wind, esp. inaudibly but pungently. Also *to drop (one's) guts*.

drop on (sb) from a (very) great height to reprimand (sb) very severely. Originally used by the armed forces, sometimes with *shit* in place of *drop*, during World War II. *See also* **shat upon 2**.

drop-out, n. a person who opts out (or **drops out**) of society. The term was applied to hippies and drug users from around 1960; since 1970 it has been in more general use.

drop out, v. to opt out of society; to become a **drop-out**.

drop them (of a woman) to be sexually accommodating. Since the mid-20th century. The word *them* refers to the woman's underwear, as in *she's not fussy: she'll drop 'em for anybody*.

drown to put too much water into whisky or brandy, as in *don't drown it!*

druggie a drug addict. Adopted from the USA around 1970 or earlier.

drugstore cowboy a young man who hangs about a corner drugstore, acting tough and eyeing up anyone he finds attractive. Used in the USA and Canada.

drum a building, house, lodging or flat, as in *to have (one's) drum done*, to have (one's) house searched by detectives. Since before 1859.

dry out to take a course of treatment for alcoholism. Hence the noun *drying out*, which is also applied to a slow withdrawal from drugs.

dry run an experimental practice or rehearsal. Since around 1950 or earlier. *See also* **dummy run**.

duck to avoid; to neglect to attend, as in *to duck a meeting*.

duck and dive to dodge work. Rhyming slang for 'skive'.

duckie *see* **ducky**, n. and adj.

duck-pond the Atlantic Ocean. Since World War II.

ducks a variant of **ducky**, n. Mainly used in London and the Home Counties.

duck weather very wet weather. Used in Australia since around 1920. From the phrase *fine weather for ducks*.

ducky or **duckie**, n. a term of endearment. Since the early 19th century.

ducky or **duckie**, adj. an expression of admiration, sometimes sarcastic or jocular, as in *she was wearing a ducky little pair of shorts*. Since around 1930.

dud worthless; useless. Since around 1895.

dude 1 a swell or dandy. Originally US; used in the UK since the late 19th century. 2 any male person; a guy or fellow. Later 20th century.

duff, n. 1 in *up the duff*, pregnant, as in *he put* (or *got*) *her up the duff*. 2 *see* **piece of duff**.

duff, adj. no good; inferior; broken. Late 19th–20th centuries.

duff up, v. to beat up or assault, as in *he got duffed up by a gang of louts*. Since around 1950.

dukes (often pronounced *dooks*) hands or fists, as in *to put up (one's) dukes* (often imperative). Since before 1874. Possibly from *Duke of Yorks*, rhyming slang for 'forks' (hence, fingers or hands).

dullsville anything dull or boring. *See also* **-ville**.

dumb blonde a very attractive but stupid girl or young woman, blonde by nature or artifice, such as the character played by Marilyn Monroe in the film *The Seven-Year Itch*. Adopted from the USA around 1940. *See also* **dizzy blonde**.

dumb cluck a stupid, foolish or dull person. Adopted from the USA by the mid-20th century.

dumbo a nickname for a slow-witted person. Probably popularized by Walt Disney's cartoon film (1941) of the same name.

dum-dum a stupid person. Adopted from the USA in the later 20th century.

dummy run a practice or rehearsal. Since around 1910. *See also* **dry run**.

dump, n. 1 a dirty, dilapidated or unpleasant place. Since around 1915. 2 as in *to have a dump*, to defecate.

dump, v. to dispose of; to abandon. From 1940.

dunny lavatory. Used in Australia since around 1880. From the dialect word *dunnakin*, lavatory.

dustbin lid child. Rhyming slang for 'kid'.

dusty in *not so dusty*, not too bad, e.g. as a semi-jocular reply to 'How are you?' Since the mid-19th century.

dusty answer a bad-tempered, uncooperative reply, as in *to give (sb) a dusty answer, to get a dusty answer*.

dyke or **dike** a lesbian. Adopted from the USA around 1935.

dykey or **dikey** lesbian. Since the late 1930s.

dynamite, adj. (of a person) alarmingly violent, brutal, drastic, autocratic, powerful or expert; (of things) extremely dangerous or sudden. From around 1914.

E

E *see* **Ecstasy**.

eager beaver a person who is excessively or conspicuously keen and diligent, but sometimes lacking in forethought or efficiency. Adopted from the USA around 1955 or earlier. Perhaps from the phrase *as busy as a beaver*, of US origin. *See also* **beaver**, v.

eagle a hole played in two strokes under par. Golfers' slang. Adopted from the USA around 1922. *See also* **albatross, birdie**.

ear 1 in *on (one's) ear*, in disgrace. Adopted from the USA around 1909. 2 in *out on one's ear*, dismissed, thrown out, as in *you'll be (thrown) out on your ear if the boss hears about this!* Since around 1920.

ear-basher a bore. Used in Australia since around 1925.

ear-bashing conversation; talking, esp. fluently and at length. Originally Australian soldiers' slang, from 1939.

early bath an unexpectedly early departure or retirement, as in *he was sent for an early bath*, the player was ordered off the field or replaced by a substitute. Mid-1980s.

earn to make corrupt or dishonest profit, as in *we can all really earn on this one*, referring to a proposed fraud or illegal scheme; 1970s. *See* **earner**.

earner 1 any situation that can be turned to corrupt or dishonest advantage, as in *we're on to an earner here!* 1970s. *See* **earn**. 2 a particularly lucrative job, scheme or situation, esp. one in which money is made easily or dishonestly. Often used in the phrase *a nice little earner*.

ear to the ground, keep (one's) be alert to what is going on, and to what is likely to happen. Possibly since around 1950.

earwig, v. to eavesdrop.

ease up! steady!; slow down! From before 1923.

easy esp. in *I'm easy*, I don't mind one way or the other. Since the late 1930s.

easy as pie, as very easy to do, solve, etc. Perhaps a shortening of the phrase *as easy as apple-pie*, which dates from around 1920 and may have originated in the abecedarian mnemonic *A is for apple-pie*. . ..

easy as taking candy from a baby, as very easy indeed. Of US origin. Also *as easy as taking money* (or *toffee*) *from a child*, used in the UK in

the late 19th–20th centuries; *as easy as taking pennies from a blind man.*
easy on the eye   (of a person) good-looking. Probably adopted from
  the USA in the 1930s.
easy-peasy   very easy, usually with an undertone of contempt or dim-
  inution, as in *anybody can do that: it's easy-peasy!*
eat   to worry, to bother, as in *what's eating you?* From around 1919.
eating-irons   knife, fork and spoon. Since around 1920.
eat (sb) out   to perform cunnilingus on (a woman). Used in the USA
  since the mid-1950s.
eats   food; provisions.
eat shit   to submit to verbal insult or degrading treatment. Of
  US origin. Later 20th century.
'eck-as-like   *see* **heck-as-like**.
Ecstasy   an amphetamine-type drug with hallucinogenic effects. Of
  US origin. Since the mid-1980s. Often abbreviated to E.
edge   **1** antagonism; tension arising from mutual dislike. Since the
  mid-20th century.   **2** in *to have the edge on*, to have a slight advantage
  over. Adopted from the USA in the mid-20th century or earlier.
edgy   irritable; nervous. From the phrase *on edge.*
eff, v.   to use the word **fuck** and other similar expletives, esp. in the
  phrase *to eff and blind.* Hence *effing and blinding,* foul-mouthed
  swearing. Of euphemistic origin.
eff off!   go away! Originally a euphemism for **fuck off!**, the term
  established an independent identity around 1935.
egg-beater   an affectionate term for an old car. Later 20th century.
egghead   a scholar; an erudite person; an intellectual. The term is also
  used attributively, as in *the egghead press,* the serious newspapers.
  Adopted from the USA in the late 1950s.
egg on (one's) face   esp. in *to have* (or *get*) *egg on (one's) face,* to come
  out of an affair (esp. a political or commercial affair) badly, to suffer
  humiliation or embarrassment, to make a fool of oneself through
  presumption or lack of judgement, as in *they're going to end up with a
  lot of egg on their faces over this.*
egg-whisk   a helicopter. Since around 1948.
ego-trip   any activity that brings personal gratification; an opportunity
  for self-aggrandizement, as in *that political campaign of his is all just
  one big ego-trip.*
eight-ball, behind the   in an extremely difficult position; at a considerable disadvantage. Adopted from the USA around 1945; in British
  usage by 1960. From the game of pool.
elbow   in *to give (sb) the elbow,* to dismiss, jilt or otherwise get rid of (sb);
  to get the elbow, to be dismissed or jilted. Since the late 1970s. *See also*
  big E.

elephant heroin. Drug users' slang.

elephant's (trunk) drunk. Rhyming slang. Since the 19th century.

elevenses a mid-morning drink of coffee, tea, etc., and perhaps a bite to eat. 19th–20th centuries (originally dialectal).

eliminate to kill (a person) esp. in a cold-blooded way. From around 1915.

emcee, n. and v. (to act as) master of ceremonies or *MC*. The verb has been in use since around 1950; the noun is of much earlier origin.

emmet a derisive term for a holiday-maker. Used in Cornwall in the later 20th century. From the dialect word *emmet*, ant. *See also* **grockle**.

emote to be or become emotional; to show excessive emotion. Of theatrical origin; adopted from the USA around 1950. A back-formation from *emotion*.

empire a large (esp. unnecessarily large) department, usually administrative. Since around 1944.

empire-builder somebody who deliberately tries to extend his or her responsibilities, increase his or her staff, etc., so as to (appear to) merit promotion. Since around 1944. Hence the noun *empire-building*.

end 1 the glans penis. The term is often used in compounds, such as *bell-end, blunt end, red end*, etc. 2 in the phrase *to have* (or *get*) (*one's*) *end away*, (usually of a man) to achieve sexual intercourse, as in *he's been here for three weeks and he still hasn't got his end away*. Since around 1910.

end of the line, the 1 esp. in *that's the end of the line for (sb)*, (sb) is finished physically, socially, professionally, etc. Possibly from the US. Since around 1960. From the end of a railway-line. 2 the end (e.g. of a love affair), as in *it's the end of the line for us*.

enough on (one's) plate, have *see* **plate**.

enthusiastic amateur *see* **amateur**.

epic excellent; an expression of high approval. Teenagers' slang. Around 1977.

'Erbert *see* **Herbert**.

'er indoors one's wife. The term was used from the early 1980s by the Cockney character Arthur Daley (played by George Cole) in the TV series *Minder*, referring to his never-seen wife.

erk 1 a lower-deck rating. Nautical slang. Late 19th–20th century. Possibly from the verb *irk*. 2 a recruit; a person of lowest rank in the RAF. Used in the RAF since 1918. Probably short for *aircraftman*.

Ernie the electronic brain that selects the numbers of winning Premium Bonds. Since October 1956, the month before the first bonds were issued. Electronic Random Number Indicator Equipment.

even-handed (of a transaction) fair; honest. From the mid-1970s.

even Steven(s) (or **Stephen(s)**)   share and share alike. Possibly of US origin; used in the UK since the mid-20th century or earlier. The phrase was formed by reduplication of *even*, perhaps influenced by the 19th-century slang term *Stephen*, money.

ever   in *the best* (or *worst, greatest, biggest,* etc.) *ever* the best, worst, etc., that has ever been. Adopted from the USA around 1930.

ever so   very much, as in *thanks* (or *ta*) *ever so!* From around 1985. Elliptical for *ever so much.*

every which way   in every manner or direction. Often in the phrase *every which way but (the right one)*. Used in the USA since 1840 and in the UK from around 1910.

ex   former spouse or lover. Since around 1920.

ex-con   a former convict.

exec, n. and adj.   short for executive (committee) or (business) executive, as in *exec meeting*. Since the late 1950s.

expat   an expatriate, esp. a person who has chosen to live and/or work in a foreign country. Since the late 1940s.

extract the Michael   to make fun of, to jeer at. Since around 1950. A jocularly pedantic version of **take the mickey**.

eyeball, v.   to see; to meet face to face. Originally used by beatniks and on Citizens' Band radio. Later 20th century.

eyeball to eyeball   in very close, usually hostile, confrontation. Since around 1960.

eye! eye!   a call for vigilance; a pun on the nautical expression 'aye! aye!'. Since around 1920.

eyeful   **1** an attractive or striking person, esp. a woman, as in *she's a bit of an eyeful.* **2** a long steady look; as much as the eye can take in.

Eyetie (often pl.)   an Italian. Since World War I; much used during World War II. From the nonstandard pronunciation *Eye-talian.*

F

f.a. *see* **sweet f.a.**

fab wonderful; an expression of enthusiastic approval. Used by teenagers in the 1960s and revived in the 1980s. Short for *fabulous*.

face 1 a person, esp. a well-known person. Since the late 1950s. 2 a known criminal. Police and underworld slang of the 1970s. 3 *see* **put (one's) face on**.

face-ache 1 an ironically jocular term of address. 2 an unpleasant, ugly, miserable-looking or undesirable person. Since around 1960.

face like a milkman's round a long face; a disappointed or unhappy expression. Since around 1950.

face like the back of a bus a plain or ugly face. Since the late 1940s.

face the music to go through an ordeal, esp. a severe reprimand or punishment, as in *I suppose I'd better go back and face the music.* Since the 19th century. Of US origin.

factor *see* **buggeration factor; chuff factor**.

fad, n. 1 a passionate but short-lived trend or pastime, as in *a passing fad.* 2 a personal eccentricity or whim, as in *it's just a fad of his.* Since the 19th century.

fade, n. 1 in *to do a fade*, to disappear without paying the rent. Canadian. 2 in *on the fade*, evading justice, dodging the police. Australian. Since around 1920.

fade, v. to depart; to disappear. Since around 1950.

faff about to mess about, restlessly and ineffectually; to waste time, often while something urgent needs attention, as in *stop faffing about: we'll never get there at this rate!* Since around 1930. *See also* **fanny about; fart about**.

fag 1 a cigarette. From around 1887. The term originally referred to an inferior cigarette. 2 a male homosexual, esp. one who plays a passive role. Adopted from the USA around 1960. Probably short for **faggot**.

faggot a male homosexual. Since around 1960 or earlier. *See* **fag 2**.

fag-hag a woman who habitually consorts with male homosexuals. Of US origin. Since the late 1960s.

faintest, not have the not have the least idea, have no idea at all, as in *I haven't the faintest.* Since around 1910.

fair crack of the whip fair play, as in *to give (sb) a fair crack of the whip*, to deal fairly with (sb); *to get a fair crack of the whip*, to have a fair share.

fair do's a fair deal; justice, as in *fair do's all around*. Originally *fair dues* (since the 19th century); by the mid-20th fair do's had become the most common form of the phrase.

fair few, a a considerable number. Late 19th–20th centuries.

fairy story any unlikely tale; a downright lie.

fall to become pregnant; to conceive a child. Since the 19th century.

fall about to laugh immoderately, as in *if I tell them that, they'll fall about*. Since the mid-1970s. Elliptical for *to fall about laughing* (or *with laughter*).

fall down (often followed by *on*) to make a bad mistake; to fail, esp. in *to fall down on the job*, to fail badly or inexcusably at something. Used in the USA since 1870 and in the UK from around 1910.

fall guy a scapegoat, esp. one who has been specially set up. Of US origin. 1970s.

fall over (oneself) to be very eager, as in *they were falling over themselves to help us*. Since around 1920.

falsies imitation breasts; breasts enlarged by padding. Adopted from US servicemen around 1944.

family jewels, the a man's genitalia. Since the 1920s or earlier.

fancy to desire sexually, as in *I really fancy him!* Late 19th–20th centuries, esp. since around 1950.

fancy (one's) chances to act in a conceited and arrogant manner; to have an unduly high estimation of one's own importance or ability, often with the implication that the person in question (often male) will rely upon his charm or skill to see him through.

fancy pants a person who is all dressed up. Used in the UK since the mid-20th century. Popularized in the US film of that name, made in 1950, starring Bob Hope and Lucille Ball.

fanny 1 the female genitalia. From around 1860 or earlier. 2 the buttocks. Adopted from the USA around 1930, but still regarded as an Americanism in the UK.

fanny about a synonym of **faff about** or **fart about**. Later 20th century.

Fanny Adams *see* **sweet f.a.**

fantastic very good; excellent; attractive; unusual. Since the late 1940s.

fare the client of a male homosexual prostitute. Homosexuals' slang. Since around 1930.

far-out, adj. 1 extraordinary; avant-garde. 2 first-rate; wonderful. Adopted from the USA; since the 1950s.

fart about to dawdle; to waste time; to play about. Late 19th–20th centuries.

fart-arse about   a synonym of **fart about**. 20th century.

fashion victim   one who follows fashion trends blindly and with no imagination. A vogue word of the 1980s.

fast one, pull a   to cheat or deceive; to play a mean or unscrupulous trick; to malinger or evade duty. Since around 1938.

fast talker   a confidence trickster. Since around 1930.

fat   an erection of the penis. Australian. *See also* **crack a fat**.

fat cat   (often pl.)   an ostentatiously wealthy person, as in *the fat cats of the music business*. Since around 1955.

fat chance   no chance at all, as in *Do you think you'll get a promotion? Fat chance!*

fat lot of, a   very little or none at all, as in *that's a fat lot of good!*

Fatso   a nickname for a fat person. Adopted from the USA around 1950.

fave   favourite. Later 20th century.

feather-bedding   making things very easy for a person or group of people.

feather-plucker   an objectionable person. Rhyming slang for 'fucker'. Since around 1945. *See also* **pheasant-plucker**.

feature   to present prominently. Used in the USA since around 1897 and in the UK from around 1905.

feature with   to achieve sexual intercourse with. Used in Australia in the later 20th century. The term was popularized in the UK by the Australian humorist Barry Humphries in the satirical 'Barry McKenzie' comic strip.

Feds, the   1 employees of the FBI, the US Federal Bureau of Investigation.   2 hence, in the UK, police in general.

fed to the back teeth   an intensive variant of **fed up**. From around 1910.

fed up   bored; disgusted or discontented; tired (of), as in *I'm fed up with this work.* From around 1889.

feed (one's) face   to eat, esp. greedily.

feel like a boiled rag   to feel very limp or unwell. Also *to feel like a piece of chewed rag* (or *string*).

feel like shit   to feel wretched or ill. Since around 1950.

feel no pain   to be very drunk. Since around 1945. Perhaps from the song: 'I feel no pain, dear mother, now/But oh, I am so dry!'

feel (one's) oats   to get bumptious or very high-spirited. Used in the USA since around 1840 and in the UK from around 1905. By analogy with a horse that has just fed on oats.

feel rough   to feel unwell or indisposed; to have a hangover. From around 1917.

feel the draught   to have financial problems; to be short of money.

From 1925.

feel up   to caress sexually. Possibly from the 19th century.

feet under the table, to get or **have one's**   to be on very friendly visiting terms with a family, esp. if one is courting a member of the household. Since around 1925.

feisty   spirited, lively, as in *a feisty battle of wits*. Probably of US origin. From the late 1970s.

fella, fellah or **feller**   **1** a colloquial or careless pronunciation of 'fellow', as in *young fella me lad*, a jocular term of address. From around 1870. **2** boyfriend, as in *that's her new feller*.

fiddle, n.   a swindle; fraud; petty pilfering, as in *he's on the fiddle*. Since around 1920.

fiddle, v.   1 to cheat or swindle. The term was in Standard English until around 1800; it was revived by the underworld around 1840.   **2** to falsify, as in *to fiddle the books; to fiddle (one's) expenses*. Since around 1945.

fifty-fifty, adj. and adv.   equal(ly), as in *a fifty-fifty chance; they split the money fifty-fifty*. Adopted from the USA around 1914.

figure   in *it* (or *that*) *figures*, that's just what one would expect. Adopted from the USA around 1955.

figure out of the air   in *to take* (or *pluck*) *a figure out of the air*, to estimate without detailed calculation. Later 20th century. The figure may be chosen at random, or based on feeling and experience.

fill (sb) in   **1** to beat (sb) up, as in *if he does that again, I'll fill him in!* Since around 1925.   **2** to inform or instruct (sb), as in *I filled her in on what had happened*. Since the early 1940s.

fill the bill   to fill a need, to be the right thing at the right time in the right place. Since around 1950 or earlier. A variant is *fit the bill*.

filth, the   the police. Used by criminals since around 1950.

filthy, adj.   extremely unpleasant, as in *this filthy weather we've been having*. Originally dialectal but widespread since the early 1900s.

filthy, adv.   extremely or disgustingly, as in *filthy rich and good looking*. Since the late 19th century.

find, n.   a person worth knowing; a thing worth having, as in *our new cleaner was a real find*.

fine-tune   to modify, usually by making minor changes, as in *to fine-tune a procedure; the first draft of the essay is OK, but it'll need fine-tuning*. From the act or practice of tinkering with internal-combustion engines, radio/TV sets, etc.

finger, n.   **1** a gesture made with the extended middle finger, in a thrusting upward motion, meaning 'Fuck you!'. The term is most commonly used in the phrase *to give (sb) the finger*. Adopted from the USA around 1965.   **2** in *to put the finger on (sb)*, to point out (a wanted person) to the police; to inform on (sb). Adopted from the USA.

finger, v. to nominate a person for a job. Probably from the USA. Since around 1965. *See* **finger,** n. **2.**

finger-fuck **1** (of a woman) to masturbate. Since the 19th century. **2** to stimulate sexually a woman or a male homosexual, using the fingers.

finger on the pulse, (have or **keep one's)** to remain informed about something, as in *even when she's 2,000 miles away, she's got her finger on the pulse.* 20th century.

Fingers a nickname for a pickpocket; since the 1930s.

fingers crossed esp. in *to keep (one's) fingers crossed,* to hope or pray for success (or merely to avert failure, defeat or bad luck). Uncommon before 1925. A modification of the ecclesiastical sign of the Cross.

finito! an exclamation of completion. Since around 1950. From the Italian *finito,* finished.

fink **1** an unpleasant person, esp. one who is felt to be untrustworthy. Adopted from the USA around 1965. **2** an informer. **3** a strikebreaker. *See also* (for all senses) **ratfink.**

firm **1** a gang of burglars or other similar criminals. Since around 1950. **2** a gang that follows a leader, esp. a gang of young football supporters who are prone to violence. Late 1970s.

fishing expedition, on a spying or pumping others for information. Since around 1930. From Japanese fishing boats that went into foreign waters to obtain information.

fishing fleet a group of marriageable girls or young women going to India during the colonial era in the hope of finding a husband amongst the officers serving there. Around 1900–40.

fishy **1** dubious, equivocal, unsound. From around 1844. **2** hence, suspicious, as in *there's something fishy going on.* Since the mid-20th century or earlier.

fit sexually attractive, as in *she's as fit as fuck.* Used by both sexes.

fit the bill *see* **fill the bill.**

fit to be tied very angry, furious, hopping mad. Used in the USA and Canada.

fit-up a situation in which an innocent person is made to appear guilty of a crime. Since the 1930s. *See also* **frame-up.**

fix, n. the taking of a narcotic drug, esp. by injection. Adopted from the USA in the late 1950s.

fix, v. **1** to take one's revenge, esp. with an act of violence, as in *I'll fix them!* Since around 1920. **2** to prepare or plan; to arrange, as in *she's fixing to kill him.* Used in the USA and Canada. **3** *see* **fix (sb) up.**

fixed, be to have money or some other commodity, as in *how are you fixed for cash?; how are we fixed for time?* Later 20th century.

fixer   an agent, esp. Since around 1950.

Fixit, Mr   a person who is known to be able to 'fix' things, in any of the senses of the verb. Later 20th century.

fix (sb) up   1 to provide (sb) with lodgings. From around 1888.   2 to provide (sb) with other necessities, such as money, clothing, or even a romantic or sexual companion. Since the mid-20th century or earlier.

flab   flabbiness, excess fat, obesity. Originally used by slimmers. Since around 1935. A back-formation from *flabby* or an abbreviation of *flabbiness*.

flak   adverse criticism, as in *you'll get a lot of flak for saying that.* Since the late 1940s, but not widespread in the UK until around 1975. From *flak*, German anti-aircraft fire, an abbreviation of the German FLiegerAbwehrKanone, air-defence gun.

flake out   to fall asleep from sheer exhaustion or drunkenness (or, later, from the effects of narcotic drugs). Originally Australian. Since around 1945.

flaky or **flakey**   1 crazy or eccentric in behaviour. Of US origin. Since the late 1960s.   2 of poor or uneven quality. Used by the media in the later 20th century.

flaming hell!   an expletive. 20th century.

flannel, n.   empty and pretentious talk; flattery. Since around 1920.

flannel, v.   to indulge in empty and pretentious talk; to bluff or waffle; to flatter.

flap   great excitement or panic, as in *to be in a flap; there's a flap on.* Probably from around 1916.

flash, v.   to expose one's genitals, suddenly and briefly, in public. Hence **flasher**. 20th century. From the 19th-century expression *to flash (one's) meat.*

flash, adj.   fashionably smart. Used in Australia and New Zealand since the late 19th century and in the UK since the mid-20th century or earlier.

flasher   a sexual exhibitionist, esp. male. *See* **flash** v.

flash Harry   a showy or boastful person.

flatties   flat-heeled (as opposed to high-heeled) shoes. Used by women since around 1945.

flavour of the month   any person or thing that is suddenly very popular. The popularity is usually ephemeral, as in *I realized I was no longer flavour of the month.* Adopted from the USA in the 1980s. From ice-cream advertising.

flea-bag   1 a bed. Around 1835–1915.   2 hence, a sleeping-bag. From around 1909.

flea-pit   a second-rate, dirty or dilapidated cinema. Since around 1918.

flicks, the   the cinema, as in *to go to the flicks*. Since before 1927. From the slang term *flick*, a film, from the flickering effect of the early movies; *see* also **skinflick**.

flies   in the phrase, *there are no flies on him, her,* etc., he, she, etc., is no fool. Since the 19th century. Of US origin.

flip, v.   **1** to become wildly or deliriously elated. Chiefly used in the USA and Canada. From the phrase *to flip (one's) wig*. **2** (sometimes followed by *out*) to go mad; to have a mental breakdown, as in *I think she's flipped*. Adopted from the USA in the 1960s. *See also* **flip (one's) lid, flip (one's) top**.

flip, adj.   flippant. Adopted from the USA around 1950.

flip (one's) lid   to go crazy, to go to the extreme of any emotion, to lose control. Later 20th century. *See* **flip**, v. **2**.

flipping   a derogatory adjectival and adverbial intensifier, as in *the flipping car wouldn't start; I don't flipping well care!* Since around 1920. A euphemism for **fucking**, as in the exclamation *flippin' 'eck!*, fucking hell!

flip side   **1** the reverse side of a record. Adopted from the USA in the late 1950s. **2** the reverse of anything (esp. a less familiar or less desirable aspect), as in *the flip side of this argument; the flip side of La Dolce Vita*. From the early 1980s.

flip (one's) top   to become extremely angry or excited. Used in the USA and Australia.

flip (one's) wig   *see* **flip**, v. **1**.

flob   to spit. Since the 1930s. Perhaps imitative of the sound of spitting, influenced by **gob**, v.

flog   to sell, to offer for sale. Late 19th–20th centuries. The term originally referred to illicit selling.

floozie, floozy, floosie or **floosy**   a girl or young woman, esp. a disreputable or promiscuous one; a good-time girl or prostitute. Since around 1940.

flop   to (go to) sleep.

fluff   esp. in the phrase *a bit of fluff*, a girl or young woman; girls or young women considered collectively. Since around 1903.

flummoxed   confused, often by an unexpected turn of events, and uncertain what course to take. Since the mid-20th century.   **2** disappointed; outwitted; silenced; ruined. From the 1850s.

flunk   to fail in an examination. Adopted from the USA in the early 20th century.

fly a kite   to test public opinion by tentative measures. From around 1926.

fly by the seat of (one's) pants   *see* **seat of (one's) pants**.

flying   under the influence of drugs. Used in the USA since before 1942.

fold (up)   (of a business, plan, etc.) to fail or collapse. Since around 1945.

foodie   a person who is obsessed by food; a connoisseur or gourmet. Early 1980s.

footling   trivial, petty, insignificant, silly, incompetent, as in *we shouldn't argue about such a footling little thing.*

foot on the floor   in *to put one's foot on the floor*, to accelerate; *with one's foot on the floor*, driving very fast, with maximum acceleration. Motorists' slang. Since around 1920.

footy   football, as in *a game of footy; a footy match.* Of Australian origin.

for crying out loud!   an exclamation of annoyance, impatience, etc.; a euphemism for 'for Christ's sake!'. Probably of US origin. From around 1930.

for ever and a day   for an indefinite (but considerable) length of time; an intensification of 'for ever'. Since the mid-20th century.

for free   free, as in *I got it for free.* Adopted from the USA around 1954. The word *for* is superfluous.

for it, be   to be in trouble, to be liable or due for punishment. Since around 1915.

form   1 a criminal record. Since around 1925.   2 situation, position, as in *what's the form?* Since the mid-1920s.

for real, adj. and adv.   real(ly). Often used ironically as in *is he for real?*, is he being serious? Adopted from the USA around 1965.

for starters   for a start; to begin with, as in *for starters, I'd like to know what you're doing here; you can clear up this mess for starters.* Since around 1960.

four by two   a Jew. Rhyming slang; from 1914.

four-letter man   a very objectionable person. Since 1917. From *shit* or some other four-letter word that could be used to describe such a person.

four-letter word   an obscene swearword, often (but not necessarily) of four letters. Since 1929.

fourpenny one   a blow, esp. with the hand, a clip on the ear, as in *to give (sb) a fourpenny one; to get a fourpenny one.* Since around 1910. Perhaps from *fourpenny bit,* rhyming slang for 'hit'.

fox   to puzzle. Since 1939.

foxy   (esp. of a woman) seductive, sexually attractive. Originally used by Black people in the USA; adopted in the UK in the later 1970s.

frame   to incriminate an innocent person with false evidence; to present an unjustified case against (sb). Adopted from the USA around 1924.

frame-up   the act or an instance of framing (sb), as in *the whole thing was just a frame-up: he was completely innocent.* Adopted from the USA around 1940 or earlier. *See also* **fit-up**.

fraught 1 risky or dangerous. Since the early 1960s. Elliptical for *fraught with danger.* 2 very anxious or worried. Since the early 1960s. Possibly from the riskiness of the situation that causes this anxiety, perhaps influenced by *distraught.*

frazzle, to a absolutely, utterly, as in *worn to a frazzle*, exhausted. From a verb meaning 'to fray'.

freak a devotee or enthusiast, as in *computer freak.* Adopted from the USA in the early 1960s. The term is also used as a suffix, as in *eco-freak,* a person who is fanatical about ecological issues.

freak out to have a hallucinogenic experience, esp. an unpleasant one; to suffer a bad trip. Drug users' slang. Since around 1966.

freebie, n. and adj. (sth that is) free of charge, esp. a promotional give-away (e.g. a free sample), or a perk (e.g. a free trip). Adopted from the USA in the later 1970s.

freeloader a person who takes advantage of other people's generosity or hospitality; a person who gate-crashes or gains admittance to publicity lunches, cocktail parties, etc. Adopted from the USA by 1960. Also *freeloading;* the verb *freeload* is less common.

French, v. to perform an act of oral sex, esp. fellatio, on (sb).

Frenchie a condom. Since around 1910. From **French letter**.

French kiss a deep, open-mouthed kiss in which the tongue enters the partner's mouth. Since before 1923.

French letter a condom. From around 1870. The French equivalent is *capote anglaise,* English overcoat.

fresh out of having none, esp. having (just) run out of, as in *sorry, we're fresh out of bacon.* Chiefly US and Canadian.

frig 1 to masturbate. From around 1590. 2 to copulate with. Since the mid-19th century.

frigging an adjectival and adverbial intensifier.

frighteners on, put the to scare. Since around 1930.

frighten the living daylights (or **shit**) **out of** *see* **scare the living daylights out of**.

fritz, on the broken, out of order. Mainly US and Canadian. *See also* **blink, on the**.

frog a French person. From around 1790.

frog in (one's) throat, have a have phlegm in one's throat, causing hoarseness. Possibly since the mid-19th century.

front, n. 1 the seemingly legitimate or respectable façade of a criminal or radical organization. Since the late 1940s. 2 effrontery, impertinence, as in *you've got a lot of front asking me that.*

front, v. to be the leader of a band or group. Since the late 1920s.

front man a go-between; a nominal leader who lacks power but lends respectability to an organization.

front money money paid in advance for drugs. Drug users' slang. Used in the US since before 1969.

frot to rub against another person for sexual stimulation, often surreptitiously, e.g. in a dense crowd.

fruit a male homosexual. Adopted from the USA around 1937. *See also* **old fruit**.

fruit salad a large display of medal ribbons. Used in the armed forces, esp. the RAF, since around 1919.

fruity 1 amorous, sexually aroused. Since around 1955. **2** erotic, sexually stimulating.

f.u. a euphemistic shortening of **fuck-up**. Much used by servicemen during World War II.

fuck, n. 1 an act of sexual intercourse. From 1800. **2** a person considered as a sexual partner, as in *she's a good fuck*. 19th–20th centuries.

fuck, v. to have sexual intercourse (with). Since the 16th century.

fuck all nothing, as in *'What did he tell you?' 'Fuck all.'* *See also* **sweet f.a.**

fucking an adjectival and adverbial intensifier, as in *fucking hell!; it's fucking awful!*

fuck like a mink (esp. of a woman) to be very amorous and promiscuous. Used in Canada since around 1920.

fuck me! an exclamation of surprise, often wry or semi-humorous. Since the late 19th century. The phrase may evoke the jocular response 'Not now!' or 'Later!' or 'No thanks!'

fuck off to depart, to go away. Late 19th–20th centuries.

fuck off! go away!

fuck up, v. to fail dismally; to spoil utterly; to bungle or make a mess of. Since around 1930. Hence to be fucked-up (of sb or sth), to be ruined, mixed up.

fuck-up, n. a blunder; a failure, as in *to make a fuck-up of (sth)*.

fuckwit a fool, an idiot, a dim-witted or half-witted person. Used in Australia since the late 1940s.

fuddy-duddy a fussy, old-fashioned, narrow-minded person. Adopted from the USA around 1944.

full of beans vigorous; energetic; in high spirits. From around 1870.

fun, adj. amusing; interesting, as in *a fun dress; having a fun time*. The term may be applied to anything that would be fun to do, see, wear, eat, etc. Since around 1975.

fun and games 1 a very agreeable time. Since around 1921 **2** (ironic) a difficult or unpleasant time, as in *we had fun and games getting to work during the rail strike*. Later 20th century. **3** sexual intercourse. Since around 1925.

fungus-features a man with a beard; often used as a term of address.

Since around 1950.

funk an earthy, unsophisticated, melancholy kind of song and music (*see* **funky**). First used by Black jazz musicians in the mid-1950s; adopted in the UK around 1960.

funky having the style and feeling of blues or soul music. Used in the USA since around 1958 and in the UK since the early 1960s. *See also* **funk**.

funnies, the the comic strips in a newspaper or magazine. Since around 1946.

funny business a shady transaction, a dubious affair; **hanky-panky**, monkeying about. From around 1890.

funny farm a mental hospital. Since around 1970.

funny money 1 counterfeit money. Since before 1960. 2 hence, any foreign or unfamiliar notes or coins. *See also* **mickey-mouse money**.

fuzz, the the police. Adopted from the USA by 1964.

G

gab-fest a long conversation; an evening of talk (and drink). Adopted from the USA around 1955. From the German *Fest*, feast.

gaff home, house, dwelling-place, as in *they did him in his gaff*, they arrested him at home; *he screwed a gaff*, he robbed a house. Since around 1920.

gaffer the boss, the foreman, the person in command, the person who owns and/or runs an organization. Since the early 18th century.

gaga suffering from senile dementia; dotty, crazy, as in *to go gaga*. Since the 1920s.

gag me with a spoon an expression of disgust, as in *gag me with a spoon!*, oh that's disgusting; *you gag me with a spoon*, you make me sick. Early 1980s.

galah 1 a simpleton, a fool. Australian. Since around 1930. Probably from the old bush saying *as mad as a treeful* (or *gumtree full*) *of galahs*; a *galah* is a large pink-and-grey cockatoo. 2 a chap, a fellow. Australian.

gam an act of oral sex, esp. fellatio. Short for *gamaroosh* (or *gamaruche*), which dates from the 19th century and is probably of French derivation.

game as Ned Kelly, as extremely brave. Australian. Late 19th–20th centuries. From the famous bushranger, who held out against the police for two years.

game sewn up, have the to be in a position where one cannot lose; to have a monopoly. Mostly Australian. Since around 1925. *See also* **sewn up.**

gammy 1 false, spurious; forged. Since before 1839. 2 of low quality, as in *gammy gear*, inferior goods. Since the late 19th century. 3 injured; lame, as in *my gammy leg*. Since the late 19th century.

gander a look, as in *let's have a gander*. Since 1941 The term originally referred to a look over another person's shoulder at a letter, newspaper, etc, and probably alluded to a *gander* (male goose) craning its long neck.

ganga *see* **ganja.**

gang-bang sexual intercourse between one woman and several men in succession. The woman may or may not be a willing participant. Since around 1950.

gang up on (sb) (of a group of people) to combine against (sb). Since the late 1940s.

ganja, ganga or **gunja** cannabis, marijuana. Drug users' slang. Since around 1920. From Hindi.

gaol-bait *see* **jail-bait**.

gas a joke, a jest; a very amusing situation, as in *what a gas!* Since around 1945.

gash, n. 1 the female genitalia. 18th–20th centuries. 2 a girl or woman; women considered collectively as sex objects, as in *is there any gash around?* 20th century. 3 waste, rubbish; surplus. Since around 1910.

gash, adj. spare, available. Since around 1915.

gaslight, v. to create an illusion for the purpose of frightening or deceiving (sb).

gasper a cigarette. From around 1912. The term originally referred to an inferior cigarette.

gat a revolver. Of US origin; used in the UK since around 1924, thanks to gangster novels and film. From *Gatling gun,* a 19th-century machine-gun with clustered barrels.

gate-crasher a person who attends a private party or entertainment without invitation. Adopted from the USA in 1926. Hence the verb *gate-crash* and the noun *gate-crashing. See also* **crash 3**.

gate fever the restlessness that affects long-term prisoners nearing the end of their sentence. Prison slang. Since around 1920.

gay, n. and adj. (a) homosexual. In modern usage the term is more frequently applied to male homosexuals than to lesbians. This meaning is no longer slang. Used in the USA since 1945 and in the UK since around 1955. In 19th-century slang the adjective *gay* was applied to female prostitutes.

gazump 1 to swindle. Since 1934 or earlier. 2 to demand a higher price from a buyer, esp. of a house, after the purchase has been agreed (but before the contracts have been signed). The vendor may have been offered a higher price by another prospective buyer, or may simply wish to take advantage of a general rise in prices. This immoral practice, and hence the use of the term in this sense, became widespread in the early 1970s. *See also* **gazunder,** v.

gazunder or **gazunda,** n. a chamber-pot, so called because it *goes under* the bed.

gazunder, v. (of a house-buyer) to force a vendor to reduce the price of a house by withdrawing (or threatening to withdraw) from the purchase; to reduce one's offer, esp. just before the contracts are signed and exchanged. Adopted in the late 1980s, during the slump in the property market. A blend of **gazump** and *under*, perhaps influenced by the noun **gazunder**.

GBP (often ironic)   the Great British Public. Since around 1950 or earlier.

GCMG *see* **CMG**.

gear, n.   1 stolen property. Since around 1930.   2 clothes. Mostly used by young people, since around 1950.   3 drugs, esp. marijuana or heroin. Drug users' slang. Since the late 1940s.   4 supplies of drugs, syringes, etc. Drug users' slang of the 1970s.

gear, adj.   excellent. Originally Merseyside slang. Since 1955 or earlier.

gee, v.   to encourage, to incite. Since before 1932.

gee!   an exclamation of surprise, admiration, regret, etc. Mostly US. Since the mid-19th century. A euphemism for 'Jesus!', originally spelt *Jee! See also* **gee whiz(z)!**

geek   1 a foolish or contemptible person, usu. a man; 19th century.   2 a carnival performer who bites the head off a live animal; from the USA since the 1940s.   3 a (long) look. Australian. Since World War I.

gee whiz(z)!   an elaboration of **gee!** Late 19th–20th centuries.

geezer   a person, usually a man, as in *an old geezer*. Since the 1880s, when the term was more frequently applied to women. Possibly from *guiser*, a mummer, or from the Basque *giza*, man, fellow.

gelt   money. From Yiddish. Since the 17th century.

gen, n.   information. Since around 1929. From the phrase 'for the general information of . . .'.

gen up   1 to learn, esp. quickly; to swot or study, as in *I must gen up on that*. Since around 1933.   2 to inform or brief (sb), as in *have you genned her up?* Since around 1933.

George   an automatic pilot. Since around 1928.

get, n.   a fool, as in *you stupid get!* Since around 1930. From the noun *get*, offspring, bastard. *See also* **git**.

get, v.   to annoy or worry, as in *what gets me about him is his confounded complacency*. Used in the USA since around 1880 and in the UK from around 1920.

get (one's) act together   1 to take concerted and effective action, as in *if the heads of department get their act together, this college will really go places*. Adopted from the USA in the later 20th century.   2 to organize (one's) talents and abilities, as in *you won't impress any potential employer unless you get your act together. See also* **get it together; get (one's) shit together**.

get a wiggle on   (usu. imperative) to get a move on; to look lively; to hurry. Since before 1950.

get cracking   (usu. imperative) to get a move on; to respond immediately. Since around 1925. From the *cracking* of a whip.

get (sb's) goat   *see* **goat, get (sb's).**

get (one's) head down   *see* **head down, get (one's).**

get in bad with   *see* **bad with, get in.**

get in (sb's) hair   *see* **hair, get in (sb's).**

get into bed with   *see* **bed with, get into.**

get it together   to gain control of oneself, to become organized. Adopted from the USA in the early 1960s. *See also* **get (one's) act together 2; get (one's) shit together; together.**

get it up   to achieve an erection, as in *he can't get it up.* Adopted from the USA in the mid-1940s.

get knotted!   an angry or derisive exclamation of rejection, refusal, etc. Since around 1930.

get (one's) leg over   *see* **leg over, get (one's).**

get off   esp. in *to tell (sb) where to get off,* to rebuke or scold; to tell (sb) to stop (being a nuisance, being obnoxious or presumptuous, etc.), as in *he put his hand up her skirt and she told him where to get off.* Adopted from the USA around 1929.

get off on   to derive pleasure and enjoyment from, as in *she gets off on classical music.* Used in the USA since the mid-1960s and in the UK in the later 1970s.

get off with   to establish a romantic or sexual relationship with. Since around 1914.

get on (sb's) tits   to irritate or annoy.

get on (sb's) wick   to exasperate, irritate or annoy. Since around 1920. From *wick,* penis (*see* **Hampton Wick**).

get-out   an escape from a difficult or dangerous position. Since the 19th century.

get out of it!   a dismissive exclamation, directed at animals, trespassers, etc.

get (one's) shit together   a variant of **get (one's) act together 2,** or **get it together.** Adopted from the USA in the later 20th century.

get stuck in   1 to start work, esp. hard and seriously, as in *right, let's get stuck in!* Later 20th century. 2 to tuck into one's food. Later 20th century.

get stuffed!   an exclamation of contemptuous or defiant refusal or dismissal. From **stuff, v. 1.**

get the chop   *see* **chop, get the.**

get the (or sb's) drift   to understand, to follow, as in *do you get my drift?; OK, I get the drift.* Often used in a threat, as in *if you do that again, I'll flatten you. Get the drift?*

get the goods on   *see* **goods on, get the.**

get-up-and-go energy, initiative, drive, courage. The term is often used in the pun *my get-up-and-go just got up and went.* Adopted from the USA by 1950.

get up (sb's) nose *see* **nose.**

get (one's) wires crossed *see* **wires crossed.**

ghetto-blaster a portable stereo radio/cassette player, esp. when used at full volume out of doors. Since the early 1980s. *See also* **boogie-box; Brixton briefcase.**

ghost a person with no tax record, esp. one who is working in the black economy. Late 1980s.

GI a US soldier (not an officer). Adopted from the USA in 1943. Perhaps from the initial letters of Government Issue.

giddy aunt!, my an exclamation of surprise. Since 1919. *See also* **sainted aunt!, my.**

giddy limit, the the last straw, the final touch, the utmost, as much as (or more than) one can bear, as in *that's the giddy limit!* An intensification of **limit.** *See also* **dizzy limit.**

gig 1 an engagement to play at a party, dance, concert, etc., for one evening. Since around 1935. 2 Hence, a concert, usually of pop or rock music.

gimmick any device, plan or trick calculated to attract attention and/or ensure success, esp. in advertising. Since around 1946.

ginormous (pronounced *jynormous*) very large. Since World War II. A blend of *gigantic* and *enormous.*

gip or **gyp,** v. to cheat, to swindle, as in *I was gipped of a day's pay.* Adopted from the USA around 1930.

gip or **gyp,** n. in *to give (sb) gip,* to cause (sb) pain, as in *my back's giving me gip.* Since around 1905.

gippo or **gyppo** 1 a gypsy. 2 an Egyptian. Late 19th–20th centuries.

gippy (or **gyppy**) **tummy** stomach trouble, esp. diarrhoea, suffered by visitors to Egypt. Since the late 19th century. *See also* **Delhi belly.**

girlie magazine a magazine containing many pictures of female nudes or semi-nudes in provocative poses. Adopted from the USA in the late 1950s.

gism *see* **jissom.**

gismo *see* **gizmo.**

gissum *see* **jissom.**

git a fool. Since around 1920. From the noun *get,* offspring, bastard. *See also* **get,** n.

give (sth) a go to make an attempt at (sth); to experiment or try, as in *I've no idea what it'll be like, but let's give it a go anyway.* Since the early 20th century.

give (sth) a miss to refrain from or avoid doing (sth), as in *'Are you* *going down the pub?' 'No, I think I'll give it a miss tonight.'* Since around 1912. From a phrase used in billiards.

give (sb) gip   *see* **gip**, n.

give head   to perform an act of oral sex, esp. fellatio. Adopted from the USA in the later 20th century. *See also* **head job**.

give over!   1 stop it! Referring to an activity that is annoying the speaker. 2 I don't believe you! you're joking! as in *'He said he only weighs 50 kilos.' 'Give over!'*

give (sb) stick   *see* **stick 2, 3**.

give (sb) the big E   *see* **big E**.

give (sb) the brush-off   *see* **brush-off**.

give (sb) the elbow   *see* **elbow**.

give (sb) the finger   *see* **finger**, n. **1**.

give (sb or sth) the (old) heave-ho   *see* **heave-ho**.

give (sb) the shits   1 to get on (sb's) nerves; to be intensely disliked by (sb). Since the mid-20th century. 2 to frighten (sb).

give (sb) what for   to beat or thrash; to scold or reprimand. Since the 19th century.

gizm   *see* **jissom**.

gizmo or **gismo**   a gadget, device or appliance, as in *an electronic gizmo.* Adopted from the USA in the late 1960s.

gizzum   *see* **jissom**.

glad eye, the   a come-hither look, as in *give (sb) the glad eye, to get the glad eye.* Early 20th century. From an obsolete sense of *glad*, bright.

glad rags   one's best clothes, as in *get your glad rags on: we're going out tonight.* Adopted from the USA around 1906.

glam   glamorous. Since around 1950.

glammed up   all dressed up and made up, esp. for a party, dance or date. Since around 1955.

glass, v.   to hit (sb) with a drinking-glass, esp. a broken one; to cut or slash (sb) with a piece of broken glass, a broken bottle or other jagged glass edge. Since around 1910.

glasshouse   a guardroom, esp. detention barracks or cells for long-term prisoners. Army slang, from around 1905. From the *Glass House*, a nickname for the military prison at North Camp, Aldershot, which had a glass roof and was particularly dreaded for its severity.

glitch   a malfunction; a problem; a snag. The term originally referred to a small voltage surge affecting sensitive devices, and was applied to a malfunction in a spacecraft. Adopted from the USA around 1964. Possibly from a Yiddish word for 'slip'.

glitterati, the   flashy, publicity-conscious people who have achieved success in the creative arts. Since the early 1980s. Perhaps from *glitter* (or the clichéd *glittering prizes* attained by such people), punningly blended with *the literati*, scholarly people.

glitzy glamorous, flashily stylish. Adopted from the USA in the early 1980s. Possibly a blend of *glitter* (or *glamour*) and **ritzy**.

glooms, the a mood or fit of depression; gloominess, despondency. Anglo-Irish slang of the late 19th–20th centuries.

glop any viscous substance, such as blancmange, baby-food or wallpaper paste. Later 20th century.

glossies magazines printed on glossy paper. Adopted from the USA around 1945.

gnat's piss a weak, insipid beverage, esp. beer or tea. *See also* **piss**, n. **2**.

gnomes of Zurich international (originally Swiss) bankers and financiers. Later 20th century.

go, n. a try; a turn; an attempt; a chance, as in *can I have a go now?*; *you've had three goes, I've only had two*. Since the early 19th century. *See also* **give (sth) a go**.

go, v. to say. Used when reporting direct speech, as in *he goes 'I don't want to', so she goes 'well, that's it, then'*.

go a bundle on *see* **bundle**, n. **2**.

go-ahead an order or permission to proceed, as in *to give (sb) the go-ahead; to get the go-ahead*. Later 20th century.

goalie a goalkeeper.

go all the way to have full sexual intercourse, as opposed to just petting, as in *we kissed and cuddled, but we didn't go all the way; she let him go all the way*. Since around 1920.

goat, get (sb's) to annoy (sb). Adopted from the USA around 1916. Perhaps from the French phrase *prendre la chèvre*, to take the goat that was a poor person's sole source of milk.

gob, n. mouth, as in *shut your gob!* Perhaps from Gaelic. Since the 17th century.

gob, v. to spit, esp. copiously. Since the 19th century.

gobble, n. and v. (to perform) an act of oral sex, esp. fellatio. 18th–20th centuries.

gobbledygook pompous or long-winded speech or writing, heavily laced with jargon. Coined in the USA in 1944; well-known in the UK by 1951. From the fussy, self-important gobbling sound made by a turkey cock.

gobshite a fool; a contemptible person.

gobsmacked rendered speechless by astonishment, anger, etc. Originally used in north-west England, esp. Liverpool; more widespread since the mid-1980s.

God-awful an intensification of *awful*.

God-botherer **1** a parson. From around 1920. **2** an excessively pious person.

go down (or **drop**) **like flies**   to succumb to an epidemic or other adversity, as in *the workers went down like flies as the virus spread.* Probably from the effect of cold weather (or fly-spray) on flies.

go down (south) on   to perform an act of fellatio or cunnilingus on.

God slot   a religious programme on radio or TV; a period of time (esp. on Sunday) set aside for such programmes. Originally broadcasters' slang.

go Dutch   to pay one's own share instead of being treated, e.g. to drinks, a meal, an outing or entertainment, *my girlfriend and I usually go Dutch.* Possibly since the mid-20th century. From *Dutch treat.*

goer   a person who enthusiastically seeks sexual satisfaction. Since the late 1940s.

gofer   a person who runs errands for others; a general dogsbody who is told to *go for* this or that. Adopted from the USA around 1980. Perhaps influenced by *gopher*, a burrowing rodent found in the USA.

go for broke   1 to risk everything. Used in gambling, betting and other hazardous ventures since before 1930.   2 to try to crash through the broken part of a wave. Australian surfers' slang. Since around 1960.

go-getter   a person who is very active, enterprising, ambitious or pushy. Adopted from the USA around 1925. From the phrase *to go (and) get what one wants.*

gogglebox   a television set. Since around 1958.

gogo girl (or **dancer**)   a performer of erotic dances in striptease clubs. Since the 1960s. From the French *à gogo*, galore.

going for   in *to have a lot* (or *not much*) *going for one* (or *it*), to have a lot of (or not many) advantages or merits. Since around 1970.

going-over   any process (often disagreeable) applied to a person or thing, such as an examination, inspection, interrogation, physical attack, robbery, etc., as in *he got a thorough going-over*, he was badly beaten up; *they gave the house a good going-over*, they searched and robbed it.

going's good, while the   while there is still the opportunity or possibility; while things are going well, before they take a turn for the worse, as in *to go* (or *get out*) *while the going's good.* From around 1912.

gold-digger   a woman who attaches herself to a rich man. Used in the US since around 1925 and in the UK by 1930. Hence the noun *gold-digging.*

golden handshake   a large gift of money to a departing director or important employee. From around 1950. Since the late 1970s the term has been applied to any lump-sum payment to any redundant employee.

golden oldie   a hit song, tune or record that has lasted well and is still popular; a former hit that is remembered with nostalgia or is enjoying a revival. Disc jockeys' slang.

golf ball a protective, pressurized dome housing a ground radar installation. Later 20th century. From the colour and shape, seen from a distance.

golf widow a woman who is isolated by her partner's zeal for golf. From around 1920.

go native to mix with the local people, adopting their customs and way of life. The term is often applied to expatriate Britons settling in non-European or tropical countries, or to Londoners settling in the provinces.

gone in a state of ecstasy or euphoria induced by drugs, music, etc. Adopted from the USA around 1948.

gong a medal or other decoration. Since the late 19th century.

goo any semi-liquid, viscous or sticky substance. Later 20th century. Perhaps from the slang term *burgoo*, porridge or thick stew.

good and . . . properly, thoroughly, absolutely, as in *I'll come when I'm good and ready, and not before!*

good for you! well done! excellent work!; splendid news! Also *good for him!*, *good for her!*, etc. From around 1910. *See also* **good on you!**

goodie or **goody** a good person or hero in a film, story, game, etc., as in *the goodies and the baddies; she's one of the goodies. See also* **baddie**.

good on you! a chiefly Australian variant of **good for you!**

goods on, get the to learn the truth about, to get the **low-down** on. Adopted from the USA around 1943.

good thing, be on to a to stumble on or be pursuing something advantageous or profitable. Later 20th century.

good value (esp. of people) worth having. Used in Australia and New Zealand since around 1920 and in the UK in the later 20th century.

goody *see* **goodie**.

gooey 1 viscous or semi-viscous. Since the mid-1930s. From **goo**.
  2 hence, excessively sentimental; infatuated, as in *I go all gooey when he looks into my eyes*. Since 1936.

goof, n. a silly or stupid person. Since 1922 or earlier.

goof, v. 1 to blunder. Since around 1950. 2 *see* **goof off**.

goof balls drugs in pill or tablet form, taken alone or in a drink, that produce exhilaration. Of US origin. In the UK the term has been applied to barbiturates since the 1970s.

go off the deep end *see* **deep end**.

goof off to play the fool. Used in the USA and Canada.

goofy 1 stupid, dull-witted, crazy. Since around 1935. From **goof**, n.
  2 excessively sentimental; infatuated, as in *to be goofy about (sb)*.
  3 awkward, diffident, given to unintentional faux pas. Since around 1950.

gook   a Filipino. US slang. The term has also been applied to the Japanese, Vietnamese, Koreans and other peoples of the Pacific and the Far East.

goolies   testicles. Since the late 19th century. From the Hindi *gooli*, pellet.

goon   1 a stupid or dull person. Perhaps a blend of **goof** and **loon**. Since the 1930s.   2 a person with a wild, surrealist and zany sense of humour. From 'The Goon Show', a BBC radio comedy series of the 1950s, which exemplified this type of humour. Hence *goonery*, *goonish*.

goose   to jab a finger up between a person's legs or buttocks from the rear, in order to surprise or annoy. Since around 1944.

goose's (neck)   *see* **sausage**, v.

go places   1 to travel extensively; to gad about, esp. in *to go places and see* things. Adopted from the USA around 1938.   2 to become successful, as in *he's really going places*. Since the mid-20th century.

gorblimey! or **cor blimey!**   an exclamation of surprise; a corruption of 'God blind me!' Originally Cockney slang. Since 1870. *See also* **blimey!**

Gordon Bennett!   a mild expletive, sometimes used as a euphemistic replacement for 'God!' (pronounced *gawd*). Probably from James Gordon Bennett (1795–1872), founder and editor of the *New York Herald*, or his son of the same name.

go slumming   to mix with one's inferiors. Since around 1905.

go spare   *see* **spare** 1.

go steady   (usually of young people) to enter or be in a long-term romantic or sexual relationship, as in they've been going steady for several months.

go the (full) distance   *see* **distance**.

go through the motions   *see* **motions, go through the**.

go through the roof   to become extremely angry, to fly into a rage. Since around 1960. A later intensification of **hit the roof**.

go to town   to tackle with zest, as in *I went to town on the spring-cleaning; he really went to town on them*, he punished them severely. Adopted, probably from US servicemen, around 1943.

got you!   I understand, and will comply. Since around 1940.

graft   work, labour, esp. in the phrase *hard graft*. From around 1870.

gramp or **gramps**   grandfather. Mostly used by children, as a term of address, in Southern England. Since the mid-19th century.

gran   grandmother. Late 19th–20th centuries.

grand   a thousand pounds (£1,000), as in *it'll cost you fifty grand*. Adopted from the USA, where the term refers to the sum of $1,000. Since around 1940.

grand-daddy of them all, the   a person who has been pre-eminent in his or her field for a long time. Later 20th century. *See also* **daddy of them all.**

grandstand, v.   to play to the crowd; to show off. Of US origin. Hence the noun *grandstanding.*

grapevine, the   the means by which secret information or rumours are circulated, as in *I heard it on the grapevine.* Adopted from the USA around 1920.

grass, n.   **1** an informer. Since before 1933. *See also* **supergrass**. Possibly from the slang term *grasshopper*, rhyming slang for 'copper', referring to a policeman or his informer. *See* **grass**, v.   **2** cannabis, marijuana. Adopted from the USA around 1965.   **3** *see* **put (sb) out to grass.**

grass, v.   (sometimes followed by *on* or *up*) to inform on (sb). From around 1930. *See* **grass**, n. **1**.

Grauniad, the   a nickname for the *Guardian* newspaper, renowned for its typographical errors. Since around 1976. The term was coined by the satirical magazine *Private Eye.*

graveyard shift   a night shift. Since around 1915.

gravy train, the   easy money, esp. from a well-paid but undemanding job in politics, commerce or industry, as in *to ride the gravy train.* Of US origin; not widely used in the UK until the mid-1970s.

greaser   a member of a gang of rowdy or aggressive young people, esp. motorcyclists. Since the early 1960s. From the heavily oiled long hair of these people.

greasy spoon   a small, cheap and cheerful café, esp. one that specializes in cheap, fried food. Of US origin. From the state of the cutlery.

greatest, the   the best. Adopted from the USA around 1961. Popularized by the US boxer Muhammad Ali's proclamation 'I am the greatest'.

great guns   in *to go* (or *be going*) *great guns*, to get along extremely well.

great stuff   a term of approbation applied to any person, thing or situation that is excellent.

great unwashed, the   the proletariat, the masses. Since the late 18th century.

Great White Chief, the   the head of any establishment or organization. The term was originally applied to a head of department in the Civil Service. Since around 1910.

greenback   **1** a dollar bill (i.e. note). Used in the USA and Canada. From the colour of the note.   **2** a pound note. Green pound notes were issued by the Bank of England from 1917 to 1989, except for the period 1940–48, when they were blue.

green fingers esp. in *to have green fingers*, to be a successful (amateur) gardener. Since around 1925 or earlier. The US equivalent, *green thumb*, may have been the original form of the phrase in the UK.

green wellie brigade, the the county set, or those who aspire to membership of this set, esp. **yuppies** who have moved to the country. Since the early 1980s. From the green wellington boots favoured by such people. *See also* **yellow wellie.**

grey, n. a middle-aged, conventionally dressed (or minded) person. Since the mid-1960s.

grim unpleasant, as in *how did your appraisal go? It was a bit grim.* 20th century.

grind, n. 1 (an act of) sexual intercourse. Since the late 16th century. 2 daily routine; hard or distasteful work. Since the mid-19th century.

grind, v. to copulate. Since the late 16th century.

Gringo an English or Anglo-American person. Used by the inhabitants of South America. From the Spanish gringo, gibberish, referring to the language spoken by foreigners.

gripe, v. to complain, as in *what are you griping about?* Probably late 19th–20th centuries. From the pains of colic.

gripe, n. a complaint. Since around 1915.

grizzle-guts a tearfully or whiningly ill-tempered or melancholy person. From around 1875.

grockle a tourist, holiday-maker, visitor or outsider. Used in Devon since 1962 or earlier, the term became more widespread in the 1970s. Possibly from *Grock, the name of a famous clown.* Hence *grockle bait,* cheap arcades; *grockle fodder,* fish and chips. *See also* **emmet.**

grog-blossom a pimple caused by strong drink. Since before 1791.

groggy in poor health, faint, nauseous or hungover. In the 19th century it meant inebriated; from *grog,* alcoholic drink.

groove, in the 1 getting absorbed by the rhythm of music, esp. jazz, rhythm and blues, and funk. The phrase originally referred to jazz musicians and was subsequently applied to listeners. Adopted from the USA around 1940. 2 working properly, esp. after a momentary lapse of concentration or coordination, as in *to be back in the groove.* Later 20th century.

groovy excellent; a term of approbation used by teenagers in the 1960s and 1970s. Of US origin.

gross an all-purpose adjective of disapproval, as in *that's really gross!* Used by children and young people from the mid-1980s.

grot dirt, filth. Since the 1960s. A back-formation from **grotty.**

grotty bad, inferior, disagreeable, crummy, lousy, as in *a grotty flat; the weather was grotty.* Originally Liverpool slang, popularized by the

Beatles and others during the 1960s. From the adjective *grotesque*.

ground floor 1 in *to let (sb) in on the ground floor*, to allow (sb) to share in a financial or commercial speculation on equal terms. Adopted from the USA around 1900. 2 in *to be in on the ground floor*, to be in at the beginning of a project, venture, trend, development, etc. Later 20th century.

groupie a (typically teenage) camp-follower of pop or rock groups; somebody who associates with pop or rock musicians for social and sexual purposes. Since around 1965.

grouse, v.   to grumble. From around 1850.

grouse, n.   a grumble. Since around 1890.

grovel, grovel! an expression accompanying an abject apology. Later 20th century.

growler a low-lying mass of ice that is indistinguishable from the surrounding sea at night. Mostly nautical slang. Since around 1910.

grubstake an advance payment given to authors to keep them going while they write their books. Used by publishers and authors from around 1920. The term is derived from the US and Canadian practice (dating back to the mid-19th century) whereby a person with capital provides gold-prospectors with food and, if necessary, equipment. Also used as a verb.

gruesome twosome two people who are frequently inseparable. Of US origin.

grunge, n.   1 a youth movement since the late 1980s, characterized by a deliberately tattered and grimy look. Grunge anti-fashion consists of layers of flannel shirts and cardigans, baseball caps worn back to front and clumpy footwear. It is chiefly associated with Seattle where several grunge rock bands are also from, but it has become more widespread; *grunge music* is typified by thrashing guitars. 2 a devotee of grunge. *See also* **grungy**.

grungette, n.   a female devotee of **grunge 1**.

grungy dirty; unwashed and smelly; squalid. Since the early 1970s. Perhaps a blend of **grotty** and *gungy* (*see* **gunge**).

gubbins 1 rubbish. Late 19th–20th centuries. From the earlier (17th-century) meaning: fish-offal.   2 thingummy; anything that one is too lazy or forgetful to name. Since around 1918.   3 odds and ends; trimmings, as in *steak with all the gubbins*. Since around 1919.

guessing-stick a slide-rule. Since around 1950 or earlier.

gues(s)timate a rough calculation. The term is also used as a verb, meaning 'to calculate approximately'. Adopted from the USA by 1950. A blend of *guess* and *estimate*.

guff official information, as in *to give (sb) the guff on (sth)*. Since around

1945.

guiver flattery; artfulness; make-believe; pretence. From around 1880.

gum up the works to spoil or upset things. Adopted from the USA around 1915.

gun, v. to accelerate a car. This term supplanted the earlier phrase *to give (her) the gun* around 1935.

gun for esp. in *to be gunning for (sb)*, to seek sb in order to cause him or her serious trouble, or to reprimand, punish, harm or kill him or her. Adopted from the USA around 1944. From the hunting and shooting of game.

gung-ho actively and militaristically jingoistic. The term was coined in the USA during World War II by a brigadier of the US Marine Corps, as a rallying call for his battalion, from a Chinese phrase that he interpreted as 'work together'.

gunge grease; oily dirt; sticky or congealed matter. Since around 1940. Hence the verb *gunge (up)* and the adjectives *gungy* and *gunged up*.

gunja *see* **ganja**.

gunk 1 dirt; viscous or slimy matter. In the UK the term is used as a tradename for a chemical cleanser; in Canada is has been applied to chemical compounds, esp. those that provide solid fuel for space rockets. 2 rubbish or trash (in the non-physical sense). The term may be applied, for example, to a radio or TV broadcast that is technically and/or artistically deficient. Since the late 1960s.

gut, adj. arising from or typified by what is fundamental, essential or natural, as in *gut feeling or gut reaction*.

gutless cowardly. From the noun *guts*, in the colloquial sense of 'courage'. *See also* **gutsy**.

gut-rot 1 food or alcoholic drink of inferior quality. *See also* **rot-gut**. 2 pain in the stomach; intestinal trouble.

gutsy courageous. *See also* **gutless**.

gutted disgusted, fed-up. Footballers' slang of the early 1980s.

guy a man; chap, fellow, as in *one of the guys I work with*. Adopted from the USA by 1903, the term did not become popular in the UK until the 1960s. Today it is often applied to both sexes, as in *come on you guys, lets go*.

gynae gynaecology. The term is also used attributively, as in *the gynae ward; the famous gynae man*. Medical slang of the late 19th–20th centuries.

gyp *see* **gip**.

gyppo *see* **gippo**.

gyppy tummy *see* **gippy tummy**.

H

H   heroin. Drug users' slang. Adopted from the USA around 1945. *See also* **H and C; Harry**.

habdabs   *see* **abdabs**.

hack, v.   **1** to cope with, surmount or achieve a (usually) difficult task, as in *do you reckon you can hack it?* Since the late 1950s.   **2** hence, to endure boredom, danger, privation, etc., as in *we can hack it for a couple of months, can't we?*   **3** to break into a computer network. *See also* **hacker**.

hacked off   utterly bored; irritated, angry. Since the late 1950s.

hacker   **1** an unauthorized person who breaks into a computer network. Since the early 1980s.   **2** hence, any computer enthusiast.

hackette   a female journalist. Journalists' slang of the later 1970s. From *hack*, literary drudge, mediocre journalist.

hair, get in (sb's)   to annoy or irritate (sb). Adopted from the USA around 1930.

hair of the dog that bit (one)   an alcoholic drink taken as a hangover cure, esp. a drink of the same substance that caused the previous night's drunkenness. Since before 1546. Often shortened to *hair of the dog* in 20th-century usage. From an ancient notion that the burnt hair of a dog is an antidote to its bite.

hairy   **1** unpleasant; rough. Since around 1935.   **2** hence, dangerous and/or exciting. Since around 1945.

hairy-arsed   (of a man) hirsute, mature and virile. Since around 1947.

half   in . . . *and a half*, used as an intensifier, as in *it was a problem and a half*, a very tricky problem; *he's a cunt and a half*, an extraordinarily obnoxious person. Possibly since around 1930.

half a mo   half a moment, a very short time, as in *I'll be with you in half a mo*; *half a mo! I'm not ready yet!*, *wait a moment!* Late 19th–20th centuries.

half-and-half   sexual intercourse and fellatio, esp. provided by a prostitute, as in *give me a half-and-half.* Prostitutes' slang.

half brass   a promiscuous woman who does not accept money in return for her favours. Mid-20th century.

half-inch, v.   to steal. Rhyming slang for 'pinch'. Since before 1914.

half-iron   a person who associates with homosexuals but is not homosexual. Mid-20th century. *See also* **iron hoof**.

half-pint a nickname for a short person. The term is often used in a complimentary or affectionate manner. Since around 1925.

ham, n. 1 an amateur radio operator. Adopted from the USA in 1936. 2 an inferior actor, one who overacts or employs stock mannerisms. Adopted from the USA in the late 19th century.

ham, v. to be an inferior actor, to act badly. Adopted from the USA around 1939. *See also* **ham it up**.

ham-fisted clumsy, maladroit. Since the mid-1930s.

ham it up to overact, esp. deliberately. Adopted from the USA by 1945. *See also* **ham**, v.

hammer to defeat severely, as in *Southampton were hammered by Liverpool in yesterday's match*. Since around 1940.

Hampstead Heath teeth. Rhyming slang. From around 1880. Often abbreviated to **'Ampsteads**.

Hampton Wick penis. Rhyming slang for 'prick'. Late 19th–20th centuries. Often abbreviated to *Hampton*. *See also* **dip (one's) wick; get on (sb's) wick**.

H and C heroin and cocaine taken together. Since around 1965. A pun on *H and C*, hot and cold water. *See also* **C; H**.

handful a troublesome person, esp. a child, as in *her youngest is a right handful*.

hand it to (sb) to give credit to (sb); to admit the superiority of (sb), as in *you've got to hand it to him, he's a bloody good cook*. Adopted from the USA by 1914.

hand job masturbation, as in *she gave me a hand job*. Later 20th century.

handle, n. 1 a title, such as Dr, Mrs, Sir, Lady, etc. Since the mid-19th century. 2 the name or nickname by which a person is known. Later 20th century. 3 a person's call sign on Citizen's Band radio.

handle, v. to control or cope with, as in *his problem is, he just can't handle drink; when she blows her top, I can't handle it any more*. Later 20th century.

handlebar moustache or **handlebars** a moustache resembling the handlebars of bicycle. Since around 1910.

hand-out a gift of money (or food, clothing, etc.) to the needy. Adopted from the USA around 1920.

hang about! wait a moment! Since around 1960.

hang on 1 to wait. 2 (imperative) *hang on; don't be so hasty!; hang on, be reasonable!* Since the mid-19th century.

hang on by the (or **one's**) **eyelashes** (or **eyebrows**) to be near to ruin, death or defeat.

hang one on (sb) to strike (sb), esp. in the eye. Adopted from the USA in the late 1960s.

hang-up 1 any emotional or psychological problem or inhibition, as in *he's got a hang-up about undressing in front of other people.* Later 20th century. *See also* **hung up 3**. 2 any considerable difficulty, esp. if irritating or frustrating. *See also* **hung up 1**.

hang up (one's) boots to be forced by age, ill-health, etc., to stop playing football. The word *boots* may be replaced by the tools of another trade, as in *to hang up (one's) tits* (of a female impersonator).

hang up (one's) hat to die. From the mid-19th century.

hanky-panky 1 trickery. Since before 1841. 2 hence, sexual intercourse, esp. illicit sex. 20th century.

ha'p'orth 1 a term of contempt, as in *you daft ha'p'orth!* *See also* **soppy ha'p'orth**. 2 in *a ha'p'orth of (sth)*, a contemptibly small amount, as in *it won't make a ha'p'orth of difference.* A contraction of *halfpennyworth*, a very small amount.

happen to achieve success. Probably of US origin.

happen for (sb) with (sth) to be a success, as in *I hope it happens for her with this one*, I hope this one will be a success. Since around 1965.

happening, adj. presently in vogue; trendy or fashionable, as in *that new club really is the happening place.* From the USA; since the 1980s it has become a vogue word.

happy as Larry, as very happy. Late 19th–20th centuries.

happy hour a period early in the evening when a pub or bar offers drinks at less than the normal price, to boost trade. Adopted from the USA in the early 1970s.

hard knocks *see* **school of hard knocks**.

hard man a tough person; a hard case. Since around 1950.

hard-nosed 1 stubborn, unyielding. Adopted from the USA in the late 1960s. 2 full of common sense; shrewd or practical. Since the 1970s.

hard-on an erection of the penis, as in *to have a hard-on.* Since the late 19th century.

hard stuff 1 (usually *the hard stuff*) whisky or other spirits. *See also* **drop of the hard (stuff)**. 2 morphine or other hard drugs. Used in the USA since before 1955.

hard word on, put the to ask for something, esp. a loan. The phrase may be applied to any request or approach that is difficult or unpleasant to make. Used in Australia since before 1914.

hare to run very fast. Late 19th–20th centuries.

Harry heroin. Drug users' slang. Used in the USA since before 1954. An elaboration of **H**.

Harry Tate a state; emotional confusion; nervous excitement, as in *she was in a right Harry Tate.* Rhyming slang. From around 1920. *See also* **two-and-eight**.

hash 1 hashish. Drug users' slang. Since the early 1960s. 2 mess, bad job, as in *to make a hash of (sth)*, to bungle or spoil (sth). Since the mid-18th century. *See also* **hash up**.

hash tea   a concoction of herbs (containing cannabis). Drug users' slang of the later 20th century.

hash up   to spoil or ruin. Since the late 19th century. *See also* **hash 2**.

hassle, n.   fuss, trouble; a disagreement or row, as in *I don't want any hassle*. Of US origin; common in the UK by around 1975.

hassle, v.   to harass or annoy. Adopted from the USA around 1970.

hat **1** a role, post or position of responsibility, usually one of a number held simultaneously by the same person, as in *she's wearing three different hats at the moment; come and see me this afternoon when I'll be wearing my union representative's hat*. Since around 1960. **2** *see* **hat(s) off**.

hatchet job   a vicious or devastating attack in speech or writing.

hatchet man   an executive who is given the task of dismissing employees or making them redundant. Adopted from the USA around 1974. From the US underworld sense of 'hired or appointed killer'.

hate (sb's) guts   to dislike (sb) intensely. Adopted from the USA around 1937.

hat(s) off   in *take (one's) hat off to (sb)*, to compliment, praise or admire (sb), esp. for tackling something that one wouldn't (or couldn't) do oneself. Also in the phrase *hats off to (sb)*, let's compliment or praise (sb).

haul arse   to go away, esp. quickly, as in *let's haul arse out of here*. Used in the USA and Canada.

have a ball   *see* **ball**, n. **1**.

have a bash   *see* **bash 1**.

have for (or **before**) **breakfast**   *see* **breakfast**.

have had it   **1** esp. in *you've had it*, you've missed your chance, you're too late. Since 1938 or 1939.   **2** to have had more than enough, to be fed-up (with) or sick and tired (of). From 1950 or earlier. *See also* **have had it up to here**.

have had it up to here   an elaboration of **have had it 2**, usually accompanied by a gesture at the throat or at the top of the head. Since the 1950s.

have it away   to have sexual intercourse. Since the mid 1950s. From the phrase *to have (one's) end away* (*see* **end 2**). *See also* **have it away with 2; have it off**.

have it away with   **1** to steal, as in *somebody's had it away with my keys*. Since around 1925. **2** to have sexual intercourse with. Since the late 1960s. *See also* **have it away**.

have it off   to have sexual intercourse. Since around 1940.

have kittens   *see* **kittens**.

have (sb) over a barrel   *see* **barrel**, n.

have (one's) wires crossed *see* **wires crossed.**

hawkish descriptive of a person who adopts a hard, warlike line. Adopted from the USA in the late 1970s.

hay cannabis. Drug users' slang. Used in the USA since around 1920.

haymaker a swinging blow. Boxers' slang. From around 1920.

haywire in wild or utter disorder; chaotic; crazy, esp. in *to go haywire*, to become completely out of order or out of control, to go crazy. Adopted from the USA in 1914.

headbanger 1 a young person given to shaking his or her head very violently in time to very loud music, as a way of dancing. From the late 1970s. 2 an insane person. From the idea of a severely mentally ill or disabled person banging his or her head against the wall.

headcase a mentally ill person. Since the mid-20th century.

head down, get (one's) to lie down and go to sleep. Since around 1920.

head job cunnilingus or fellatio. Since around 1950 or much earlier. *See also* **give head.**

head-shrinker a psychiatrist. Adopted from the USA in the late 1950s. *See also* **shrink.**

health, for (one's) (always negative or interrogative) for nothing, with the implication that one is doing the specified thing for a particular reason, esp. for profit, as in *I'm not in politics for my health.* Used in the USA since 1904 and in the UK since around 1912.

healthy large in size or amount, as in *a healthy bruise, a healthy cheque.* From around 1920.

heap a dilapidated old car. Since the mid-20th century. From *heap of old iron.*

heap big very large, important, etc., as in *him heap big man.* Jocular use of a term associated with American Indians in Westerns. Earlier 20th century.

hear (oneself) think, can't to be subjected to excessive noise, as in *turn that damn radio down, I can't hear myself think; the noise was so deafening she could hardly hear herself think.* Since around 1916.

hearty, n. a person enjoying boisterous health, esp. a non-intellectual devotee of outdoor games and sport. Originally used by undergraduates. From around 1910.

heat 1 police activity, esp. following a crime; being wanted by the police, as in *the heat is on* (or *off*). Adopted from the USA around 1936. 2 hence, the police themselves. Later 20th century. 3 intensity, pressure; coercion, esp. in *to take the heat off,* to relieve the pressure (on), *to put the heat on,* to threaten. 4 *see* **pack heat.**

heater revolver, pistol. The term is chiefly associated with US gangster films and crime fiction.

heave 1 to vomit; to retch. Since the 19th century. **2** to discard, to throw away. Used mostly in Australia since around 1920, the term became more common in the UK in the later 20th century.

heave-ho, the (old) in *to give (sb or sth) the (old) heave-ho,* to dismiss, jilt, reject or expel; *to get the (old) heave-ho,* to be dismissed, jilted, rejected or expelled.

heavy, n. a bodyguard. Later 20th century.

heavy, adj. 1 important; prominent. Adopted from the USA in the late 1960s. **2** sexually aroused, as in *he was getting heavy.* Later 20th century.

heavy-duty seriously and ardently committed, as in *the place was full of heavy-duty feminists.* Mid-1980s. From *heavy-duty* tyres, clothing, etc.

heavy metal a type of very loud rock music that uses electric musical instruments, drums and many amplifiers. Also used attributively, as in *a heavy-metal band.*

heavy mob, the 1 the prison police. Prison slang. Since around 1944. **2** a gang that specializes in large-scale robberies. Mid-20th century.

heavy petting petting that is very passionate and stops just short of full sexual intercourse. Originally teenagers' slang. Adopted from the USA in the late 1940s.

heck-as-like or **'eck-as-like** in such phrases as *did he heck-as-like!,* of course he didn't; *would they heck-as-like!,* it is highly unlikely that they would. Since the mid-19th century or earlier.

heebie-jeebies, the a fit of nervous depression, irritation or anxiety. Of US origin. Since 1927 or 1928.

heel an objectionable person, esp. one who is untrustworthy or treacherous. Adopted from the USA around 1938.

Heinz: (one of the) 57 varieties a mongrel dog. Since around 1925. An allusion to the 57 varieties of tinned food manufactured by the Heinz company.

heist a robbery. Adopted from the USA around 1965. From the verb *hoist,* in the slang sense of 'steal', perhaps via Yiddish.

hell and high water, between in great difficulty.

hell's angel a member of an intimidating gang of young men on powerful motorcycles, typically wearing black leather jackets decorated with metal studs. Popularized by the US film *The Wild Ones* (1954).

hell's bells! an exclamation of surprise, annoyance, etc. Late 19th–20th centuries. An elaboration of *hell!*

hell's own an adjectival and adverbial intensifier, as in *I had hell's own job unlocking the door.* Since around 1930.

hell's teeth! an exclamation of annoyance, surprise, etc. Since the late 19th century. An elaboration of *hell!*

helluva   hell of a; extremely, as in *it's a helluva problem; we had a helluva good time.* From around 1919 or earlier.

helter-skelter   an air-raid shelter. Rhyming slang, mostly used by Londoners during World War II.

hemp   marijuana. Drug users' slang. Used in the USA since around 1930 and in the UK from around 1955.

hens' teeth, as scarce (or **rare**) **as**   very scarce (or rare) indeed. *See also* **rocking-horse manure.**

hep   **1** in the know; having good taste. Used by jazz musicians and jazz-lovers. Adopted from the USA around 1945. From the US *hep*, lively, alert, shrewd; also used as a command to a team of horses. *See also* **hep cat**; **hip**. **2** hence, alert, progressive and well-informed. Used by beatniks and other young people in the late 1950s and early 1960s.

hep cat   a jazz fiend, a lover of swing music. Adopted from the USA around 1935. The term was superseded in 1950 by **hipster**. *See* **hep 1**.

herb   cannabis. Drug users' slang of the later 20th century.

Herbert or **'Erbert**   a chap, a fellow; a simpleton or fool, as in *you stupid Herbert!*

het   a shortening of **hetero**.

hetero, adj. and n.   heterosexual. Since the late 1940s. Also **het**.

het-up   excited, angry, agitated, in a state, as in *there's no need to get het-up about it.* Adopted from the USA around 1935. From *het*, heated.

hex   a spell, as in *to put a hex on*. Adopted from the USA around 1950. From the German *Hexe*, a witch.

hiccup   a fault in administration. Since around 1965.

hickey   **1** a thingummy; a gadget; an unnamed thing. Used in the USA and New Zealand. Late 19th–20th centuries. Also *do-hickey, doohickey.* **2** a love-bite; a long, hard, sucking kiss that raises a blister (or the blister so caused).

high, n.   **1** (a period of) exhilaration produced by drugs, as in *to give (sb) a high.* Adopted from the USA around 1960. **2** hence, any feeling or period of exhilaration, however produced or inspired, as in *she gets a real high from helping others.* Since the early 1970s.

high, adj.   **1** intoxicated by alcohol. Since before 1627. **2** under the influence of an exhilarating drug. Since around 1930. **3** overexcited. Since the mid-1970s.

high as a kite, as   **1** extremely drunk; an intensification of **high**, adj. **1**. Since around 1944. **2** an intensification of **high**, adj. **2**. Since the early 1970s. **3** an intensification of **high**, adj. **3**. Since the mid-1970s.

high jump, be for the   to be about to face a difficult or very unpleasant task; to be about to undergo a difficult or very unpleasant experience; to be about to receive a severe reprimand or punishment. Since around 1912.

high-octane of high quality; powerful, as in *a high-octane management course*. Later 20th century. A jocular metaphor, from *high-octane* fuel.

high-roller a big gambler (originally with dice, then on the racetrack). Used in the USA and Canada.

high spot the outstanding part or feature, as in *the high spot of the evening's entertainment*. Adopted from the USA around 1925.

high-tail (sometimes followed by *it*) to make off speedily without looking behind; to bolt, as in *we high-tailed it out of there*. Mainly used in the USA and Canada. From the stiffly upright tails of bolting cattle.

high-up a person of high rank, as in *one of the high-ups in the company*. Since around 1937.

hike a sharp lift or rise, esp. a rise in pay, prices, etc. Journalistic slang. Adopted from the USA in the mid-1970s. Probably influenced by **hoick**.

Hill, the the Notting Hill district of London. Late 19th–20th centuries.

hip 1 an alteration of **hep 1**. Used by jazz musicians and jazz-lovers in the 1950s. 2 hence, aware, realistic and worldly. Since the early 1960s.

hipster a jazz fiend, a lover of jazz and swing music. Adopted from the USA around 1950. *See also* **hep cat**.

hit, n. a killing by gangsters, spies, etc. Adopted from the USA around 1965. *See also* **hit-man**.

hit, v. to go to, travel along, arrive at, etc., as in *to hit the high spots; to hit the road; to hit town*.

hit (or **knock**) **for six** to rout decisively in argument, business, etc; to stun or overwhelm. Since around 1920. From cricket.

hit-man a hired killer. Underworld slang. Adopted from the USA around 1955. *See also* **hit**, n.

hit (**the**) **pay-dirt** to strike it rich. The term may be applied to any enterprise that suddenly becomes financially rewarding and is also used figuratively, e.g. in research. Adopted from the USA around 1975. From prospecting for minerals.

hit the deck to fall or throw oneself to the ground (e.g. to avoid injury). Later 20th century. *See also* **deck**.

hit the roof to become very angry, to flare up. *See also* **go through the roof**.

hit the sack to go to bed. Perhaps from the 19th-century nautical slang term *sack*, hammock.

hit the wall to reach the point of exhaustion. The term is used by athletes, esp. long-distance runners, in the later 20th century.

hobo a tramp, esp. one who works. Of US origin, the term has been used in the UK since 1905 but is still widely regarded as an Americanism.

hock to pawn. Hence *in hock*, in pawn.

hog to appropriate greedily, as in *the boys tend to hog the computers; stop hogging the chocolates: hand them round!* Used in the USA since 1887 and in the UK from around 1912.

hog-whimpering extremely and incoherently drunk. Used by **Sloane Rangers** and **yuppies** since the early 1980s. Elliptical for *hog-whimpering drunk*.

hoick a swift, jerking movement.

hokum anything designed to make a melodramatic or sentimental appeal; **bunkum**. Used in the USA since 1920 and in the UK by 1926. Probably a blend of *hocus(-pocus)* and *bunkum*.

hold down to do (sth, esp. a job) satisfactorily, keeping abreast of the problems and difficulties; to manage to keep (a job). Used in the USA since around 1890 and in the UK from around 1910.

hold it! 1 stay in precisely that position! From around 1895. 2 wait! Also, in the later 20th century, *hold everything!*

hold no brief for not to support, defend or sympathize with. Since around 1910.

hold out on (sb) to keep something (esp. money or important information) back from (sb). Adopted from the USA around 1924.

hold the fort to deputize or substitute for a person who is temporarily away, as in *will you hold the fort while I nip to the loo?*

hole in the head in *to need (sth) like a hole in the head*, not to need (sth) at all, to be better off (or happier, safer, etc) without (sth). Adopted from the USA around 1950.

hole up to hide; to remain hidden or secluded, as in *I was holed up in this dreadful hotel.* Of US origin; used in the UK in the later 20th century.

hollow-legs 1 applied to a thin person who habitually eats a great deal. The term is also used in the phrase *to have hollow legs*, as in *she must have hollow legs.* Since the 19th century. 2 hence, a person (often male) who habitually drinks a considerable quantity of beer. Since World War II.

hols holidays. Mainly schoolchildren's slang of the 20th century.

holy Joe any ostentatiously pious person. Late 19th–20th centuries.

holy mackerel! a mild oath. Adopted from the USA around 1944. Probably a euphemism for 'holy Michael!', but perhaps with a hidden dig at Roman Catholics, called *mackerel snappers* in the USA because they were supposed to eat fish on Fridays.

homework, do (one's)   to do all the preliminary work necessary for the completion of any task, esp. preparatory research, as in *if you'd done your homework, you'd wouldn't have made a stupid mistake like that*; the speaker had done his homework, and he had a ready answer. From around 1955.

homo   a (usually male) homosexual. Since around 1925.

honcho   the person in charge, the chief, the boss. Used in Australia, adopted from the USA. From the Japanese *hancho*, group leader.

honestly!   (often preceded by *oh!* or *well!*) an expression of exasperation, disgust, etc. Later 20th century.

honest-to-God (or **-goodness**), adj. and adv.   real(ly), genuine(ly); thorough(ly). Used in the USA since before 1916 and in the UK from 1921.

honey-bun (or **-bunch**)   an attractive girl or woman. Also used as a term of endearment. Adopted from US servicemen around 1943.

honk, n.   a bad smell. Used in Australia since around 1925. Perhaps from the Maori *haunga*, ill-smelling.

honk, v.   **1** to vomit. Since around 1940. Imitative of the sound of vomiting. **2** to stink. Used in Australia since around 1925. From **honk** n.

Honkie or **Honky**   a White person. Used by Black people in the USA and also in the UK, possibly since the mid-1960s.

honky-tonk   jangling piano music; noisy jazz. Adopted from the USA (where the term is applied to a low place of amusement or show) around 1950.

honours, do the   to take on the duties of a host, esp. to assume responsibility for pouring drinks, as in *shall I do the honours?* Possibly since around 1950. The drinks may be alcoholic, soft, cold or hot; compare the phrase *to be mother*, (*see* **mother 2**).

hooch or **hootch**   alcoholic liquor, esp. spirits that have been illicitly distilled. Adopted from the USA during World War I. From *Hoochino(o)*, (a very strong drink made by) an Alaskan tribe.

hood   a hoodlum; a (usually petty) gangster. Adopted from the USA around 1965.

hoodoo   any person or thing that causes bad luck; an adverse charm, such as the evil eye. Used in the USA since 1881 and in the UK from around 1910. Perhaps a corruption of *voodoo*.

hooey   nonsense. Adopted from the USA around 1937. Perhaps from **ballyhoo**.

hoof, v.   (sometimes followed by *it*) to dance. From the mid-1920s.

hoo-ha or **hoohah**   an argument or row; a fuss, as in *to make a (big) hoo-ha*.

hook, off the   relieved of responsibility, blame, etc.; out of danger or

difficulty, as in *to let (sb) off the hook*; *to get off the hook*. Since the 1920s
or earlier. By analogy with the release or escape of a fish.

hooked 1 (hopelessly) addicted to drugs. Adopted from the USA by
1945. **2** hence, addicted to anything, such as chocolate, sailing, etc.
Later 20th century.

hooker a prostitute. Of US origin.

hook up with to join forces with; to encounter. Since around 1910.

hooley or **hoolie** a party, esp. a wild or lively one. Anglo-Irish slang.
Perhaps a variant of the Gaelic *ceilidh.*

hoor (pronounced *hooer*) whore; a jocular mock-Scottish pronunciation, as in *ye dirty wee hoor*. Also used as a term of abuse to a person
of either sex (esp. male), as in *get out of here, you drunken hoor!*
19th–20th centuries.

hooray! goodbye. Used in Australia and New Zealand since around
1930.

Hooray Henry an upper-class or upper-middle-class young man who
behaves in a rowdy, exhibitionistic or excessively hearty manner.
Journalistic slang. From the late 1970s. The term *Hooray Henrietta* is
occasionally applied to the female of the species.

hoosh a thick soup or stew. From 1905.

hoot a cause for laughter, as in *what a hoot!* The term is also used
sarcastically, as in *that's a hoot!* Since around 1940. From the sound
of laughter, as in the verb *hoot* (with laughter).

hootch *see* **hooch**.

hooter nose. Since around 1940.

hop, n. 1 a stage of a long journey by air, as in *we did it in two hops*.
Since around 1925. **2** opium. US drug users' slang of the 20th
century. **3** *see* **hops**.

hophead a drug addict, esp. a marijuana user. Adopted from the USA
in the later 20th century. The term was originally applied to opium
users (*see* **hop**, n. **2**) in the USA, in the early 20th century.

hop it, v. to depart quickly, as in *hop it!*, go away! From around 1912.

hops in *on the hops*, on a drinking spree, on the beer. Around 1920–50.

Horlicks in *to make a (right) Horlicks of (sth)*, to make a complete mess
of (sth). Early 1980s. From the well-known brand of soporific beverage, used in this sense as a euphemism for **bollocks**.

horn in (often followed by *on*) to interfere; to intrude, as in *he's trying to
horn in on my province*. Used in Australia since the late 19th century and
in the UK since the early 20th century. An allusion to horned cattle.

hornswoggle, v. to cheat, to deceive. Used in the USA since 1852.

hornswoggle, n. nonsense. Of US origin. From around 1860.

horny sexually aroused; disposed for sex, esp. in *to feel horny*. 19th–20th
centuries.

horrors, the 1 delirium tremens. 19th–20th centuries. 2 acute psychosis caused by amphetamines; withdrawal symptoms from amphetamines or heroin. Later 20th century.

horse, n. heroin. Drug users' slang. Adopted from the USA around 1945. Perhaps an allusion to the kick obtained from heroin.

horse around, v. to play practical jokes; to indulge in horseplay. Since 1939 or earlier.

hostie an air hostess. Used in Australia since around 1955.

hot 1 regarded as likely to win, esp. in the phrase *hot favourite*. Used in horse-racing slang from 1894 and in more general contexts – sporting, political, etc. – since around 1905. 2 extremely skilful, esp. in *to be hot on* (or *at*) *(sth)*. From around 1895. 3 stolen. Adopted from the USA around 1935.

hot air boastful, empty or exaggerated talk. Adopted from the USA around 1910. Hence *hot-air merchant* (or *artist*), a person who indulges in such talk.

hot and bothered, all *see* **all hot and bothered**.

hot-dogging 1 fast turns and fancy stunts in surfing. Surfers' slang, adopted in Australia from Hawaii around 1960. A *hot dog* is a type of surfboard. 2 hence, fancy skiing. Skiers' slang of the later 20th century.

hot-foot (often followed by *it*) to hasten; to run or walk very quickly; to depart speedily, as in *I hot-footed it to the bank*.

hot potato a political or sociological problem that is particularly difficult to handle. Adopted from the USA around 1954. From the phrase *to drop (sth) like a hot potato*, to abandon with (often callous or unseemly) alacrity.

hot rod a very fast car, esp. one with a modified engine. Adopted from the USA around 1950.

hots, the esp. in *to have the hots for*, to lust after. Later 20th century.

hot seat esp. in *to be in the hot seat*, to be in a very difficult or dangerous position, esp. of responsibility. Adopted from the USA around 1950.

hot stuff a person or thing that is remarkable, striking, exceptional, out of the ordinary, etc.

hottie a hot-water bottle.

hot to trot ready and eager to go; ready and eager for sex.

hot under the collar annoyed or angry, esp. in *to get hot under the collar*. Since around 1920.

hot-wire, v. to start a car by bypassing the ignition system, esp. in order to steal it. Later 20th century.

how! a salutation with the right hand raised, palm forwards, and an expressionless face. From the greeting used by Native American Indians, esp. in Westerns.

how come? why?; how does (or did) that come about? Adopted from US servicemen around 1943.

how-do-you-do or **how-d'ye-do** a source or an instance of trouble; a quarrel; a fuss; a difficult situation, as in the ironic phrase *that's a nice how-do-you-do!*

how's-your-father or **howsyerfather** sexual activity, esp. illicit sex, as in *a spot of howsyerfather behind the haystack.*

huddle, go into a to go into secret or private conference. Since around 1930.

hug-me-tight a jumper, a pullover. Used in Glasgow since before 1934.

hump, v. to have sexual intercourse. The term was originally used in 18th-century English, transported to the USA, and revived in the UK in the later 20th century.

Hun 1 (usually *the Hun*) the Germans; the enemy. Since World War I, esp. during World War II. 2 a very objectionable person.

hunch a suspicion, intuition or premonition. Adopted from the USA by 1916. *See also* **play a hunch**.

hungry determined to win, to overcome all opposition. Adopted from the USA in the late 1960s.

hung up 1 annoyed, irritated, irritable, tense, esp. because of delay, difficulty or dilemma. Adopted from the USA around 1960. *See also* **hang-up 2**. 2 obsessed; addicted, as in *to be hung up on ambition, revenge, etc.* Adopted from the USA around 1965. 3 having a hang-up or hang-ups, as in *to be hung up about (sth).* *See* **hang-up 1**.

hunk an attractive boy or young man. Teenage girls' slang of the later 20th century. Hence the adjective *hunky*.

hunky-dory fine, as in *everything's hunky-dory*. Adopted from the USA around 1938.

hush-hush secret, as in *it's all very hush-hush, so don't tell anybody.* Since World War I.

hustle 1 to cadge or scrounge. Adopted from the USA in the late 1970s. 2 (of a prostitute) to solicit.

hustler a prostitute (of either sex). Adopted from the USA around 1970.

hype, n. intensive publicity; a publicity stunt, as in *that movie's been getting a lot of hype.* Adopted from the USA in the early 1970s.

hype, v. to publicize intensively; to promote by means of a publicity stunt. From **hype,** n.

hyped up 1 over-publicized; exaggerated. 2 highly stimulated; over-excited.

I

ice diamonds. Adopted from the USA around 1925. From the icy sheen of diamonds.

icky excessively sentimental, corny. Originally US jazz musicians' slang. From around 1935. Perhaps from *sticky*.

idea in *the (very) idea!*, an exclamation of disapproval, often in response to a preposterous remark or suggestion.

idiot board an autocue, teleprompter or similar device. Used in the world of television since around 1970.

idiot box or **idiot's lantern** a television set. Since around 1955.

iffy 1 uncertain; unsound; risky. Since around 1920. 2 doubtful; dishonest; stolen. Underworld slang of the later 20th century.

ignorant ill-mannered, as in *well, he always was an ignorant bastard.* Since around 1950 or earlier.

illywhacker a trickster, esp. a con-man. Used in Australia since around 1930. From *to whack the illy*, to trick or swindle.

imposs impossible. From the early 1920s.

I'm sure! 1 certainly; it certainly is/was/will be, etc. From around 1870. 2 used for emphasis, as in *oh, beg pardon, I'm sure!*, said ironically or jocularly in response to an unjustified rebuke. From the mid-20th century.

in, n.   a way or means of getting inside, literally or figuratively, as in *I think I've found an in*. Later 20th century.

in, adj. 1 fashionable, as in *the in thing; it's no longer in.* Probably elliptical for *in fashion*. 2 accepted by a group of people as a welcome member. Mainly Australian. Since around 1920. 3 restricted to a particular group of people, as in *an in-joke*.

indulge to take alcoholic drink, esp. habitually, as in *he doesn't indulge.* Late 19th–20th centuries.

info information. Since around 1930.

in my book *see* **book**, n.

innards the internal mechanism of any mechanical or electronic appliance.

in on participating in; admitted to (a share of) some thing or affair, as in *to be in on a deal, secret, etc; do you want to be in on this?* From around 1919.

inside job a crime, esp. a burglary or robbery, committed by (or with the help of) somebody living or working on the premises. Since around 1920.

in stitches *see* **stitches.**

intense serious; soulful. From around 1878.

in the picture *see* **picture.**

in the pipeline *see* **pipeline.**

in the works *see* **works 2.**

into in *to be into (sth)*, to be very interested or involved in (sth), and hence enthusiastic about it, as in *she's into yoga.* Adopted from the USA in the 1970s.

iron hoof a male homosexual. Rhyming slang for 'poof'. Often shortened to *iron* in the later 20th century; *see also* **half-iron.**

ironmongery arms, weapons. Since World War I.

iron out to put right, as in *a few minor problems to be ironed out.* Since around 1930.

is all that is all, as in *I'm tired, is all.* Chiefly used in the USA and Canada.

is it fuck! of course it isn't! An emphatic negative, as in *is that justice? Is it fuck!*

it sex appeal. From around 1920.

itchy feet a desire to travel or move on, esp. in *to have* (or *get*) *itchy feet,* to be restless. Later 20th century.

it just isn't true *see* **true.**

J

jab an injection, esp. a vaccination or inoculation. Since 1914.

jack in to abandon, to give up, as in *he had a good job at the paint factory, but he jacked it in*. Since around 1910. *See also* **pack it in 2**.

Jack Jones esp. in *on (one's) Jack Jones* (sometimes shortened to *on (one's) Jack*), alone, on (one's) own. Defective rhyming slang.

jack off (of men) to masturbate. Adopted from the USA in the mid-1940s. *See also* **jill off**.

jackpot exceptionally good luck, as in *to hit the jackpot*. Adopted from US servicemen in 1943.

jacksie or **jacksy** buttocks; anus, as in *up your jacksie!* Late 19th–20th centuries.

Jack the lad a (likeable) rogue; a light-hearted trouble-maker or philanderer. Since the mid-1970s.

jake, n. methylated spirits. Mostly tramps' slang. From around 1920.

jake, adj. honest, upright; equitable, correct; OK, all right; excellent. Since 1910 or earlier.

jail-bait or **gaol-bait** a girl under sixteen (the age of consent). Adopted from the USA by 1950.

jalopy or **jaloppy** a cheap or old car. The term also implies some degree of dilapidation. Adopted from the USA around 1950.

jam 1 a difficulty, an awkward situation, a mess, as in *to be in a jam; to get into a jam*. From around 1920. 2 *see* **jam on it**.

jam jar a car. Rhyming slang. Since around 1925.

jammy phenomenally lucky, esp. in *jammy bastard* (or *sod, bugger, devil*, etc.), often said with ill-concealed envy.

jam on it esp. in *to want jam on it*, to want or demand something extra, over and above what is reasonable; to be dissatisfied with what has been offered or given, as in *I've said I'm sorry – do you want jam on it?* Since around 1920. From the phrase *what do you want – jam on it?*, originally a response to complaints about food.

jam-packed (usually of a crowd) jammed together, closely packed. Since around 1950.

jam sandwich a police car. From the prominent red stripe along the side of a white police car.

jar a glass of beer, as in *we had a few jars*. Since around 1950.

J. Arthur Rank   an act of masturbation. Also used in such phrases as *not worth a J. Arthur Rank*. Rhyming slang for **wank**. From the mid-20th century.

jaw-jaw   talking; discussion, esp. in the phrase *jaw-jaw is better than war-war*, a remark that has been attributed to Churchill (1954) and Macmillan (1958).

jay-walker   a person who crosses the street at a place where it is dangerous or illegal to do so. Adopted from the USA in 1925. From *jay*, foolish person. Hence the noun *jay-walking*.

jazz   **1** nonsense. Adopted from the USA around 1957. **2** stuff, paraphernalia, esp. in the phrase *all that jazz*.

jazz up   **1** to modernize; to add decorative touches to. Since around 1950. **2** to enliven, esp. to convert classical music into pop. Since around 1945.

jazzy   brightly coloured, gaudy, flashy, loud. Since around 1935.

jeepers creepers!   an exclamation; a euphemism for 'Jesus Christ!'. Adopted from US servicemen around 1944.

jelly   gelignite. Since around 1918.

jerk   a foolish or contemptible person. Adopted from US servicemen around 1943. *See also* **creep**.

jerk off   (often reflexive) to masturbate. 18th–20th centuries.

Jerry, n. and adj.   German, esp. (of) a German soldier or the Germans collectively. From 1914. From *German*, perhaps influenced by *jerry*, chamber-pot (the steel helmet worn by German soldiers resembled a chamber-pot).

Jessie   an effeminate man. Used in Glasgow since before 1934.

Jesus boots   sandals. Since the early 1960s.

jet set, the   rich socialites who travel by air from one fashionable place to another. Since the early 1960s. Hence *jet-setter*, a member of this set.

jill off   (of women) to masturbate; a feminine form of **jack off**.

Jim Crow   racial prejudice, esp. against Black people. Since around 1955.

Jiminy Cricket!   an exclamation; a euphemism for 'Jesus Christ!'. Mainly US and Canadian.

jim-jams   pyjamas.

Jimmy Riddle   an act of urination, as in *to have a Jimmy Riddle*. Rhyming slang for 'piddle'. Late 19th–20th centuries.

jissom, jissum or **jism**   semen. Adopted from the USA around 1970. There are numerous variant spellings, including *gism, gissum, gizm, gizzum* and *jizzum*. Perhaps from Yiddish.

jitters, the   a feeling (or bout) of nervousness, as in *to get the jitters*. From around 1930.

jittery   very nervous, on edge. Adopted from the USA in 1935 or 1936.

jive, n. talk or conversation esp. where it is deliberately misleading. Of US origin since the 1930s.

jive, v. to dance the jive, esp. to jazz or rock-and-roll music.

jizzum *see* **jissom**.

joanna piano. Rhyming slang (for the pronunciation *pianna*).

job **1** a crime, esp. a robbery. Since the 18th century. **2** any person or thing, as in *who was that blonde job I saw you with last night?*; *he's got a new car, a three-litre job*. **3** in *on the job*, copulating, engaged in sexual intercourse. **4** *see* **big jobs**.

jobsworth any petty official who delights in turning down requests with the phrase 'it's more than my job's worth'. Since the early 1950s.

jock a male athlete, a sportsman, a male physical education student. Of US origin; used in the UK since the early 1980s. From *jockstrap*, an athletic support worn by men.

Jock a Scot; often used as a nickname.

Joe Soap a person whose willingness and/or lack of intelligence is exploited by others; a stooge or scapegoat. Rhyming slang for 'dope'. Since around 1930.

john **1** (contemptuous) a prostitute's client. **2** (usually *the john*) lavatory. 20th century.

Johnny-come-lately a newcomer; a novice. Mainly used in Australia and New Zealand.

John Thomas penis. Since the late 19th century.

joint a marijuana cigarette, as in *to roll a joint; we smoked a few joints*.

jollies pleasure, thrills; (sexual) gratification, esp. in *to get (one's) jollies*. Since around 1950.

jolly a pleasant excursion, as in *they went off on a jolly; an expenses-paid jolly to Florida*. Mid-20th century.

jolly d. jolly decent, very good. Originally public-school slang.

josh to tease; to banter; to joke. Used in the USA since the 1880s and in the UK by 1935.

journo a journalist. Used in Australia since around 1940.

joy satisfaction; luck; success, esp. in *any joy?*; *no joy*. Since around 1930.

judy a girl or woman. Since the late 19th century.

jugs a woman's breasts. Used in Australia since around 1920 and in the UK in the later 20th century.

juice **1** petrol. From 1909. *See also* **step on the gas**. **2** electricity. Originally electricians' slang; in general usage from around 1920.

juicy excellent. From 1916.

jump, n. an act of sexual intercourse, esp. in *to have* (or *get*) *a jump*. Since the 17th century.

jump, v. **1** to get a free ride on (a train, lorry, etc.). **2** to attack, esp.

suddenly and without warning, as in *they jumped me from behind.*

jumping   lively, as in *the joint was jumping.* Used in the USA since the 1930s.

jungle juice   any strong alcoholic liquor, esp. cheap and/or low-quality liquor.

junk   any narcotic drug; narcotic drugs in general. Adopted from the USA around 1945.

junkie or **junky**   a drug addict. Adopted from the USA around 1955.

K

K **1** knighthood of any order (e.g. *KBE*, *KCVO*, etc.), as in *I see old Smithers has got his K at last.* **2** a thousand pounds, as in *a salary of 50K.*

kaput or **caput** finished, no more; broken, no longer functioning, as in *the engine's kaput.* Since 1915. From the German *kaputt*, ruined, done for.

karsy, karzi or **karzy** *see* **kharsie**.

Kate and Sidney steak and kidney, as in *Kate and Sidney pie.* Since 1914.

Kate Carney or **Karney** the Army. Defective rhyming slang. Since the late 1890s. Often shortened to *Kate*, as in *he's in the Kate.* Kate Carney was a very popular comedian of the 1890s.

kazi *see* **kharsie**.

KCMG *see* **CMG**.

kecks trousers. Liverpool slang of the 19th–20th centuries.

keen excellent; highly desirable. Mainly used by US and Canadian teenagers.

keep (one's) fingers crossed *see* **fingers crossed**.

keep (sb) guessing to keep (sb) in a state of uncertainty or ignorance. Adopted from the USA around 1910.

keep (one's) nose clean (often imperative) to keep out of trouble. Since around 1925.

keep tabs on to observe (sb) closely, over an extended period of time, esp. in order to *see* what he or she is up to. Adopted from the USA in the early 20th century.

keep (sth) under (one's) hat (often imperative) to say nothing about (sth), as in *it's all very hush-hush: keep it under your hat.* Late 19th–20th centuries.

keep up with the Joneses to hold one's own in the rat race of conspicuous consumerism; to emulate others (esp. one's neighbours) in the acquisition of material possessions. Since around 1950.

keester or **keister** buttocks; anus. Mainly US and Canadian.

kerb-crawling the practice of driving slowly, close to the pavement, on the lookout for a prostitute. Since around 1925.

kerfuffle a fuss, a to-do, as in *what a kerfuffle!* Since 1939. From the Scottish verb *fuffle*, to throw into disorder.

kharsie, kharzie, khazi or **kazi** lavatory. Cockney slang. Since around 1870. There are numerous variant spellings, including *carsey, carsie, carsy, carzey, carzie, carzy, karsy, karzi, karzy* and *kazi*. Possibly from the slang term *case*, brothel, which is related to the Spanish and Italian *casa*, house, and the French *case*, hut.

kibitz to watch; to be an onlooker, esp. an inquisitive or interfering one. Adopted from the USA around 1962. Of Yiddish origin, from the German *Kiebitz*, peewit.

kibosh on, put the to thwart or frustrate; to prevent; to ruin; to put a stop to. Since before 1836.

kick a thrill, as in *just for kicks; to get a kick out of (sth)*, to find (sth) exciting, pleasurable, satisfying or absorbing. Since around 1925.

kick in to contribute to a kitty, collection, etc. Later 20th century.

kick up to cause trouble. Since the late 1940s. Elliptical for *to kick up a fuss*, which probably dates from around 1880.

kick up (one's) heels to enjoy oneself in an uninhibited manner, to have a high old time. Perhaps from dancing, or an allusion to livestock that have just been released from their pens.

kiddiwinks or **kiddywinks** children. Since around 1930.

kiddo a person (esp. a young man); fellow, chap, as in *he's a bright kiddo*. Also used as a term of address, as in *look here, kiddo!* From the mid-20th century.

kiddology or **kidology** humbug, deception. Later 20th century. A pseudo-scientific coinage, from the verb *kid*, to deceive for fun.

kiddywinks *see* **kiddiwinks**.

kidology *see* **kiddology**.

kief or **kif** cannabis. Drug users' slang of the later 20th century.

kike a Jew. Adopted from the USA around 1935. Perhaps from the Yiddish *kikel*, circle: illiterate Jewish immigrants to the USA would sign their names with a circle (rather than a cross).

kill 1 to suppress or discard, as in *to kill a story*. Journalistic slang. Since around 1910. 2 to switch off, as in *kill that light!* Since around 1930.

kinell! or **'kinell!** an exclamation; short for *fuckin' 'ell!* Late 19th–20th centuries.

kink an odd or eccentric person.

kinky related to unusual, abnormal, deviant or perverted sexual practices. Since around 1930.

kip, v. to sleep; to lodge. From around 1880.

kip, n. sleep, as in *two hours' kip*.

kisser mouth; face. Originally boxing slang. Since the 19th century.

kiss of death, the an action that brings trouble or destruction, esp. an action that is apparently benevolent or advantageous. Since around 1950. From the kiss with which Judas Iscariot betrayed Jesus Christ.

kit a drug addict's equipment or paraphernalia. Used in the USA since before 1959.

kite a worthless cheque.

kitsch art that is inferior, pretentious, in poor or dubious taste, devoid of aesthetic value, etc.; rubbish. Also used to mean sth is fashionably vulgar. Since the late 1960s. From the German *kitschen*, to throw together, esp. hastily.

kittens, have to become nervous or agitated, as in *she'll be having kittens if we're not back soon; he nearly had kittens when he found out.* Since around 1933.

Kiwi a New Zealander. Used in the UK since World War II.

kludge anything that is assembled in a makeshift, jury-rigged manner, but which may well work. Later 20th century.

klutz or **clutz** a stupid lout. Adopted from the USA around 1960 or 1970. Via Yiddish from the German *Klotz*, blockhead.

knackered 1 (of a person) physically exhausted. 2 (of a thing) worn out and beyond repair.

knackers testicles. Since the 19th century.

knees-up a jovial evening or boisterous party, esp. with some kind of dancing, as in *we had a knees-up to celebrate his release.* From the song (and dance) 'Knees up, Mother Brown'.

knickers in a twist, get (one's) to get agitated or flustered; to panic; to become angry or upset, esp. in *don't get your knickers in a twist!* Since around 1950.

knob penis. Since the 19th century.

knob-end an irritatingly foolish person. Later 1980s. Perhaps with reference to the glans penis (*see* **knob**).

knock, n. 1 an act of sexual intercourse. Since the 16th century. Also used as a verb; *see* **knocking shop**. 2 in *on the knock*, (of canvassers, market researchers, etc.) calling at houses, going from door to door. Since the late 1940s.

knock, v. to disparage, as in *don't knock it – it pays the bills.* Adopted from the USA around 1943.

knock along to get through life without too much difficulty, though perhaps in reduced circumstance, as in *oh, we'll knock along all right.* Later 20th century.

knock around with to keep company with, as in *who's she knocking around with now?; he generally knocks around with his mates from the club.*

knock-back, n. a refusal; a great disappointment.

knock back, v. 1 to cost, as in *that'll knock you back a fiver.* 2 to refuse; to reject. 3 to drink or (less commonly) eat, as in *knock it back and I'll buy you another.* From around 1912.

knockers a woman's breasts. From the 1940s or 1950s.

knock for a loop to astound. Since around 1910 or earlier. *See also* **throw for a loop.**

knock for six *see* **hit for six.**

knocking on (a bit) middle-aged or elderly. Since around 1930.

knocking-shop (or **-joint**) a brothel. Since the 19th century. *See* **knock,** n. 1.

knock it off! stop it! ('it' being anything that is annoying the speaker). Since the late 1930s.

knock it on the head! shut up!; stop it! Used in Australia since around 1920. From the killing of a snake.

knock-off, n. 1 something that has been stolen (*see* **knock off,** v. 1). Since the mid-20th century. 2 a cheap copy of a fashionable item or best-selling line, e.g. in clothing. Commercial and industrial slang of the later 20th century.

knock off, v. 1 to steal. 2 to have sexual intercourse with, often adulterously or illicitly, as in *he's been knocking off his neighbour's wife.* In common usage in the UK by 1960.

knock-on effect the effect that an event has on (a series of) subsequent events, esp. an indirect or cumulative effect. Late 1970s.

knock out to impress profoundly, as in *her performance knocked me out.* Since the early 1960s.

knock-out drops a drug that is used to make a person fall asleep or lose consciousness. The term often refers to a liquid drug that is (secretly) added to the person's drink. Used in the USA from 1876 and in the UK from 1904.

knock seven shades of shit out of (sb) *see* **seven shades of shit.**

knock up to make a girl or woman pregnant, intentionally or unintentionally.

know (sb) from a bar of soap, not to have no idea what (sb) looks like. Used in Australia since before 1918.

know-how skill; knack, as in *he hasn't got the know-how.* Adopted from the USA around 1943.

knowledge, the close familiarity with the streets of London, esp. routes across the city, required for the examination leading to a taxi-driver's licence.

know the score to know the risks involved, esp. in personal relationships.

knuckle sandwich a punch from a fist, esp. on the mouth or jaw, as in *to give (sb) a knuckle sandwich.* Since around 1920.

knuckles on the ground applied to a person (esp. a young man) of low intellect and primitive (i.e. ape-like) appearance, as in *a right thickie, with his knuckles on the ground.*

k.o., v. and n.   to knock out; a knock-out. Mostly boxers' slang; of US origin.

Kraut, n. and adj.   German. Since World War II. From *sauerkraut,* a German dish of pickled cabbage.

L

lab laboratory. Originally school and university slang, now in general use. Late 19th–20th centuries.

la-di-da, lah-di-dah or **lardy-dah** excessively or affectedly genteel of voice or manners, as in *she always puts on her la-di-da voice on the telephone.* From around 1860.

lads, the a convivial group of men on equal terms with each other, usually friends, team-mates, work-mates, etc., as in *one of the lads; to have a drink with the lads.*

lady-in-waiting a woman who is noticeably pregnant. Used mainly in Canada since the early 1960s; adopted in the UK around 1965.

Lady Muck a pretentious or affected woman, as in *who do you think you are: Lady Muck?* Since the 1890s. *See also* **Lord Muck**.

lah-di-dah *see* **la-di-da**.

laid back relaxed, easy-going, unhurried. Adopted from the USA around 1977.

lairy 1 vulgar, flashy or showy, esp. of dress. Mainly Australian. 2 conceited. Teddy-boys' slang, from the mid-1950s.

laking being out of work. Used in the North Country, esp. Yorkshire, since around 1920. From the dialect verb *lake*, to play.

lallies legs. The term was popularized in the 1960s and early 1970s by Kenneth Williams and Hugh Paddick in the BBC radio comedy series 'Round the Horne'.

lam, on the on the run from justice, making an escape, deserting from the armed forces. Originally US and Canadian slang; adopted in the UK around 1944.

lame-brain a person of feeble intellect, a stupid or foolish person. Adopted from the USA.

lame-brained stupid, foolish; dull-witted, as in *a lame-brained individual; a lame-brained idea.*

lamp, v. 1 to see, to gaze at, to stare. Adopted from the USA around 1920. 2 to attack with one's fists or with a weapon. Teddy-boys' slang, used in the mid-1950s.

lardy-dah *see* **la-di-da**.

last knockings, be on the to be nearing the end of a job or undertaking. Since around 1925.

latch-key kid   a child whose parents are out at work all day, and who must therefore use a key to get back into the home after school. Later 20th century.

latch on   to understand. Usually intransitive, as in *he didn't latch on.* Since around 1919. From the dialect verb *latch,* to catch, seize or grasp.

laughing, be   to be in a safe or fortunate position, as in *he's got a job at head office, so he's laughing.*

laughing all the way to the bank, be   to have great financial success, esp. in the face of long odds or disapproval. Adopted from the USA around 1965. Originally to *cry all the way to the bank,* a response to adverse criticism attributed to the successful pianist Liberace.

laughing boy   a morose, surly or gloomy-looking person.

laugh like a drain   to laugh heartily and noisily. Since around 1950.

laughs, for   in *just for laughs,* as a joke, for the fun of it. Since around 1950. Also in the singular, as in *I only did it for a laugh.*

launder   to legitimize something acquired illegally, such as money or arms. Since around 1975.

lav   lavatory. Since the late 1970s. *See* **loo.**

law   (usually *the law*) the police; a police officer. Since around 1945.

lax   lacrosse. Schoolgirls' slang since around 1950.

lay, n.   a person (usually female) considered as a sexual partner, esp. in *an easy lay; a good lay.* Adopted from the USA around 1955.

layabout   a lazy person who does no work; a loafer. Since around 1932.

lay by, v.   to purchase an item by making a deposit and paying for it in instalments. Used in Australia since around 1925.

lay-by, n.   in *I bought it on the lay-by,* I bought it on hire-purchase.

lay down tracks   to put songs on records. A term used in pop and rock music since the mid-1960s.

lay it on the line   to explain directly and thoroughly; to be frank and honest, as in *lay it on the line, doc, am I going to die?*

lay off!   stop it!; leave (me) alone! Referring to an activity that is annoying the speaker.

lazyitis   laziness, used as a pretext for shirking. Since around 1945. A jocular use of the medical suffix *-itis.*

lead in (one's) pencil   sexual vigour, as in *that'll put lead in your pencil!* (referring to a drink of strong liquor).

lead off   to lose one's temper, be angry. From around 1910.

lead-pipe cinch   an absolute certainty. Used in Canada since around 1945. From the effectiveness of a short length of lead-pipe as a weapon.

lead-swinger   a loafer; malingerer. From **swing the lead.**

lead (sb) up the garden path   to entice or mislead (sb). Since the early 1920s.

leak   an act of urination, as in *to take a leak; to have a leak.*

leaky   tearful, apt to weep. Since around 1923.

lean on   to bring pressure to bear, often accompanied by threats, as in *my creditors are leaning on me.* Originally underworld slang, referring to the use of force to persuade or convince. Since around 1940.

lean over backwards   to do more than normal or expected in order to please or satisfy, as in *we leant over backwards to help them, and what thanks do we get?* Since around 1945.

leather-jacket   a young motorcyclist of rough appearance and behaviour. Later 20th century. From the leather jackets characteristically worn by such motorcyclists.

leave (sb) cold   to fail to impress or please (sb), as in *I'm sorry, but your offer leaves me cold.*

leave it out!   stop it!; shut up! Since the early 1980s.

lech or **letch**, n.   a lecherous person (usually male), as in *he's a real lech.*

lech or **letch**, v.   esp. in to lech after/for/over, to lust after, to behave lecherously towards, as in *to lech for young girls; she was leching after her boss.*

lecky, adj.   electric, as in *lecky blanket; lecky kettle.* Later 20th century.

left carrying the can, be   to be made the scapegoat; to be burdened with unwanted responsibility. Since the mid-20th century. *See also* **carry the can.**

left-footer   a Roman Catholic. The term was originally used by Protestants in Northern Ireland, referring to the Catholics' turf-cutting style: Catholics traditionally used spades with the lug on the left side, whereas Protestants used spades with the lug on the right.

lefty   a socialist or communist. From 1936.

legal eagle   a lawyer. Adopted from the USA in the late 1940s.

leg it   to run or hurry; to run away or escape, as in *when they saw the police, they legged it.* Since before 1859.

legit, adj. and adv.   legitimate(ly), as in *don't worry, it's all legit.*

legless   **1** extremely drunk, as in *I got completely legless last night.* Since around 1965.   **2** (of a film) unsuccessful, a flop. *See* **legs, have.**

leg-opener   a strong drink, esp. gin, given to a woman in the hope that it will make her a willing (or unresistant) sexual partner. Since around 1945.

leg over, get (one's), v.   to have sexual intercourse. Later 20th century.

leg-over, n.   sexual intercourse, as in *a bit of leg-over.* Later 20th century.

leg-pull   a good-natured, innocuous hoax or deception. Since the later 19th century. From **pull (sb's) leg.**

legs, have   (of a film) to have staying power at the box-office. *See also* **legless 2.**

leg-up   assistance, esp. in *to give (sb) a leg-up,* to assist (sb); also in figurative sense of to assist. Late 19th–20th centuries.

lemon 1 something undesirable or useless, such as a car that has many defects. 2 a foolish or embarrassed person, as in *I felt a bit of a lemon*.

les (pronounced *lez*) a lesbian. Since around 1930.

letch *see* **lech.**

let (one's) hair down to relax and enjoy oneself thoroughly; to behave in an uninhibited way. Since around 1925, but not very common in the UK before around 1950.

let off steam to give vent to pent-up exuberance or anger.

level to speak or act honestly or frankly. Adopted from the USA around 1950. In British usage *to level with* is more common, as in *I'll level with you; I don't think he's levelling with us.*

level money the most appropriate exact multiple of £100. A term used by second-hand car dealers since around 1945.

liberate to gain illicitly or deviously; to steal. From around 1944.

lickety-split at full speed, in a great hurry. Adopted from the USA around 1918.

lie down on the job to loaf. Used in Australia since around 1925; later used in the UK with the added implication of inefficiency.

life of Riley (or **Reilly**), **the** a carefree and comfortable life, esp. in *to live the life of Riley*. Possibly of Anglo-Irish origin.

lig, v. to freeload; to take advantage of free drinks, free admittance to concerts and parties, etc. A term used by the media and in pop and rock music since the early 1980s. Hence *ligger*, a freeloader, and *ligging*, freeloading.

lights on – no one home of below average intelligence. Since the later 1970s.

like, adv. as it were; somewhat. Used at the end of a phrase or sentence to express vagueness or hesitation, as in *it was a bit dark, like; he was just standing there, like.*

likely story, a an ironic expression of profound disbelief, as in *he said he found the money lying in the street: a likely story!*

likewise I agree; I share the sentiment. Used in the UK to reciprocate a compliment (or an insult), also in the phrase *likewise, I'm sure!*

limb, out on a in a dangerous situation; at a grave disadvantage. Adopted from the USA around 1945.

limey an British person; a British sailor. Used in the USA and Canada since the early 20th century and adopted in Australia around 1943. An abbreviation of *limejuicer*, a US term derived from the practice of serving lime juice on British ships to prevent scurvy.

limit a person or thing that is (beyond) the extreme of what one can bear, as in *that's the limit!* Adopted from the USA around 1908. *See also* **dizzy limit; giddy limit.**

limo (pronounced *limmo*)   a limousine. Motorists' slang, since around 1960. Also, in the later 1980s, *stretch limo,* a particularly long limousine.

line   a measure of powdered drugs laid out in a narrow strip on a mirror or similar surface for easy inhalation.

line of country   one's vocation or profession; one's particular interest or hobby, as in *what's your line of country?; that's not my line of country, you'd better ask Mary.*

lip   cheek, impudence, as in *don't give me any more of your lip, young man!*

liquid lunch   a lunchtime drinking session, usually in place of a 'solid' meal.

lit or **lit up**   **1** slightly drunk. From around 1930. **2** under the influence of drugs. Originally US, since before 1938.

little black book   a notebook in which the telephone numbers of potential partners are kept. Used mainly in Australia since about 1930. In British usage the term may refer to any secret list of names, as in *you'd better watch out, or he'll have you down in his little black book.*

little boys' (or **girls'**) **room, the**   the (men's or women's) lavatory. Euphemism adopted around 1944 from US servicemen.

little friend   the menstrual period, considered a welcome sign of non-pregnancy. Canadian and Australian euphemism. Since around 1920.

little girls' room   *see* **little boys' room.**

little number   **1** any object or gadget, as in *I bought this little number for Nigel.* Later 20th century. **2** a dress, as in *a classy little number.* Later 20th century. **3** a young woman, esp. as regarded sexually, as in *she's a hot little number.* Since around 1945.

little something, a   **1** a dash of spirits, as in *would you like a little something in your coffee?* **2** a snack between meals. The phrase was popularized from 1926 by A. A. Milne's Winnie-the-Pooh, as in *time for a little something.*

littlies   young children, as in *the littlies' ballet class.* Since around 1965.

lit up   *see* **lit.**

live over the brush   (of unmarried lovers) to cohabit.

loaded   **1** very rich, having plenty of money, as in *her parents are loaded.* Since about 1945. **2** slightly drunk. Adopted from the USA around 1958 and used esp. by beatniks. **3** intoxicated by drugs. Drug users' slang. Later 20th century.

loaf   the head, esp. the brains, as in *use your loaf,* use your common sense. Rhyming slang (originally *loaf of bread*). Since the late 19th century.

local yokel   (contemptuous or jocular) an indigenous inhabitant of the area where one is a visitor or temporary resident. Since around 1950.

loco

loco insane; crazy. Adopted from the USA in the mid-20th century. The term refers to the effects of the **loco weed**, which derives its name from the Spanish *loco*, mad.

loco weed cannabis. Drug users' slang. Used in the USA since around 1931.

lolly money. Originally Cockney; in general use in the later 20th century. From *lollipop*, rhyming slang for *drop*, a tip or gratuity.

lolly-water soft drink, esp. if coloured. Used in Australia, esp. by those who prefer something stronger. From around 1945.

long as (sb's) arm, as very long, as in *he's got a criminal record as long as your arm.* Since the late 19th century.

long-hair an intellectual; a highbrow. Australian, adopted from the USA around 1944. Also used in the UK, esp. in the contemptuous phrase *long-haired intellectuals,* until long hair became fashionable for men in the 1960s.

loo (usually *the loo*) lavatory. Late 19th–20th centuries, esp. later 20th century. Possibly from the French *lieux (d'aisances)*, lavatory, or *l'eau*, (the) water; or even from the place-name *Waterloo*. *See* **lav.**

looker an attractive young woman, as in *she's a real looker.* Since around 1920. Short for *good looker.*

look-in a chance of success; an opportunity to participate. In sporting use from the 19th century. In the later 20th century it is usually doubtful or negative, as in *do you think he has a look-in?*; *I never even got a look-in.*

look to be to seem as if; to look as though, as in *there's been an accident, and it looks to be a bad one.* Used by sports commentators since around 1976; in more general use since around 1979.

loon or **loon about**, v. to fool about. Adopted from the USA in the early 1960s. Probably from *lunatic*, perhaps influenced by the US and Canadian bird-name *loon.*

loon or **loony**, n. a foolish, eccentric, crazy or insane person.

loony bin a mental hospital, a lunatic asylum. Since the later 19th century. *See also* **bin.**

loopy slightly mad. Late 19th–20th centuries.

loppy louse-infested; infected. Used in the armed forces around 1930–45. From Yorkshire dialect.

lord and master a woman's husband, as in *my lord and master will be home soon; would you like to speak to the lord and master?*

Lord love a duck! a mild expletive.

Lord Muck a pretentious or snobbish man. The male counterpart of **Lady Muck**, as in *they think they're Lord and Lady Muck.* Since the 1890s.

lose a meal to vomit. Australian euphemism. Since around 1942. *See also* **burp a rainbow; technicolour yawn.**

lose (one's) marbles *see* **marbles**.

lose (one's) rag to lose (one's) temper. Since around 1934. From *to get (one's) rag out*, to become angry.

loud-mouth a person who speaks loudly, boastfully or indiscreetly. Adopted from the USA around 1944.

louse up to ruin an opportunity, plan or operation; to spoil anything. Since around 1919. Often in *to louse it up*.

lousy with full of, having plenty of, as in *lousy with money*.

lovely, n. a very pretty young woman, as in *one of the local lovelies*. From around 1930.

lover boy a man who is (likely to be) in love; a would be Romeo or Casanova. Often used contemptuously or with mock affection. Adopted from the USA around 1960.

lover's nuts *see* **blue balls**.

lowbrow, n. and adj. a person who is not, or does not claim to be, intellectual. Adopted from the USA around 1923. The opposite of *highbrow*.

low-down, the information, esp. incriminating or scandalous information, as in *she gave me the low-down on what had happened*.

luck out to strike it lucky, as in *he sure lucked out on that one!* Mainly US. Since the late 1970s. The term can also be used ironically to mean the opposite, to run out of luck, as in *boy, you really lucked out that time!*

lug-hole or **lug-'ole** ear-hole. Often used in the catch-phrase *pin back your lug-holes*, listen carefully. Since the mid-19th century. Much used by certain comedians in the mid-20th century.

lulu anything spectacular, exceptional, very attractive, very profitable, etc., as in *it's a lulu*. Adopted from the USA around 1925.

lumber, n. trouble, as in *I got into a bit of lumber, he's in dead lumber*. Since around 1935.

lumber, v. to land a person with an unwelcome burden or a thankless task. Later 20th century. Also in *to be* (or *get*) *lumbered*, as in *I got lumbered with the washing-up*.

lunatic soup strong drink. In Australia it refers specifically to cheap red wine. Since around 1940.

lurgi *see* **dreaded lurgi**.

lush, n. 1 beer; strong drink. Since the late 18th century. 2 hence, a very heavy drinker. Since the 19th century; re-adopted from the USA in the later 20th century.

M

mac or **mack** mac(k)intosh. Late 20th century. *See also* **dirty mac brigade**.

Mac a term of address to a man whose name is unknown to the speaker. Of US or Canadian origin; used in the UK since the mid-1960s.

macho, n. and adj. applied to a display of male bravado. Adopted from the USA in the 1970s. From the Spanish *macho*, male.

mack *see* **mac**.

mad as a meat-axe, as extremely angry; dangerously crazy. Used in Australia since the 1920s.

made, get it or **have it** to be assured of success, as in *with her looks and talent she's got it made.*

mad money 1 money carried by a girl or young woman on a date, esp. for her return fare, in case she quarrels with her boyfriend or has to flee his amorous advances. Since around 1918. 2 money saved up or set aside for extravagant spending while on holiday or on some other special occasion. Since around 1950.

maggoty very drunk. Anglo-Irish slang.

magic excellent, first-rate; an expression of general approbation. The term was popularized in the mid-1970s by the TV character Selwyn Froggitt (played by Bill Maynard). The opposite of **tragic**, as in *Liverpool are magic, Everton are tragic!*

mainline to inject (a narcotic drug) intravenously. Drug users' slang. Adopted from the USA around 1950 or earlier. Hence the nouns *mainliner*, a confirmed drug addict who injects drugs directly into a vein, and *mainlining*, the practice.

major in to specialize in or to have as a chief characteristic, as in *an office staffed by floozies who major in looks rather than talent.*

make to manage to attend on, at, as in *can you make Friday? I couldn't make the last meeting*

make, on the 1 opportunistic. Adopted from the USA since the 1870s. 2 in search of a sexual partner. Adopted from the USA since the 1930s.

make a bomb (or **packet**) to become rich; to earn a lot of money; to make a considerable profit, as in *I sold the house just at the right moment* *and made a bomb on it.* Since around 1945. *See also* **cost a bomb.**

make a break (for it)   to run away (from the police, from prison, etc.). Since before 1932.

make a (good, poor, etc.**) fist at** (or **of**)   to do (or attempt to do) well, badly, etc., as in *he made such a fist of it that I joined in to help.* Since the early 19th century.

make a go of (sth)   to succeed, to be successful in (a business, marriage, etc.), as in *do you think you can make a go of it?*

make a meal of (sth)   to be over conscientious, to put an unnecessary amount of effort into (sth), as in *there's no need to make such a meal of it.* Later 1970s.

make a monkey (out) of (sb)   to make a fool of (sb); to dupe, ridicule. Adopted from the USA around 1930.

make an honest woman of   to marry. The term implies that the unmarried couple have a sexual relationship, as in *you've been living with her for five years: isn't it about time you made an honest woman of her?*

make good   to succeed. Adopted from the USA around 1913. In the later 20th century, often used in phrases such as *local boy makes good,* parodying clichéd newspaper headlines.

make (sb's) hair curl   to cause (sb) to shudder. The phrase is sometimes applied to a particularly potent drink, as in *this'll make your hair curl,* this will do you good. Since before 1931.

make it   to succeed; to become prosperous, famous, etc. Adopted from the USA around 1933.

make like . . .   to act like, to imitate, as in *to make like a bird,* to go away; *to make like an oyster,* to make no noise. Chiefly US and Canadian.

make the grade   to meet a standard, to come up to scratch. Adopted from the USA around 1930.

make waves   to upset established or accepted routine or procedure; to stir up (usually unnecessary) trouble. Since around 1972. The phrase is similar in meaning and usage to **rock the boat.**

make with   to make, produce, use, etc., as in *make with the beer!; make with the accelerator!* Adopted from the USA around 1959.

-making   an adjectival suffix, as in *sick-making, blush-making, shy-making.* Since the 1930s.

malarkey   nonsense; risible exaggeration; bullshit, as in *to come the old malarkey,* to tell a tall story.

mammoth   huge, as in *mammoth sale* (advertised on a poster). From around 1920.

manky or **mankie**   dirty; rotten; inferior or worthless. Originally Cockney slang. Perhaps from the French *manqué,* failed.

manor   **1** a police division, area or district, as in *he's superintendent of this manor.* From around 1920.   **2** the area or district where a gang operates. **3** the area or district where one lives. Since the late 1940s.

marbles sanity or wits, esp. in *to lose (one's) marbles*, to go mad; *to have all (one's) marbles*, to be no fool. Since around 1950.

mare an unpleasant and bad-tempered woman.

marge or **marg** margarine. From around 1905.

mark (sb's) card to give (sb) the information he or she needs; to tell or warn (sb); to tip (sb) off. Since around 1945.

marmalade a less common synonym of **scrambled egg(s)**. Since around 1940.

max maximum, as in *max effort*. Later 20th century. From the Standard English abbreviation, used esp. in technological jargon.

max out, v. to reach its limit, as in *my credit card has just maxed out.*

mazuma money, esp. cash. Of US origin, from Yiddish.

MCP male chauvinist pig. Adopted from the USA in the late 1970s.

meal ticket a person regarded or used as a source of financial support, as in *he was using her as a meal ticket*. Adopted from the USA in the mid-1970s.

mean superlatively good, as in *he plays a mean trombone*. Adopted from the USA since the 1920s.

meanie **1** a mean or miserly person; a person who is reluctant to pay his or her share. Since around 1930. **2** a disobliging person; a spoilsport. Since the mid-20th century.

meat-head stupid person; a derogatory term of abuse. Adopted from the USA in the mid-1940s.

meat rack a place where homosexuals (esp. male prostitutes) gather. Adopted from the USA in the 1970s.

mega an adjectival or adverbial intensifier or superlative, as in *he's mega boring, a mega party*. Adopted from the USA in 1983.

megabucks a vast sum of money. Adopted from the USA since the 1940s.

mercy buckets thank you. Originally schoolchildren's slang; also used by adults in the later 20th century. From the French *merci beaucoup*, thank you very much.

meshuga crazy. Jewish slang. Since the mid-19th century. Via Yiddish from the Hebrew *meshuga*, error.

message, get the to understand; to take the hint, as in *OK, I get the message!; we dropped some pretty obvious hints, but she didn't get the message*. Since the late 1940s.

Met, the **1** the Meteorological Office. Since around 1925. Hence the noun *Met man*, meteorologist. **2** the Metropolitan Police.

meter maid a female traffic warden. Since around 1970.

Mick an Irishman. Adopted from the USA around 1890.

Mickey Finn a drink (usually alcoholic) containing chloral hydrate or some other drug, intended to make the drinker lose consciousness. Adopted from the USA around 1943.

mickey-mouse money any unfamiliar currency, such as Scottish pound notes, the 20p coin (when first introduced), etc. Adopted from the USA in the later 20th century. *See also* **funny money 2**.

middle name in . . . *is (sb's) middle name*, referring to a characteristic quality, tendency, etc., as in *generosity is my middle name*.

mike a microphone. Since around 1927.

mileage something extra; benefit, advantage, profit, use; substance, as in *the writer gets some dramatic mileage out of keeping the audience guessing; there's no mileage in that argument*. Since the early 1970s.

miles away, be to be daydreaming or lost in thought. Since around 1910.

milk round a series of visits to universities made by recruiting teams from industry, the Civil Service, banking, insurance, etc., in search of graduate talent. Since around 1960.

mill around (of people, esp. in crowds) to move about in an aimless or confused manner, as in *people were milling around outside the shop, waiting for the sale to start*. Since the 1940s.

min a minute (of time), as in *wait a min!*

minces or **mincers** eyes. Rhyming slang (short for *mince-pies*). Since the late 19th century.

mind-bender 1 a knotty problem. 2 something (esp. a drug) that changes one's thinking. Adopted from the USA in 1974. Hence (for both senses) the adjective *mind-bending*.

mind-blowing 1 (of a drug) hallucinogenic, psychedelic, producing ecstasy or euphoria. Since around 1966. 2 amazing, astounding. Since the 1970s. *See also* (for both senses) **blow (one's) mind**.

mind boggles!, the a comment on anything that is too absurd, complicated or confusing to imagine or comprehend. Since the late 1950s. Hence the adjective *mind-boggling*.

minder 1 a bodyguard. 2 an aide or assistant.

mind-fuck an experience that challenges previously held beliefs. Of US origin. The term is also used as a verb.

minge the female genitalia. Late 19th–20th centuries. From Romany.

mingy miserly, mean; stingy; disappointingly small. Since 1910 or earlier. Perhaps from *mangy*, or a blend of *mean* and *stingy*.

mis (pronounced *miz*) miserable, as in *this plant's looking rather mis: have you watered it lately?*

miss one's (female) teacher, as in *I'll tell miss!* Used by schoolchildren. *See also* **sir**.

miss, give (sth) a to avoid (sth), as in *I'm giving that lecture a miss*.

miss a trick (always negative) to miss a chance, opening, etc., as in *she* *never misses a trick.* Since the mid-20th century. From card games.

Miss Clean   *see* **Clean.**

miss out (on)   to miss; to lose an opportunity, as in *you missed out on all the excitement; he's afraid of missing out.* Adopted from the USA in the mid-1940s.

miss the boat   to be too late.

mitt   hand (often plural), as in *that's mine: keep your mitts off it!* Adopted from the USA around 1918.

mix it   to fight vigorously. Since before 1916.

moan   to complain or grumble, esp. habitually. Since 1915 or earlier.

mob-handed   in a group, gang or mob; in force, as in *the police came mob-handed.*

mockers   in *to put the mockers on,* to thwart or frustrate; to put a jinx on; to ruin or destroy; to prevent. Perhaps from Yiddish.

mod   a member of a group of fashion-conscious teenagers (esp. of the 1960s), as opposed to a **rocker 1**. From *modern* or *modernist.*

mod con   a modern convenience (such as central heating), esp. in the phrase *all mod cons.* Since around 1945. From estate agents' jargon.

mog or **moggy**   a cat. Late 19th–20th centuries. Of dialectal origin.

mole   an agent of infiltration and subversion. The term was originally used in espionage (since the late 1940s) and subsequently in the Civil Service, trade unions, etc. (since the later 1970s).

moll   **1** a woman of easy virtue and low social status; a prostitute. 17th–20th centuries.   **2** a female companion or accomplice, as in *a gangster's moll.* Since the early 19th century.

Molotov cocktail   an incendiary device that consists of a bottle containing flammable material and fitted with a fuse. From the name of a Soviet statesman.

money, in the   receiving good wages or a large salary; enjoying the proceeds of a large win. Since around 1934.

monkey   £500 (or, in the USA, $500). Since before 1856.

monkey on (one's) back, have a   to be addicted to drugs. Chiefly US and Canadian.

mons   in *da mons,* money. Used in the motor trade since around 1920.

Montezuma's revenge   a severe attack of diarrhoea. Since the 1950s or earlier. *See also* **Aztec two-step.**

moo   esp. in *silly (old) moo,* stupid woman; a term of mild abuse. Originally Cockney slang of the 19th–20th centuries, the term was popularized in the 1960s and early 1970s by the character Alf Garnett (played by Warren Mitchell) in the BBC TV comedy series *Till Death Us Do Part.*

moolah or **moola**   money, esp. ready money. Adopted from the USA by the mid-20th century.

moon, v. to display one's naked buttocks as a coarse gesture of defiance or derision. Since the late 1970s. Hence the noun *mooning*.

Moonie a member of the Unification Church, a sect founded in South Korea in 1954 by the Revd Sun Myung Moon, which spread to the USA in 1959 and had reached the UK by early 1977.

moonlighter a person who has two paid jobs at the same time. Adopted from the USA in the mid-20th century. Hence the noun *moonlighting* and the verb *moonlight*, as in *some of the teaching staff moonlight as bartenders in the evenings*.

morning glory sexual intercourse first thing in the morning. Australian. Later 20th century.

mosey (often followed by *along, over*, etc.) to stroll idly, as in *I think I'll just mosey over to the bar – anyone coming?* Used in the USA since before 1836 and in the UK since the late 19th century.

moshing, n. the activity of dancing frenetically and passing people over the head of the crowd at rock concerts. Of US origin, since the early 1990s.

most, the the very best, superlatively good, extremely attractive, as in *he's the most*. Since around 1957.

mostest, with the having every attraction, esp. in the phrase *the hostess with the mostest*, from the musical *Call Me Madam*. Adopted from the USA around 1959.

MOT'd (of a motor vehicle) having passed its MOT (Ministry of Transport) test. The term is also used jocularly of other things or people, such as a partner of some years' standing. Since the late 1960s.

mothball to set aside for possible future use or consideration, as in *the project was mothballed for two years because of lack of funds*. Later 20th century.

mother 1 an offensive term of abuse. Adopted from the USA in the later 1970s. Short for **mother-fucker**. 2 in *to be mother*, (of a person of either sex) to assume responsibility for pouring out the tea or dispensing other (usually hot) drinks, as in *shall I be mother?* Possibly since around 1950. From the mother's role at the traditional tea-table. Compare the phrase *to do the honours* (*see* **honours**).

mother-fucker an offensive term of abuse. Adopted from the USA in the early 1970s. *See also* **mother 1**.

mother's ruin gin. Late 19th–20th century.

motions, go through the to give the appearance of doing something, without actually doing it (or without doing it wholeheartedly). From around 1920 or earlier.

motor, v. 1 to travel at speed. From the mid-20th century. 2 hence, to go very well indeed, to make very good progress. Later 20th century.

mousetrap ordinary or inferior cheese. From the (type of) cheese used to bait a mousetrap.

mouth like the bottom of a birdcage an unpleasant taste or feeling in one's mouth and other after-effects of a drinking bout, esp. on waking up the next morning. Since around 1920. Variants of the phrase include. . . *like the bottom of a baby's pram* (or *crow's nest*) and . . . *like the inside of a Turkish wrestler's jockstrap* (also in *an Arab's underpants*).

mouthy excessively talkative, bombastic, loquacious. Since around 1930.

movie a film, a moving picture. Used in the USA since 1906 and in the UK from around 1913.

movies the cinema, as in *we're off to the movies tonight.* Used in the USA since before 1913 and in the UK from around 1917.

mozzy or **mozzie** a mosquito. Used in Australia since the late 19th century and in the UK since around 1925. Hence *mozzy net,* mosquito net.

Mr Big the head of a criminal gang. Adopted from the USA around 1930.

Mr Clean *see* **Clean.**

Mr Fixit *see* **Fixit.**

Mrs Mopp (or **Mop**) a female cleaner, esp. one who uses a mop. Since around 1944. From the famous 'Mrs Mopp' of Tommy Handley's radio comedy series, *ITMA,* broadcast during World War II.

muck about to play the fool, esp. in an irritating way, as in *stop mucking about!* Since the mid-20th century or earlier.

mucker a friend; mate, pal. Since around 1917. From **muck in.**

muck in 1 to share work or duties with others, as in *if everybody mucks in, we'll be finished by lunchtime.* 2 to share rations or sleeping quarters with others.

mucky pup an affectionate term of disapproval addressed to a dirty child (or occasionally adult).

muff-diver a person who performs an act of cunnilingus. Hence the noun *muff-diving,* cunnilingus. From the slang term *muff,* the female genitalia, which dates back to the 17th century.

mug, n. 1 a fool; an easy dupe. 2 face. Since the early 18th century.

mug, v. to rob with violence in the street. The term has been used in this sense in the UK since the early 1970s; in the late 19th century it referred to robbery by the garrotte and in the early 20th century it simply meant 'to garrotte'. Hence **mugger,** and also *mugging,* the crime.

mugger a person who robs with violence in the street. Adopted from the USA in the early 1970s.

muggins a simpleton or fool; a person who is taken advantage of. The term is often applied to oneself, as in *and who got lumbered with clearing up the mess? Why, muggins here, as usual.* Adopted from the USA around 1880. From *mug*, n. 1, influenced by the surname *Muggins*.

mug-shot 1 a head(-and-shoulders) photograph of a prisoner or suspected criminal. Police and professional criminals' slang. Adopted from the USA around 1955. From **mug**, n. 2. 2 any portrait photograph. Photographers' slang.

mule a drug carrier or drug smuggler. Adopted from the USA in the later 1970s.

mumsie stereotypically motherly. Since 1970 or earlier.

munchies hunger, as in *I've got the munchies*, I'm hungry. From the early 1980s.

murky containing secrets; shady; sinister; discreditable, as in *I don't want to know about his murky past.* From around 1920.

Murphy's law a euphemism for **Sod's law**. Adopted from the USA around 1975.

muscle in to intrude by force or violence on another's activities, esp. on something successful and/or profitable; to poach on another's preserves. An abbreviation of *to muscle one's way in*, as in *he tried to muscle his way in on the act, but we weren't having any.* Adopted from the USA around 1928.

mush (pronounced to rhyme with *push*) 1 mouth. Since the late 18th century. 2 a friend or companion; mate, pal. Often used as term of address, not necessarily in a friendly manner, as in *hello, my old mush!* (friendly); *look here, mush!* (hostile, aggressive, provocative).

musical fruit any fruit or vegetable (esp. beans) that produces flatulence.

must, n. something that must be done, seen, heard, bought, etc., esp. in order to keep up to date. Since the early 1950s.

mutt 1 a fool. Adopted from the USA around 1918. From *mutton-head*, an earlier synonym. 2 (affectionately disparaging) a dog. Since the mid-20th century or earlier.

mutton dagger penis. *See also* **beef bayonet, pork sword**.

MYOB mind your own business. Also *MYOBB*, mind your own bloody business.

my foot! a direct denial of a statement or suggestion just made, as in *'She said she was sorry.' 'Sorry, my foot! She couldn't give a damn!'*

mystery a homeless girl on the streets of London (or elsewhere), esp. a runaway or one who has come from the provinces in search of a job. Since the late 1940s.

N

naff vulgar, tasteless; rubbishy, contemptible. Since the late 1960s.

naff all nothing. A euphemism for **fuck all**.

naffing an adjectival and adverbial intensifier, as in *the naffing photo-copier has broken down again!*; *I'll do as I naffing well please!* A euphemism for **fucking**.

naff off! go away! A euphemism for *fuck off!*

nana (pronounced *nahna*) **1** a banana. Nursery slang. Late 19th–20th centuries. **2** a fool, as in *he's a right nana; you stupid nana!* Since around 1930.

nancy boy, nancy or **nance** a homosexual; an effeminate man or boy. Since the 19th century.

narc a drug-squad detective. Adopted from the USA around 1970. Short for *narcotics*.

nark, n. a police spy; an informer, esp. in the phrase *copper's nark*. Since before 1864. From the Romany *nak*, nose.

nark, v. to annoy, to exasperate. Since before 1888.

narked annoyed, irritated, peeved; angry. Late 19th–20th centuries.

narky irritable; ill-tempered. Since around 1910.

nasty, n. anything bad, unpleasant, undesirable or offensive, as in *video nasties*, violent or pornographic videos.

nasty, adj. ill-tempered, disagreeable, dangerous or unpleasant, as in *to turn nasty*.

natch! of course! Since 1945 or earlier. From *naturally!*

natter, n. a chat, a conversation, as in *my neighbour came round for a natter*. Since the late 1930s.

natter, v. to talk aimlessly, endlessly or irritatingly; to chat, as in *stop nattering and get on with your work!* Since around 1938.

natural in *for* (or *in*) *all (one's) natural*, for (or in) all one's life; ever. Elliptical for *all (one's) natural life*.

nature calls I need to go to the lavatory.

NBG or **nbg** no bloody good.

neat very pleasing or attractive. Chiefly used by young people in the USA and Canada.

nebbish pitifully unfortunate. Perhaps via the Yiddish *nebekh*, from the Czech *neboky*.

neck, n.   impudence; audacity; very great assurance. *See also* **brass-neck**.

neck, v.   to indulge in **necking**, as in *there were couples necking all over the place*.

necking   kissing and cuddling, petting. Adopted from the USA around 1928.

necktie party   a hanging. From 1932.

need (sth) like a hole in the head   *see* **hole in the head**.

needle   resentment, dislike or anger, as in *he's got the needle with me*. Since before 1887.

neither use nor ornament   *see* **use nor ornament, neither**.

nerd or **nurd**   a foolish person. Adopted from the USA in the late 1970s.

nerk or **nurk**   an unpleasant or objectionable person; a foolish person. Since the mid-1950s. Perhaps a blend of **nit** and **berk**.

nervous Nellie (or **Nelly**)   a naturally timid or cowardly person. Adopted from the USA around 1970.

Newky   Newcastle Brown Ale. Later 20th century.

newted   (very) drunk. From **pissed as a newt**.

nibble   a tentative or non-committal approach by a buyer, as in *I see your house is up for sale – had any nibbles yet?* From the Standard English sense of fish nibbling at bait.

nice as pie, as   (of a person) very polite and agreeable, as in *the next time we met, she was as nice as pie*, referring to a previously unpleasant person. Since around 1910.

nice little earner   *see* **earner 2**.

nick, n.   **1** in the phrase *in good nick*, (of a thing) in good condition and/or working order; (of a person) physically fit. **2** (usually *the nick*) prison; police station. From around 1910.

nick, v.   **1** to arrest, as in *to get nicked*. Since the 18th century. **2** to steal. Since the early 19th century.

nicker   a pound sterling; pounds, as in *it cost twenty nicker*. Since the early 20th century.

niff, n.   an unpleasant odour. Of dialectal origin.

niff, v.   to smell unpleasant. From the late 1890s. Of dialectal origin.

niffy   having a foul smell. From around 1890. Of dialectal origin.

nifty   agile; nimble. Since around 1950.

niggle   to nag in a petty, finicky manner.

niggling   (of a thing) irritating because of the amount of minor detail or precision involved; petty; (of a person) irritating because of over-attention to detail; fussy. Since the mid-20th century.

niggly   bad-tempered, esp. about matters of little importance. Since around 1910.

nignog or **nig-nog** **1** a fool; a raw recruit; an unskilled person or novice. A mildly contemptuous but good-humoured term (compare sense **2**). Late 19th–20th centuries. **2** a Black person; a coloured immigrant. From *nigger.*

nimby, Nimby or **NIMBY** from an acronym of Not In My Back Yard. The term is applied to (the attitude of) a person who acknowledges the possible need for a new factory, airport, dump for nuclear or noxious waste, etc., but wants it to be sited somewhere else, well away from that person's home. Adopted from the USA in the early 1980s.

nineteenth hole, the the bar-room of a golf club-house. Golfers' slang. From 1927 or earlier.

Nip a Japanese person. The term is often used in the plural. Adopted from the USA around 1941. From *Nipponese.*

nit a simpleton, a fool, as in *you stupid nit!* Since around 1950. Probably from *nit*, head-louse.

niterie a nightclub or nightspot, as in *London's niteries.* Advertisers' and journalists' slang. Adopted from the USA around 1975. From a phonetic spelling of *night.*

nit-picking, n. and adj. quibbling, petty fault-finding. Since around 1960. From the act of picking nits (head-lice) from a person's hair.

nitty-gritty, the the essentials, the fundamental truth, the hard facts or harsh realities, esp. in *to get down to the nitty-gritty.* Adopted from the USA in 1967.

nobble **1** to tamper with a racehorse, esp. by drugging it. From the 19th century. **2** hence, to (attempt to) bribe or otherwise tamper with a person, esp. a juror. Later 20th century.

nobody's business, like an adverbial intensive, as in *she's been spending money like nobody's business.* Since around 1939.

noddy a fool, a simpleton. The term has been used since the 16th century or earlier, but since the mid-20th century it has been associated with *Noddy*, the hero of a series of children's stories by Enid Blyton.

noddy('s) guide a simplistic guide, manual, handbook or textbook.

noddy suit protective clothing to be worn under conditions of NBC (nuclear, biological, chemical) warfare. Used in the armed forces since the late 1960s.

no-go area an area that is temporarily out of use; an area that certain (groups of) people are forbidden to enter or prevented from entering. The term is also applied to a subject that must not be brought up in conversation.

no-hoper a useless person, a hopeless case; a person who lacks drive, ambition, or any attribute likely to bring success. Later 20th century.

noise (usu. pl.) **1** in the phrase *to get* or *make (all) the right noises,* to get or make conventional remarks or unexceptionable platitudes that are polite and politic. Since around 1950. **2** in the phrase *to make noises about*, to talk about or discuss, often privately or indirectly; to indicate the possibility of or desire for, as in *they're making noises about taking it to a higher authority.* Since the early 1970s.

nonce   a sexual deviant or pervert, esp. one who assaults children. Later 20th century.

no-no   anything forbidden or impossible, as in *that's a no-no.* Later 1970s-80s.

nookie or **nooky**   sexual intercourse, as in *a bit of nookie.* Late 19th–20th centuries.

nope   a variant of the semi-exclamatory *no*, as in *'Have you heard from Mike?' 'Nope.'* Of US origin; used in the UK since 1918.

nose   in *on the nose*, exactly; a bull's-eye. Adopted from the USA in the early 1970s.

nose, to get up (sb's)   to disgust, irritate annoy or anger. Since around 1935, but in widespread use only since around 1970.

nosh, n.   food; a meal or snack. From around 1958. The term originally referred to food eaten between meals (*see* **nosh**, v.).

nosh, v.   to eat, esp. heartily. Since the 1960s. The term originally referred to the furtive or surreptitious sampling of food, esp. between meals. Perhaps via Yiddish from the German *naschen*, to eat on the sly, to nibble secretly.

not a dicky-bird   *see* **dicky-bird 2**.

not a sausage   *see* **sausage 2**.

not a snowball's   *see* **snowball's**.

not backward in coming forward   *see* **backward in coming forward**.

nothing on earth, like   esp. in *to feel like nothing on earth*, to feel wretched or ill; to look like nothing on earth, to look ill or ludicrous. Since before 1927.

not know from a bar of soap   *see* **know (sb) from a bar of soap**.

not on   not acceptable, tolerable, practicable or permissible, as in *it's just not on.* Since around 1940.

not short of a bob or two   *see* **short of a bob or two**.

not so dusty   *see* **dusty**.

nuddy, in the   naked. Since around 1960 or earlier. From the phrase *in the nude.*

nuke, n.   a nuclear missile. Probably of US origin. Since around 1960 or earlier.

nuke, v.   to attack with nuclear weapons.

nurd   *see* **nerd**.

nurk   *see* **nerk**.

nut, n.   **1** head, esp. in contexts of violence (*see also* **nut**, v.). From 1858 or earlier. **2** an eccentric or crazy person; a foolish or stupid person; a nutcase, as in *what do you take me for – some kind of nut?* **3** *See* **do (one's) nut**.

nut, v. to butt with the head. Since around 1920.

nutcase a mentally ill or mentally disabled person; a crazy or foolish person. Adopted from the USA around 1959. *See also* **nutter**.

nut-house a mental hospital, a lunatic asylum. Adopted from the USA around 1925.

nuts, n. **1** testicles. Since the 18th century. **2** *see* **nuts!**

nuts, adj. crazy, as in *you're nuts!* Used in the USA since around 1905 and in the UK since 1929.

nuts! **1** nonsense! Adopted from the USA around 1945. **2** an exclamation of defiance, as in *nuts to them – I'm going anyway!* Since the mid-20th century.

nutter a synonym of **nutcase**. Since around 1961.

nutty as a fruitcake eccentric, crazy or insane. Probably of US origin; used in the UK since around 1943.

nympho a nymphomaniac. Since around 1910.

O

ocker a boorish or uncultivated Australian; a person (usu. male) who is constantly disparaging, whose assurance matches his ignorance and prejudice. Used in Australia since the early 1970s. Possibly from the name *Oscar*, or from the phrase *a knocker*, a disparager.

OD **1** to take an overdose of a drug, accidentally or deliberately, leading to mental derangement, severe ill health or death, as in *she OD'd on heroin*. From Over Dose. **2** to indulge in anything to excess, as in *to OD on heavy-metal music; to OD on cream cakes*.

oddball, n. and adj. (an) eccentric. Adopted from the USA around 1950.

odd bod an odd-man-out. Since World War II.

odds and sods miscellaneous people or things. Since around 1915.

ofay a White person. Used by Black people, esp. in the USA. Since the late 1960s.

off, v. to kill, as in *he offed himself by blowing out his brains*. Adopted from the USA in the late 1970s.

off-beat unconventional. Adopted from the USA around 1960.

off-colour impolite; indecent; distasteful, as in *some of her jokes were a bit off-colour*. Since the mid-20th century.

off the cuff or **off-the-cuff** spontaneous, extempore, impromptu, improvised, as in *an off-the-cuff reply*. Since the 1920s. From a note scribbled on a shirt-cuff.

off the deep end, go *see* **deep end**.

off the hook *see* **hook, off the**.

off the wall or **off-the-wall** unusual, eccentric, weird, not normal. Chiefly US. Since the 1960s.

oil, on the on a drinking bout, as in *to go on the oil*. Earlier 20th century.

oiled drunk. Since the early 18th century. The synonym *well-oiled* is more common in the 20th century.

oil-rag *see* **oily rag 2**.

oily rag **1** a cigarette. Rhyming slang for 'fag'. Often shortened to *oily*. **2** in *to live on the smell of an oily rag* (or *oil-rag*), to (be able to) survive on minimum food or income. Used in Australia since the late 19th century. From Anglo-Irish.

okey-doke or **okey-dokey** O.K; used as an expression of agreement.

Since the mid-1930s.

old battleaxe   *see* **battleaxe.**

old battleship   *see* **battleship.**

old bean   a term of address. From 1914. Since around 1935 the term has been largely restricted to jocular usage.

old boot   a sluttish and not necessarily old woman. Since the mid-20th century.

old boy network, the   social and esp. business connections between former pupils of public schools, providing reciprocal advantage and professional advancement. The term is also applied to other groups of people who have previously studied or worked together: at university, in the armed forces, etc. From the early 1950s.

old buzzard   *see* **buzzard.**

old China hand   a person who has spent many years in China in commercial or civil service or as a missionary. Since around 1910.

old-fashioned look   a look or glance of quizzical disapproval.

old fruit   a jocular term of address. Since the early 20th century. *See also* **fruit.**

old hat   old-fashioned, out of date. Since around 1945.

oldie   any old person or thing, such as an old trick, story, film, play, song, record, etc. Since around 1925. *See also* **golden oldie.**

oldies   one's parents (and others of their generation). Used by children and young people since around 1955.

old man   **1** any head, chief, commander, employer, etc.   **2** one's husband.   **3** one's father.

old thing   a person of either sex, as in *she's a funny old thing.* Also used as a familiar term of address.

on about, be   to talk at some length in an irritating or boring way, often on a subject that is not entirely understood by the listener, as in *what are you on about?* Since around 1950.

once-over   a quick glance or examination, esp. in *to give (sb or sth) the once-over* (or *a quick once-over*). Adopted from the USA in 1919.

oncer   **1** a pound note or (later) pound coin. Since the early 20th century.   **2** something that is available or occurs only once. Mostly Australian. Since around 1925.

one-armed bandit   a fruit machine. Adopted from the USA in the late 1950s. From the lever at the side of the machine, resembling an arm, which is pulled down to operate it; *bandit* alludes to the odds against the user.

one-eyed trouser-snake   *see* **trouser-snake.**

one for (sth), a   a devotee, admirer or champion of (sth), as in *he's certainly a one for his Sunday morning golf!* Since around 1930.

one in the oven, have   to be pregnant. From the phrase *to have a bun* *in the oven* (*see* **bun in the oven**).

one-night stand a sexual liaison that lasts only for one night; a single sexual encounter that does not develop into a relationship or affair. Since around 1930.

one-off something that happens once only and is unlikely to be repeated; a unique occurrence, product, action, service, etc. Later 20th century.

one off the wrist (an act of) male masturbation, as in *to have one off the wrist*, to masturbate. Later 20th century.

one of the best a good fellow or chap. From around 1920.

one over the eight 1 one drink too many, as in *to have one over the eight*. Since before 1914. 2 hence, slightly drunk.

one up on (sb), be to have scored an advantage over (sb).

on the blanket *see* **blanket**.

on the blink *see* **blink**.

on the dot *see* **dot**.

on the fritz *see* **fritz**.

on the job *see* **job 3**.

on the nose *see* **nose 2**.

on the pig's back *see* **pig's back**.

on the town *see* **town 2**.

on to, be to be aware of or alert to a person or plan, esp. where something secret or illicit is involved, as in *I think they're on to us*. Perhaps since the mid-19th century.

oo-er an exclamation of surprise, dismay, etc.

oo-la-la esp. in *a bit of the old oo-la-la*, erotic excitement, sexual pleasure, as in *going to Paris, eh? For a bit of the old oo-la-la, I'll bet!* From a French exclamation of surprise or delight.

oomph sex appeal. Adopted from the USA around 1941. Perhaps imitative of the sound of a bull's mating bellow.

op 1 any surgical operation, as in *she had her op yesterday*. Since around 1900. 2 any military operation.

open a can of worms *see* **can of worms**.

oppo a friend or companion; mate, chum, pal, as in *my oppo*. Chiefly used in the armed forces. Since before 1914. From the phrase *opposite number*.

orbit in *to go into orbit*, to panic, to be very angry.

orft a jocular mispronunciation of *off*, as in *well, I'm orft then*. Popularized by the radio broadcaster Jimmy Young in the phrase *orft we jolly well go!* Later 20th century.

or three *see* **three**.

other half, the a return drink, a second drink. The phrase originally referred to drinks served or bought in half-measures.

OTT an abbreviation of **over the top**, as in *that's a bit OTT*; *their performance was totally OTT*.

our kid the eldest boy in the family. Chiefly used in the North of England. 20th century or earlier.

out, adj. **1** utterly impracticable, as in *that's right out!* Since the late 1940s. **2** no longer in fashion, as in *short skirts are out this season*. **3** not (or no longer) concealing one's homosexuality. *See* **come out**.

out, v. to disclose publicly the homosexuality of someone (esp. a celebrity or well-known person). The practice or result of this is known as *outing*; it was begun in the USA by gay rights activists in 1990.

outasight *see* **out of sight**.

out for the count fast asleep; utterly tired out. Since around 1920. From boxing.

outing *see* **out**, v.

out like a light unconscious, esp. in *to go out like a light*, to fall asleep or become unconscious very suddenly and deeply. Since around 1930.

out of (one's) box *see* **box 3**.

out of commission *see* **commission**.

out of it oblivious to one's surroundings, by reason of intoxication with drugs or alcohol. Later 20th century. Elliptical for *out of (one's) head* (or *skull, gourd*, etc.).

out of sight or **outasight** excellent. Adopted from the USA in the mid-1960s.

out of (one's) skull *see* **skull**.

out of sync *see* **sync**.

out of (one's) tree *see* **tree**.

out on a limb *see* **limb**.

out on (one's) ear *see* **ear 2**.

outs the out-patient department of a hospital. Medical slang. Since before 1933.

out (of) the window *see* **window**.

out to lunch **1** crazy, mad. Adopted from the USA in the late 1970s. **2** intoxicated by drugs and/or alcohol.

over my dead body! a declaration of strong resistance, as in *'They're going to close the village school.' 'Over my dead body!'*

over the hill old, past one's prime, getting on (in years), long in the tooth, as in *they seem to think you're over the hill at forty*.

over the moon delighted, extremely pleased, happy or excited, as in *I was over the moon when I found out; she's not exactly over the moon about it*. Since the early 1970s.

over the top highly exaggerated, as in *to go over the top; that's a bit over* *the top.* Since the early 1980s. *See also* **OTT.**

over the wall   *see* **wall 3.**

own goal   a self-damaging blunder or counter-productive error of judgement, as in *the government has scored an own goal on this issue.* The term has also been applied to terrorists killed by their own bombs. Since the 1970s. From football, where an *own goal* is scored by a player who accidentally puts the ball into his own side's goal. *See also* **shoot (oneself) in the foot.**

ownsome, on (one's)   by oneself, alone. Since around 1920. Perhaps a blend of *on (one's) own* and *lonesome.*

owny-o (or **ownio**), **on (one's)**   by oneself, alone. From a fanciful italianization of *own,* e.g. to rhyme with the name *Antonio.*

oy!   a call for attention; an exclamation of protest or reproof, as in *oy! Stop that!; oy! Come here, you!; oy! Look out!* 20th century or earlier. From *hoy!*

oyster   a gob of phlegm. Late 18th–20th centuries.

Oz, n. and adj.   Australia (n). Later 20th century. From the abbreviation *Aus.*

P

pack a punch to be powerful. The phrase may be applied to a car or motorcycle, or to ballistic weapons; it may even refer to a sermon. Later 20th century. From boxing.

packet 1 a large sum of money, as in *to win a packet*. From the mid-1920s. 2 *see* **cop a packet**.

packet of three a packet of condoms. An old-fashioned euphemism that resurfaced with the AIDS scare in the 1980s.

pack heat to carry personal firearms. Adopted from the USA in the later 20th century.

pack it in 1 (often imperative) to stop talking; to cease some foolish or annoying practice. 2 to give up one's job, as in *I'm packing it in: it's too much like hard work!* Since the late 1940s. *See also* **jack in**.

pack up 1 (of a person) to stop working or trying; to retire; to die. Since World War I. 2 (of a machine) to stop working, to cease to function, to fail, as in *the engine packed up on the way home*. Since around 1937.

pad a bed or bedroom; living quarters, room, flat, house, as in *I stayed at my brother's pad for a couple of weeks*. Used by beatniks, jazz-lovers and drug-users in the 1950s, and subsequently brought into more general use, though *pad* has been a slang term for 'bed' from around 1570.

paddy wagon a van for the conveyance of prisoners. Of US origin; also used in Australia. Perhaps from *Paddy*, a nickname for an Irishman, from the prevalence of Irishmen in the US police force (or among the prisoners); perhaps from the slang term *paddy*, a padlock or a padded cell.

page three (or **3**) **girl** an attractive young woman exhibiting a stereotypical form of female sexuality, notably an abundance of glossy hair, breasts of above-average size, and either a pout or a vacuous smile; a 'glamour' model.

pain short for **pain in the neck**, as in *at first it's a bit of a pain, but you get used to it; the glasses have to be washed by hand, which is a pain*. Since around 1975.

pain in the neck a tedious, boring, irritating or annoying person or thing; a nuisance, as in *he's a real pain in the neck*. Since around 1910. From the phrase *to give (sb) a pain in the neck*, to bore or irritate (sb). The word *neck* may be replaced by *arse, bum, backside, balls*, etc. *See also* **pain**.

Paki (pronounced *packy*) a Pakistani immigrant. The term is loosely applied to natives of the Indian sub-continent (or their British-born descendants). Later 20th century.

palsy-walsy jovially, excessively or hypocritically friendly. Since around 1934. Often used ironically in the later 20th century. From *pally*, friendly, and *(to be) pals*, (to be) friends.

pan, v. to criticize adversely, as in *the show was panned by the critics*. Of US origin; used in the UK since the mid-20th century.

pan, n. in *down the pan*, ruined, with no chances left. Since the 1930s. From the lavatory *pan*.

panda (car) a police patrol car. Since 1966. From the original colouring and stripes on the bodywork, which resembled the markings of the giant panda.

panhandler a beggar.

panic button any switch or button used to operate a safety device, summon help, etc., in an emergency. Hence the figurative phrase *to press the panic button*, to panic, to demand immediate action. Later 20th century.

pansy, n. an effeminate man or boy; a homosexual. From around 1925.

pansy, adj. effeminate; homosexual. From the late 1920s.

pants *see* **bore the pants off (sb)**.

paper-tearer a clerk; a pen-pusher; an administrative official. Later 20th century.

para 1 a paragraph, esp. as part of a book, article, etc. 2 a paratrooper. Since World War II.

parachute in to bring in somebody from outside an organization to do a job or fill a post within the organization. Of US origin.

paralytic extremely drunk. From around 1910.

park to place, put or position, as in *where shall I park my suitcase?*; *she parked herself in front of the fire*; *park your arse* (or *carcass*), sit down. Adopted from the USA around 1915.

park a custard to vomit. Since around 1930.

parkie a park-keeper. Mostly children's slang. Since around 1920.

party line, the the official version or story, to be adhered to whether truthful or not, often with the implication of a cover-up. Since around 1920.

party-pooper a spoilsport or wet blanket; a person who seeks to ruin a lively party. Of US origin.

pash an infatuation, esp. a schoolchild's infatuation for a fellow pupil (usually older) or for a teacher, often of the same sex. A phonetic abbreviation of *passion*.

pass in a crowd to be average, as in *it'll pass in a crowd.*

passion-killers female underwear that is not designed to arouse sexual desire or facilitate sexual activity, esp. standard-issue or 'sensible' knickers. Since 1940.

passion-wagon a young man's car, esp. when used for courting, seduction or sex. Since World War II.

pass out to lose consciousness, to faint.

pass the buck to shift the blame from one's own shoulders onto somebody else's; to evade responsibility, usually by passing a job, problem, etc., on to somebody else. Adopted from the USA around 1938. From the game of poker. *See also* **buck-passing.**

pasties covers pasted over a showgirl's nipples. Of US origin; used in Australia since around 1965.

past it too old or infirm to perform a specified or unspecified task, as in *he used to be able to cycle 50 miles a day, but he's past it now, I'm not past it yet, you know!*

patch the area or district for which a police officer, social worker, etc., is responsible; the territory of a street-gang, drug-dealer, prostitute, etc., as in *Jones will deal with the problem: it's on his patch; get off my patch!* Since around 1920.

path pathology, pathological, as in *path lab,* pathology laboratory. Medical slang of the late 19th–20th centuries.

patsy a dupe or scapegoat, a fall guy. Adopted from the USA in the later 20th century.

paws off! (keep your) hands off!; addressed, for example, to children picking the icing off a cake.

payola money. The term often refers to bribery or extortion. Adopted from the USA in 1961. From *pay* plus *-ola,* a slang suffix of Spanish or Italian origin.

PDQ pretty damn(ed) quick. Since 1900 or earlier.

peachy very pleasant. Adopted from the USA around 1925.

pea in a colander, like a flustered, agitated, jumpy; running round in circles. Variants include *like a pea in a rattle, like a fart in a colander* and *like a fart in a bottle.*

peanuts a very small sum of money; a trifle, as in *I'm fed up with working for peanuts.* Since around 1950.

peasant a person of a social position lower than one's own; an uncouth person; an uncultured person. Since World War II.

pebble on the beach, not the only not the only desirable or remarkable person available, as in *you're not the only pebble on the beach,* there are plenty of other people who are equally suitable, deserving, etc.

pee, n. **1** urine; an act of urination, as in *to have a pee*. Since the 18th century. Probably a euphemism for **piss**. **2** penny, pence, as in *you owe me fifty pee*. Since the decimalization of British currency in 1971 From *p*, the written abbreviation of *penny* or *pence*.

pee, v. to urinate. Since the 18th century.

peep a word, as in *one more peep out of you and I'll smash your face in!* Adopted from the USA around 1945.

peeve peevishness; irritation, vexation, as in *a pet peeve of his*, something that particularly irritates him. Since around 1930.

peeved annoyed, cross, as in *she was pretty peeved about it*. Since 1918. From *peevish*, irritable.

peg-leg a person with an artificial leg, esp. a wooden one. 19th–20th centuries.

peg out to have one's strength fail, esp. during a sporting endeavour; to collapse; to die, as in *he pegged out on the last lap*. Perhaps from cribbage or croquet. Since before 1870.

peke a Pekinese dog. From around 1910.

pen penitentiary; prison. From around 1820; chiefly US and Canadian in 20th-century usage.

pen and ink stink. Rhyming slang. From around 1858.

penguin suit formal evening dress, a black suit worn with a white shirt and black bow tie. Since the late 1950s.

penny packet (usu. pl.) a small number, as in *it's no use sending the tanks in penny packets*. Mainly used in the armed forces.

pep energy, vitality. Used in the USA since around 1914 and in the UK from 1920. An abbreviation of *pepper*.

pep pill a stimulant drug in tablet form. Since the late 1940s.

peppy energetic; spirited. From around 1921.

pep talk a talk or speech intended to improve morale. Since around 1925.

pep up to infuse with new life, spirit, courage, etc. Adopted from the USA around 1927.

per permission, as in *I say, have you got per?* Mainly used in public schools and the armed forces.

perc a coffee percolator. Since around 1920. *See also* **perk**.

percentage profit; advantage, as in *there's no percentage in it*, there's nothing to be gained by it. Since around 1940.

Percy penis, esp. in the phrase *to point Percy at the porcelain*, to urinate, used in Australia since around 1945 and popularized in the UK by the 'Barry McKenzie' comic strip (*see* **beef bayonet**).

perfect delightful; pleasant; amusing. From around 1910.

period! that's final!; that's all!; without further discussion, extension, modification, mitigation or repeal, as in *you're not getting a pay rise, period!* Of US origin. Since around 1945. From *period*, full stop.

perishing 1 a general pejorative, as in *damn the perishing thing!* 2 very cold, as in *it's perishing out there!* Late 19th–20th centuries.

perk to percolate, as in *the coffee won't be long: it's perking nicely.* Since around 1955. Probably from *percolator* rather than *percolate*; *see* also **perc**.

perv a pervert; a lascivious person, esp. a man who likes watching young girls and women. Used in Australia since around 1930 and in the UK from the mid-1950s or earlier.

perve to practise sexual perversion; to behave in a lascivious manner, esp. to watch naked or scantily-clad young women. Used in Australia since around 1930.

pervy perverted; lascivious; erotic.

petal a term of endearment.

PG a paying guest. From around 1910.

pheasant-plucker (jocular or derisive) an unpleasant person, usually male. From around 1920. A contrived spoonerism of *pleasant fucker*, used ironically. *See also* **feather-plucker**.

phoney fraudulent; false, fake. Adopted from the USA around 1920. Perhaps from *fawney* (probably from the Irish *fáinne*), a ring; an elliptical allusion to a fraudulent practice involving a fake gold ring.

phooey! an expression of utter disbelief, contempt, distaste, disgust, etc. Adopted from the USA around 1959. Perhaps from Yiddish.

photie, photy or **photey** photograph, as in *do you want to see my holiday photies?*

pic or **piccy** picture; photograph; illustration. Since the early 20th century. *See also* **pix**.

pick up fag-ends to eavesdrop on a conversation. From around 1910.

pick up the tab to pay for or bear the expense of something, such as a meal or entertainment. Adopted from the USA around 1960. From *tab*, bill.

picture, in the aware of what is going on, as in *to put (sb) in the picture; is she in the picture?* Since around 1935.

piddle to urinate.

piddling trivial; insignificant.

piece of ass a woman considered as a sex object; sexual intercourse. Chiefly US and Canadian. *See also* **ass 2**.

piece of cake anything that is very easy to do, handle, achieve, obtain, etc., as in *opening the safe was a piece of cake; don't worry, it'll be a piece of cake!* Since around 1938.

piece of duff a boy or young man who is available for homosexual sex.

piece of piss a variant of **piece of cake**, often used contemptuously. Since around 1940.

piece of work a person, esp. in *a nasty piece of work*. From around 1920.

pie-eyed drunk. Adopted from the USA around 1943. Perhaps from *pie-eyed*, unable to focus the eyes, or from *pied*, disordered.

piffling trivial; feebly foolish.

pig a police officer. Since around 1810; revived in the 1960s.

piggy bank one's savings, as in *I'll have to raid the piggy bank again*. Since around 1930. From a child's moneybox in the traditional shape of a pig.

piggy (or **pig**) **in the middle** a person caught in the middle of a dispute. Since around 1960. From a game played by three people in a row, in which the middle player has to intercept a ball thrown back and forth between the players at each end.

pig-ignorant very ignorant. Since around 1945.

pig in the middle *see* **piggy in the middle**.

pig's back, on the in luck's way; successful. Anglo-Irish slang. Since before 1903.

pig's ear in *to make a pig's ear of (sth)*, to blunder; to bungle or botch (sth). Since around 1945. *See also* **sow's ear**.

pig-sick extremely irritated, annoyed or disgusted, as in *it makes me pig-sick*. Mainly Londoners' slang.

pile into (of an individual, usually unarmed) to attack, as in *he piled into his tormentor with fists flying*. Since the mid-20th century or earlier.

pile-up a road accident involving several cars, esp. on a motorway. Since around 1955.

pill 1 (of a person) a bore. Since 1897 or earlier. 2 in *the pill*, an oral contraceptive, esp. in *to be on the pill*. Since around 1960.

pillock 1 penis. 2 an idiot, a stupid or foolish person. Since around 1950 or earlier.

pillow-biter a male homosexual. Since 1979.

pill popper a person who uses drugs in pill form, esp. barbiturates or amphetamines. Drug users' slang.

pimp, n. 1 a man who solicits for a prostitute and lives off the profits. 2 an informer or spy (chiefly Australian). 3 a male prostitute. Of US origin, since the 1940s.

pimp, v. to pander or procure for prostitutes. *See* **pimp, n. 1**.

pinhead a fool. Since around 1920. A small head contains few brain cells.

pink, n. close-up shots of the open vagina used in pornography.

pink, adj. mildly socialist, left-wing. From *red*, communist. *See also* **pinko**.

pinkie 1 the little finger. Used in Scotland since the 19th century; also used in the USA and Canada. **2** a White person. Used by Black people since the late 1950s.

pinko a person who holds wishy-washy left-wing views. *See also* **pink**, adj.

pin (sth) on (sb) to justify an accusation or suspicion; to place the blame on (sb), as in *I don't see how we can pin this one on her*; *he tried to pin the blame on one of his colleagues.* Later 20th century.

pinta a pint of milk. Since around 1960. From the slogan *drinka pinta milka day.*

pint-sized (of a person) short, of small build. Since around 1920 or earlier.

pin-up 1 (a picture of) a sexually attractive young woman. Adopted from US servicemen in 1944–5. **2** hence, (a picture of) a handsome man, esp. an actor or pop star admired by teenage girls. From around 1955.

pip a star on the sleeve or shoulder of an officer's uniform.

pipeline, in the already prepared, begun, in train or in progress. Since around 1965.

pip emma p.m.; in the afternoon, as in *three-thirty pip emma.* Since around 1915. From the army signallers' alphabet, where *pip* = P and *emma* = M. *See also* **ack emma**.

pipped at the post, be to fail or be defeated within reach of success or victory. Of sporting origin.

pipsqueak an insignificant person or thing. Since 1910.

piss, n. **1** urine; an act of urination, as in *to have a piss.* The term was in Standard English until the 19th century, since when it has been considered a vulgarism. **2** any drink of poor quality. Since around 1920. *See also* **gnat's piss**. **3** in *on the piss*, drinking alcoholic liquor, esp. heavily, as in *he's always on the piss, that bloke, to go on the piss,* to start drinking heavily. Since around 1910. **4** *see* **piece of piss; streak of piss; take the piss**.

piss, v. to urinate. *See* **piss**, n. 1.

piss about to potter; to fritter one's time away; to stall for time; to waste time; to mess about.

piss and wind empty talk, unsubstantiated boast(s), as in *he's all piss and wind!*

piss artist a habitual drinker. Since the late 1940s. *See also* **artist**.

pissed (very) drunk, as in *to get pissed.*

pissed as a newt, as very drunk indeed. Possibly from the tight skin of the amphibian, *as tight as a newt* being an earlier variant of the phrase.

pissed off disgruntled, fed up; highly displeased or annoyed, as in *I'm getting pissed off with the way they treat us; she was pretty pissed off about it.*

Since the late 1940s. *See also* **piss off 2**.

piss-head   a habitually heavy drinker; an alcoholic. Since around 1955.

piss money against the wall   to squander money, esp. on liquor.

piss off   **1** to depart, esp. quickly, as in *piss off!*, go away!   **2** to irritate or annoy, as in *it really pisses me off when she does that.* Since the late 1940s. *See also* **pissed off**.

piss-poor   bad, feeble, ineffective, disgusting, etc.

piss-taking   mockery; the act of taking the piss (*see* **take the piss**). Since around 1930.

piss-up   a drinking bout. Hence the phrase *(sb) couldn't organize a piss-up in a brewery*, applied to an ineffectual administrator.

pit   one's bed, as in *the lazy bastard spent all day in his pit.* Possibly since around 1925.

pits, the   the very bottom, the depths, the nadir, as in *you are the pits!* Adopted from the USA in the late 1970s and popularized in 1981 by the US tennis player John McEnroe, who called a Wimbledon umpire 'the pits of the world'. Perhaps from *armpits*.

pix   pictures; photographs; illustrations. A written variant of *pics* (*see* **pic**).

pixilated or **pixillated**   drunk. Since around 1930.

pizzazz or **pizazz**   glamour, sparkle, style, vitality, as in *to have (no) pizzazz.* Used in the world of entertainment. Adopted from the USA in the early 1970s. Also **bezazz**; **bezzazz**; **pzazz**.

placky, plaggy or **plazzy**   plastic, esp. in *placky/plaggy/plazzy bag.* Since the late 1960s.

plain Jane   a plain-looking woman; a woman who is staid, capable and/or unassuming. Late 19th–20th centuries.

planky   dull-witted, stupid. Since around 1955. From the phrase *(as) thick as two short planks.*

plastic, n.   credit cards, as in *do you take plastic?*, can I pay by credit card? Later 20th century.

plastic, adj.   artificial; ersatz; bogus, as in *plastic teds*, young people aping the teddy-boys of the 1950s; *plastic milk*, powdered milk; *a plastic smile*, an insincere smile. Since around 1960.

plate, on (one's)   esp. in *to have enough* (or *too much*) *on (one's) plate*, to have as much as (or more than) one can manage, referring to work, problems, etc. Since around 1939.

platinum blonde   a woman with silver-blonde or gold-grey hair. Adopted from the USA by 1933.

plausy   smooth-tongued, over-polite and deceitful. Anglo-Irish slang of the late 19th–20th centuries. From the adjective *plausible*.

play a hunch   to act on an intuitive idea. Adopted from the USA around 1945. *See also* **hunch**.

play-away   a weekend staying with somebody in the country. Used by Sloane Rangers since the early 1980s.

play ball   to co-operate; to reciprocate. Since around 1937.

play chicken   *see* **chicken**, n. **2.**

play footsie   to touch another person's foot flirtatiously with one's own, usually under a table. Late 19th–20th centuries.

play for time   to employ delaying tactics. Since the early 1920s.

play hard to get   to resist amorous advances, with the intention of eventual acquiescence. Adopted from the USA by 1945.

play it by ear   to proceed or make adjustments according to (changing) circumstances, needs or demands; not to plan or decide in advance; to handle a situation as seems best at the time. Since the late 1940s. From a musician playing a tune with no written music as guide.

play it (or **(one's) cards**) **close to (one's) chest**   to be secretive or cagey. Used in the USA and Canada since around 1925 and in the UK in the later 20th century. Sometimes shortened to *to play it close*. From poker players holding their cards close to their chest so that nobody can *see* them.

play it cool   to act calmly, to control one's emotions. Since around 1955. *See also* **cool**, adj. **2.**

play silly buggers   to mess about; to cause trouble or inconvenience. Since World War II.

play up   (of people, animals, machines, ailments, etc) to be troublesome; to cause trouble, inconvenience, discomfort, etc. as in *the camera's playing up again; my rheumatism plays up something rotten this weather*. Late 19th–20th centuries.

plazzy   *see* **placky**.

pleased as a dog with two choppers, as   delighted, esp. at unexpected good fortune. Late 19th-20th centuries. From **chopper 1**; variants include as pleased as a dog with two cocks (or *dicks*).

pleb (often pl.)   a plebeian, used rather contemptuously to refer to a working-class or unsophisticated person, as in *one of the plebs; to keep the plebs happy*. Since 1823 or earlier. Short for *plebeian*, from the Latin *plebs*, the common people.

plod   a police officer; the police. Probably from *PC Plod*, a character in Enid Blyton's Noddy stories (*see* **noddy**).

plonk, n.   wine, esp. cheap or inferior wine, as in *a bottle of plonk; Spanish plonk*. Used in Australia and New Zealand since around 1930 and in the UK since the mid-20th century.

plonk, v.   to put, place or set, esp. heavily, as in *he plonked it down in front of me*. Since before 1914.

plonker 1 penis, as in *to pull (one's) plonker*, to masturbate. Since around 1917.   **2** a stupid or foolish person.

pluck a figure out of the air   *see* **figure out of the air.**

plug, v.   to publicize, recommend or boost, esp. in the media. Originally advertising slang. Since around 1930. Perhaps from *plug away at,* to persevere with.

plug, n.   **1** a piece of publicity. Since around 1935.   **2** *see* **pull the plug.**

plug-ugly   a ruffian or thug; any tough, brutal-looking, violent character, such as a gang-leader's bodyguard. Adopted from the USA, possibly around 1940.

plum in the (or **one's**) **mouth**   an affected manner of speech, as in *to have a plum in one's mouth; to talk with a plum in the mouth.* From the notion that people who speak in this manner sound as if they have plums in their mouths. Hence the adjective *plummy,* as in *a plummy accent.*

po   a chamber-pot. 19th–20th centuries. From the pronunciation of *pot* in the French *pot de chambre,* chamber-pot.

pocket-billiards   esp. in *to play pocket-billiards,* (of a boy or man) to manipulate one's genitals through the pocket(s) of one's trousers. Since around 1910.

poets' day   Friday; (an excuse for) leaving work early on Friday. Since the early 1960s. An acronym of *piss* (or *push*) *off early – tomorrow's Saturday.*

po-faced   with blank or immobile features; with an expression of disapproval, disdain, superciliousness or lack of amusement. Since around 1900.

point Percy at the porcelain   *see* **Percy.**

poison dwarf   an objectionable person (esp. a small person); a general term of abuse. Later 20th century. Probably from a nickname given by the inhabitants of a German town to a Scottish regiment stationed there in the 1950s.

poisonous   objectionable; extremely unpleasant; a pejorative adjectival intensifier, as in *he's a poisonous beast.* From around 1905.

poke   **1** horsepower, as in *with all that poke under the bonnet.* Motorists' slang. Since around 1945.   **2** an act of sexual intercourse. Since the 18th century.

poker-face   a face or expression that betrays no emotion. Since the later 19th century. From the face of a bluffing poker player. Hence the adjective *poker-faced.*

Polack   a Pole; a person of Polish descent.

pole, v.   (of a man) to copulate with, as in *he poled the girl.* Anglo-Irish slang.

polish off   to finish, get rid of or defeat, esp. summarily, as in *to polish off a meal.* Since 1829 or earlier.

polish the apple to curry favour by sycophancy. Adopted from the USA around 1945. *See also* **apple-polishing.**

politico a politician, esp. an ambitious and/or unscrupulous one; any politically-minded person. Of US origin; used in the UK in the later 20th century.

polone a girl or woman. Theatrical slang. Since the mid-19th century.

poly a polytechnic, as in *the local poly; Oxford Poly.* Later 20th century.

pommie, pommy or **pom** a British person, esp. a British immigrant or visitor to Australia or New Zealand, as in *whingeing pom* (*see* **whinge**). Also used attributively, as in *pommy bastard.* Since the late 19th century. Perhaps from a blend of *pomegranate* and *immigrant.*

Pompey 1 Portsmouth. Since the late 19th century. **2** hence, Portsmouth Association Football Club.

ponce, n. **1** a man who solicits for a prostitute and lives off her earnings; a pimp. From the early 1870s. **2** a dandified, ostentatious or effeminate man. From around 1930.

ponce, v. to sponge, scrounge or cadge. Since around 1915.

ponce about to live in an idle, aimless, irresponsible or luxurious way; to behave in an ostentatious or effeminate manner. Possibly since around 1950.

ponce up to smarten up, esp. flashily, as in *to ponce oneself up; the house had been ponced up for the photographs.* Since around 1925.

poncy or **poncey** flashy, ostentatious. Since the early 20th century.

poo *see* **poo(h).**

pooch a dog. Adopted from the USA in the mid-20th century. Perhaps from the German *Putzi,* a common name for a lapdog.

poodle, v. to go, as in *we poodled off to the pub; I think I'll poodle over and see* Jane. Since the mid-20th century or earlier.

poodle-faker a man who cultivates the society of women; a ladies' man. Since the early 20th century. An allusion to lapdogs.

pooey *see* **poohy.**

poof or **pouf** a male homosexual. From the earlier 20th century. *See also* **poove.**

poofter or **pooftah** a male homosexual; an effeminate man; a general term of abuse, as in *move over, yer pommie poofter!* Of Australian origin; in fairly general use in the UK by around 1970.

poo(h)! an exclamation of disgust, esp. in response to an unpleasant smell.

poo(h), poo(h)-poo(h) or **poop,** n. faeces; defecation, as in *dog poo; to do a poo.*

poo(h), poo(h)-poo(h) or **poop,** v. to defecate, as in *the cat's pooped on the carpet.*

poohy or **pooey** faecal; disgusting. Since around 1935.

poontang 1 the female genitalia. 2 hence, sexual intercourse, esp. with a coloured woman. 3 homosexual relations.

poop or **poo-poo** *see* **poo(h)**, **poo(h)-poo(h)** or **poop**.

poor man's. . . an inferior substitute, a pale reflection of the specified person or thing, as in *the poor man's Noël Coward*.

poor-mouth, v. to disparage, to damn with faint praise. Adopted from the USA in the late 1970s.

pootle to go, as in *to pootle along*, *to pootle off*, to depart. Perhaps a blend of **poodle** and **tootle**.

poove a male homosexual; an effeminate man. The term is possibly a back-formation from the plural of **poof**.

pop 1 father. Of US origin. From *papa*. *See also* **pops**. 2 hence, any old or middle-aged man. Adopted from US servicemen around 1944.

pop (one's) clogs to die. Perhaps from *pop*, to pawn, or from *pop off*, to die.

pop-eyed having bulging eyes, or eyes opened wide in surprise. Used in the USA since around 1820 and in the UK by around 1910.

poppycock nonsense. Adopted from the USA around 1905. From the Dutch *pappekak*, soft faeces. *See also* **cock**, n. 2.

pops father. Rare before 1919. *See also* **pop 1**.

popsy or **popsie** a girl or young woman, esp. an attractive one. Since around 1935. From *poppet*, a term of endearment.

pop the (or **sb's**) **cherry** *see* **cherry-popping**.

pork-pie a lie. Rhyming slang. Since the mid-1980s. *See also* **porky**.

pork sword penis. Since around 1950. *See also* **beef bayonet**, **mutton dagger**.

porky short for **pork-pie**.

porn or **porno** pornography. Since the late 1940s.

porridge imprisonment; a term in prison, as in *to do porridge*. Since around 1930. The term was popularized in the early 1970s by the BBC TV comedy series *Porridge*. Perhaps from a pun on **stir**.

posh stylish, smart, as in *posh frock*. Since the early 20th century.

pot marijuana. Adopted from the USA around 1947. Mostly drug users' slang. Perhaps from the Mexican *potiguaya*.

potatoes in the mould cold. Rhyming slang of the late 19th–20th centuries. Often shortened to *potatoes, taters in the mould* or *taters*, the last-mentioned being the most frequent form in the later 20th century.

pot-head a habitual smoker of cannabis. Later 20th century.

potty, adj. foolish; silly; crazy. From around 1910. *See also* **barmpot**.

pouf *see* **poof**.

pound the beat to walk the streets as a prostitute. Used in Australia in the later 20th century.

pour to see or help a person who has had a lot (or too much) to drink into or onto a taxi, train, plane, ship, etc., as in *we poured old Nobby into his plane about three in the morning.*

poured into wearing very tight-fitting clothing, to the greatest enhancement of one's figure, as in *she was poured into a black dress.* From the simile *she looked as if she had been poured into.* . ..

powder 1 cocaine, amphetamine sulphate or other drugs in powdered form; heroin. 2 *see* **take a powder.**

powder (one's) nose to go to the lavatory. A euphemism used by women since around 1940.

poxy inferior, unpleasant or unattractive; rotten, disgusting or deplorable.

pram, out of (one's) very angry or overexcited, as in *OK, there's no need to get out of your pram!* Since around 1950.

prang, n. 1 a crash-landing in an aircraft. Since around 1935. 2 a crash or accident in a motor vehicle.

prang, v. 1 to crash-land an aircraft. Since around 1935. 2 to damage or destroy a motor vehicle in a crash or accident, as in *she's pranged her Porsche.*

prat 1 buttocks. Since the 15th century. *See also* **pratfall.** 2 the female genitalia. 19th–20th centuries. 3 a stupid or foolish person. Since the mid-20th century or earlier.

pratfall a fall on one's buttocks. Adopted from the USA by around 1950. From **prat 1.**

preggers pregnant. Since around 1920.

premie (pronounced *preemy* or *premmie*) a premature baby. Used in the UK by 1930.

preppy typical of the manners, attitude, values, dress, etc., of a US preparatory school student.

pressie or **prezzie** (pronounced *prezzie*) a present. Originally Australian and Merseyside slang; in general use in the later 20th century.

press the panic button *see* **panic button.**

pretty boy an effeminate young man.

pretty please an intensification of *please,* often as a wheedling request.

previous, n. a previous conviction (or previous convictions, collectively, as in *has he got any previous?* Police and underworld slang. Since around 1930.

previous, adj. premature or presumptuous, as in *that's a bit previous, isn't it?*

prezzie *see* **pressie.**

pricey or **pricy** high-priced, expensive. Used in Australia and New Zealand since around 1910 and in the UK since the early 1940s.

prick 1 penis. The term was in Standard English until around 1700. 2 a foolish or obnoxious person (usually male), as in *I feel a right prick in this outfit; you prick!* Late 19th–20th centuries.

prick-teaser or **prick-tease** a woman who arouses a man sexually but does not allow him to have sexual intercourse with her. Since the late 19th century. *See also* **cock-tease**.

pricy *see* **pricey**.

prissy effeminate; fussy; prim; prudish. Since around 1943. Perhaps a blend of *prim* and *sissy*.

private eye a private detective. Adopted from US servicemen around 1944 (or earlier, from the novels of Raymond Chandler). Perhaps a pun on *private investigator* (with reference to the initial letter of the second word).

pro 1 a professional, as opposed to an amateur. Since 1867 or earlier. 2 a prostitute. Since World War I. In this sense the term may be an abbreviation of *prostitute* or *professional* (i.e. a person who makes money from sex, as opposed to an enthusiastic **amateur**).

prob a problem, as in *no prob!* Later 20th century.

prod a Protestant, as opposed to a Catholic.

prole (often pl.) a member of the proletariat; a lower-class or uncouth person, as in *he's a bit of a prole.*

promise, on a awaiting a (promised or expected) gift, money, information, personal services, sexual favours, etc. Later 20th century.

promo anything used to promote a product, esp. a promotional video for a pop record.

prong, n. penis. Since the 1970s.

prong, v. (of a man) to have sexual intercourse. Later 20th century.

pronto promptly, quickly, at once. Adopted from US servicemen in 1918. From the Spanish *pronto,* promptly.

prop propeller. Aviators' slang. From around 1915.

proper do a very fine party or wedding reception. Since around 1910. *See also* **do**, n. 1.

proposition a matter, as in *that's quite a different proposition.* Of US origin.

prospect a person who is more or less likely to take out an insurance policy; any potential client or customer. Perhaps from the mining term *prospect,* a place where gold, etc., is likely to be found.

prossie a prostitute. Used in Australia since the late 19th century; also used in the UK.

protection racket the extortion of money, services, etc., from shopkeepers or other business people, in return for leaving them and their property unmolested. Adopted from the USA in the early 20th century.

prowl car a police patrol car. Adopted from the USA in the mid-20th century.

pseud a pseudo-intellectual; a phoney; a poseur; an affected or pretentious person. Originally public-school slang; in general use since the mid-1960s. Popularized by 'Pseuds' Corner', a regular feature in the magazine *Private Eye*. From *pseudo*, false, not genuine.

psycho a psychopath. Since around 1945.

psych out to intimidate or scare, as in *you must try to psych out your opponent.* Adopted from the USA around 1974.

psych up to prepare (oneself or another) mentally for an ordeal, difficult task, contest, performance, etc., as in *she's psyching herself up for the race, patients had been psyched up for operations and then told to go home.* Adopted from the USA around 1973.

pubes (pronounced to rhyme with *tubes*) pubic hair. Since around 1950. Probably a deliberate mispronunciation of the disyllabic noun *pubes.*

pudding club the state of pregnancy, as in *to join the pudding club, to be in the pudding club. See also* **club, in the**.

pukka genuine; certain, reliable; properly done; of good quality, excellent. Of Anglo-Indian origin. Since around 1770. From the Hindi *pakka*, substantial.

pull 1 to arrest. Since 1811. 2 to attract or seduce a potential sexual partner. Since around 1955.

pull a fast one *see* **fast one**.

pull a stroke to be faster, smarter and more deceitful than one's opponent. Since around 1945.

pull down to earn (money). From around 1920.

pullie or **pully** pullover, jumper, sweater, as in *woolly pully*. Possibly since around 1930.

pull (sb's) leg to fool or tease (sb), as in *I haven't really lost the key: I was just pulling your leg*. Also in the phrase *pull the other one - it's got bells on!*, an exclamation of disbelief. Since before 1888. From the act of tripping (sb) up. *See also* **leg-pull**.

pull out all the stops to apply all one's energy to the task in hand; to spare no effort. An allusion to the stops of an organ.

pull (one's) pud (of a man or boy) to masturbate. Since the later 19th century.

pull (one's) punches (often negative) to exercise moderation, esp. in criticism or punishment, as in *she pulled no punches*. Of boxing origin; in general use since around 1950.

pull rank to exercise superiority of rank (or the authority accruing from seniority) in order to achieve a purpose, get something done, get one's own way, etc., as in *he pulled rank on me, and I had to give in.*

Possibly from around 1918.

pull (one's) socks up   to try harder, to make more effort, as in *pull your socks up!*; *if she doesn't pull her socks up, she'll be out on her ear.* Since around 1910.

pull strings   to use one's influence, esp. secretly or unofficially, in order to gain an unfair advantage for oneself or another. 20th century.

pull the plug   to withdraw support, as in *the banks are pulling the plug on small businesses.*

pull the rug out (from under)   to disturb or unsettle; to put at a disadvantage; to betray or expose; to deprive of support or defence. Since around 1970.

pully   *see* **pullie**.

punch-up   a fight with bare fists. From around 1920.

punchy   aggressive, looking for a fight. Later 20th century.

punt   in *to take a punt at*, to have a go at, to attempt. Used in Australia since the late 1940s.

punter   a customer or client. Later 19th–20th centuries.

puppy-fat   fattiness of childhood or adolescence. Since around 1910.

purge   to dismiss from employment. Since around 1930.

purler   1 something exceptionally good. Used in Australia since around 1910.   2 a headlong fall.

purple heart   a purple-coloured heart-shaped amphetamine tablet. Drug users' slang. Adopted from the USA around 1960. Perhaps from 'Purple Heart', a US decoration awarded to men who have been wounded in action.

push   to sell drugs. *See also* **pusher**.

push-bike   a foot-propelled bicycle, as opposed to a motorcycle. From around 1910.

pusher   a person who sells drugs to others (rather than taking them himself or herself). Drug users' slang, adopted from the underworld around 1955. *See also* **push**.

pushing . . .   getting on for . . ., approaching the specified age, as in *she's pushing 60.*

push (one's) luck   to take a risk or chance, to rely too much on good fortune or goodwill, as in *don't push your luck!* Since the 1930s.

pushover   something that is very easy to do or achieve; a girl or woman who is easy to seduce; a person who is easy to take advantage of, a mug, as in *it'll be a pushover; he thinks I'm a pushover.* Adopted from the USA around 1925.

push the boat out   1 to pay for a round of drinks. Since around 1924.   2 hence, to be generous, lavish or extravagant; to splash out, as in *it was a great party: they really pushed the boat out!*

pushy   thrusting, forceful, aggressively assertive or ambitious. Since
around 1925.

pussy   1 the female genitalia. Since the 17th century.   2 women considered collectively as sex objects, as in *is there much pussy in this town?*
3 a male homosexual; an effeminate boy.

put down, v.   to reject or snub; to humiliate or crush; to belittle.
Adopted from the USA around 1960 or earlier.

put-down, n.   a snub. Since around 1960.

put (one's) face on   to apply make-up, as in *I'll just go upstairs and put
my face on.*

put (one's) hands up   to surrender. Later 20th century.

put it (or **oneself**) **about**   to be sexually promiscuous, as in *he was a
man who had always put it about a bit, she's been putting herself about.*
Possibly since the late 1940s.

put (sb) on   to fool, deceive, tease or con, as in *are you putting me on?*
Adopted from the USA around 1960.

put on dog   to show off. Earlier 20th century.

put (sth) on hold   to put off or delay (sth) for a while. Perhaps since
the 1920s. From telephonists' jargon.

put out   to be sexually promiscuous. Mainly US and Canadian.

put (sb) out to grass   to retire (sb). Since around 1955. An allusion to
old horses, esp. retired racehorses.

putrid   a pejorative adjectival intensifier.

put the acid on   *see* **acid** 3.

put the bite on   *see* **bite**.

put the boot in   *see* **boot in**.

put the heat on   *see* **heat** 3.

put the skids under (sb)   *see* **skids**.

put up (one's) dukes   *see* **dukes**.

pyjams   pyjamas. From around 1910.

pzazz   *see* **pizzazz**.

Q

quack   (usu. *the quack*) any doctor of medicine, as in *you'd better go and see the quack*. Since around 1912.

queen   a homosexual, esp. an effeminate and/or ageing homosexual. Late 19th–20th centuries.

queer, n. and adj.   homosexual, esp. male. Since around 1920. *See also* **raging queer**.

queer-bashing   assaulting male homosexuals either for gain or for perverse pleasure. Later 20th century.

queer fella, the   the man who happens to be in command; anybody whose name is momentarily forgotten. Late 19th–20th centuries.

quick and dirty   hastily compiled (and published or used before correction). Originally used in the world of computers. Adopted from the USA in the late 1960s.

quickie   a quick drink, question, story, act of sexual intercourse, etc., as in *have we got time for a quickie?*

quid   a pound sterling (£); pounds, as in *it cost thirty quid*. Since the 17th century.

quids in   doing well; in an advantageous position, as in *I'm quids in!* 20th century.

quim   the female genitalia. Since the 17th century.

quit   to give up or abandon in a very lazy or cowardly manner. Of US origin.

R

rabbit and pork, n. and v. (to) talk. Rhyming slang. Often shortened to *rabbit*, as in *she can't arf rabbit, stop rabbiting and listen!* *See also* **rabbit on**.

rabbit food vegetable salad, esp. lettuce. Since around 1920.

rabbit on to ramble on, esp. boringly or complainingly, as in *he's been rabbiting on about the government all evening.* Since around 1960. *See also* **rabbit and pork**.

rabbit punch a blow, usually from behind, on the nape of the neck.

rabbits perquisites; anything free of charge. Since around 1920.

rack off to go missing, as in *rack off!*, get lost! Used in Australia since around 1975.

rad, n. radiator. From around 1905.

rad, adj. superlatively good. Teenagers' slang of the 1980s. Short for **radical**.

raddled (of a person's face) heavily made-up; showing the signs of age or dissipation. From the verb *raddle*, to paint the face with rouge, from *ruddle*, red ochre.

radical excellent. Used by young people, esp. surfers and skateboarders, since the late 1970s. *See also* **rad**, adj.

Raff, the the Royal Air Force. Since 1918. From the abbreviation *RAF*.

raft a (very) large number, as in *a raft of people attended the meeting.* Used in the USA before 1861.

rag, on the menstruating. From *rag*, sanitary towel.

ragga shortened form of *ragamuffin*. A type of macho, confrontational, Jamaican rap music that focuses on materialism and violence. Adopted from the USA since the mid-1980s. *See also* **rap**.

ragged unwell; suffering from nervous exhaustion, as in *those bloody kids – they're running me ragged.* Late 19th–20th centuries.

raging queer a particularly ostentatious or importunate male homosexual. Mid-20th century. *See also* **queer**.

rag top a convertible car. Car-dealers' slang of the later 20th century.

rag trade tailoring, dressmaking, the clothing trade. From around 1880.

rain-check any request or promise to accept an invitation at a later date; a postponement of any arrangement, as in *we'll have to take a rain-check on that one.* Adopted from the USA around 1970. From the receipt, usually a ticket stub, given to spectators at a rained-off baseball match (or similar event), allowing them to see another game at a later date.

rake-off   a profit or commission, esp. illegal or excessive, as in *a rake-off of 40 per cent*. Adopted from the USA around 1920. Perhaps from the croupier's rake at the gaming-table.

rambustious or **rambunctious**   *see* **rumbustious**.

rammy   *see* **clash**.

randy   lecherous; sexually aroused, as in *to feel randy*. Since around 1780. Perhaps from the verb *rand*, to rave, and possibly influenced by the Hindustani *randi-baz*, a lecher.

rap, n.   a charge; a case, as in *a murder rap*. Adopted from the USA in the 20th century.

rap, v.   to talk, esp. much or excitedly. Adopted from the USA in the late 1960s. Hence *rap (music)*, a style of rock music where the words are spoken to the beat rather than sung.

raring (or **rarin'**) **to go**   eagerly impatient to get started. Of US dialectal origin. A variant of *rearing to go*, originally used of horses.

raspberry   **1** a fart-like noise made with the lips and tongue as an expression of disapproval or contempt. Probably of theatrical origin. Since before 1880. Short for *raspberry tart*, rhyming slang for 'fart'. **2** *see* **raspberry ripple**.

raspberry ripple   a cripple. Rhyming slang of the later 20th century. Sometimes shortened to *raspberry*.

rat-arsed   drunk. Since the early 1980s. *See also* **ratted**.

ratbag   **1** an ill-disposed, unpleasant, disreputable or despicable person. Of Australian origin; used in the UK since around 1960.   **2** an eccentric. Used in Australia since around 1910.

rate   (usually negative) to think highly of, as in *she didn't rate him*, she didn't think much of him, she rated him low on her personal scale.

ratfink   a particularly treacherous or despicable **fink**.

rat on   to betray; to inform on, as in *he'd never rat on a friend*. Of US origin.

rat race, the   fierce competition to make a living, to be successful, etc.; the hectic or competitive routine of working life or professional advancement, as in *to get out of the rat race*. Since around 1945.

rat run   a back alley between buildings; a side street used by commuter traffic.

ratted   drunk. Since the early 1980s. *See also* **rat-arsed**.

rattler   the London Underground. Taxi-drivers' slang. From around 1905.

raunchy   earthy; *risqué*; pornographic. Adopted from the USA around 1965.

rave 1 an enthusiastic notice in the press. The term is also used attributively, as in *a rave review*. Originally theatrical slang. Since around 1920. **2** a party or dance. Young people's slang. Since the late 1950s. *See also* **rave-up.**

raver 1 a confirmed party-goer. Originally beatniks' slang of the late 1950s. **2** a person who leads a wild or uninhibited social life. Later 20th century.

rave-up a variant of **rave 2**. Sometimes used ironically by middle-aged people, as in *are you going to the rave-up at the vicarage after evensong?*

raw, in the naked, as in *to sleep in the raw*. Adopted from the USA around 1943.

raw deal harsh or unfair treatment, as in *to get a raw deal*. Adopted from the USA around 1930. From card games.

razoo a small coin; any very small sum of money. Usually negative, as in *I haven't a razoo*. Mainly used in Australia and New Zealand. Probably a corruption of the Maori *rahu*.

razzamatazz or **razzmatazz** showy or extravagant activity or publicity, as in *the razzmatazz of a US presidential campaign*.

readies money in banknotes (or other currency); cash, as in *two thousand pounds in readies; have you got the readies?* Since before 1935. *See also* **ready.**

read the riot act 1 to warn or reprimand severely or threateningly. From the reading of the Riot Act (1715) to unruly crowds, who had to disperse within the hour. **2** to read the Fire Arms Act to prisoners about to be discharged. Prison slang. Since around 1920.

ready (usually *the ready*) money, esp. money in hand, available for immediate use; ready money, as in *I haven't got enough of the ready*. Since the 17th century. *See also* **readies.**

ready up to prepare or contrive, illicitly or not honourably. Used in Australia since 1893 or earlier.

real McCoy, the the real thing; something completely authentic, as in *now that's the real McCoy!* The phrase *the real McCoy* is the US version of *the real Mackay*, of Scottish origin, which dates from the later 19th century.

rear up to become extremely angry. Late 19th–20th century.

rebound, on the recovering from a relationship that has recently ended, as in *to catch (sb) on the rebound; to get married on the rebound*, to marry soon after being refused, rejected or jilted by another. From around 1908.

recce (pronounced *recky*), n. reconnaissance, as in *to go on a recce*. Since around 1920.

recce (pronounced *recky*), v. to reconnoitre, to go on a reconnaissance. Since around 1935.

reckon (usually negative) to esteem; to have a high opinion of, as in *I don't reckon him*. Since the late 1940s.

reckon (oneself) to be conceited; to overestimate one's own abilities, as in *she reckons herself a bit*. Since the mid-1940s.

red, in the in debt. Since around 1920. From the use of red (rather than black) ink in book-keeping to indicate debt. *See also* **black, in the**.

red eye a flight that takes off late at night and arrives very early in the morning, its passengers emerging with eyes red from lack of sleep. Adopted from the USA in the 1980s.

red hot sexually aroused.

red-necked excessively martial and/or chauvinistic. Adopted from the USA around 1977.

Reds (usu. *the Reds*) communists, esp. communists of the former Soviet Union. Since 1917 or 1918.

redundo redundancy payment, as in *he could pick up several thousand in redundo*. Londoners' slang.

reefer a marijuana cigarette. Adopted from the USA around 1935.

ref, n. and v. (to) referee. Sporting slang.

refained excessively refined and genteel. Since around 1920. From a 'refained' pronunciation of *refined*.

reg (pronounced *rej*) the year of registration of motor vehicle, shown by a letter on the registration plate, as in *a J-reg Volvo*. Later 20th century.

rehab a rehabilitation ward or department in a hospital. Since around 1945. From the official abbreviation *rehab*.

Rene or **Renee** a girlfriend; a young working-class woman. Since around 1980.

rent a man or boy who charges for his homosexual services. The term is also used adjectivally, as in *be careful of that one, he's rent*. Since around 1930 or earlier. *See* **rent boy**.

renta- hired or impersonal, as in *rentamob*, a crowd of people specially assembled at a political demonstration; *rentamissive*, a form letter. Since the late 1960s. From commercial usage of the prefix in such terms as *Rentavan, Rentavilla*, etc.

rent boy a boy who hires himself out to homosexuals. Since around 1970. *See* **rent**.

rep, n. 1 repertory theatre, as in *she spent six years in rep*. Mainly theatrical slang. From around 1920. 2 a trade-union representative. Since around 1920. 3 a travelling salesman, a commercial traveller; a firm's representative. Since the mid-20th century.

rep, v. to act as a representative, esp. for a commercial firm (*see* **rep**, n. 3). Since the mid-20th century.

repro (pronounced *reepro*)   reproduction, as in *a repro carriage lamp*.
reptile an objectionable or contemptible person. Of US origin. *See also* **creep**; **jerk**.
result in *to get a result*, to secure one's objective. Originally football slang, subsequently adopted by the police; now in general usage.
rev (usu. pl.)   an engine's revolution, as in *to increase the revs*; *3000 revs a minute*. Probably since before 1914.
revved up esp. in *all revved up*, very excited, very tense. Since around 1960.
rhubarb nonsense, as in *that's a load of rhubarb!* Later 20th century. From *rhubarb, rhubarb, rhubarb*, the muttering of actors simulating the sound of a crowd.
rib to make fun of; to fool or tease, as in *they ribbed him something rotten*. Since around 1925.
Richard the Third a turd, a lump of excrement. Rhyming slang.
ride an act of sexual intercourse. 19th–20th centuries. From the much older use of the verb in this sense.
ride shotgun to take the front seat in a vehicle, next to the driver; to ride as escort to a driver; to escort in any way. Since around 1950. From the days when a man armed with a shotgun would ride next to the driver of a stagecoach at risk of a hold-up.
rig a large lorry or truck. Since around 1980. From Citizen's Band radio jargon.
right safe, under control, in good order, all right, esp. in *she'll be right*, an expression of general reassurance and optimism. Australian. From the earlier 20th century.
righto! or **righty-ho!** certainly!; gladly!; all right!; very well!; agreed!
right on 1 used as an interjection to indicate approval. Since the 1970s, associated particularly with left-wing rhetoric. 2 used as an adjective to describe people and attitudes that are broadly liberal, socially conscious or politically correct.
rim to perform anilingus. Homosexuals' slang. Adopted from the USA.
ring a bell to sound familiar, to bring something to mind, as in *that rings a bell*. Adopted from the USA around 1925. Perhaps from fairground games (or Pavlovian experiments). *See also* **ring the bell**.
ring-a-ding sure-fire, certain to succeed. Later 20th century.
ring-burner a very hot curry. Later 20th century. From *ring* in the slang sense of 'anus', referring to the sometimes painful after-effect of eating such a curry.
ringer 1 a person who steals vehicles and alters their appearance for sale; a vehicle that has been altered in this way; any fake that appears genuine. The term was originally applied to horses or greyhounds

that had been similarly disguised. **2** *see* **dead ringer for, be a.**

ring-snatcher   a person who commits buggery.

ring the bell   to bring one's female sexual partner to orgasm. Since around 1920. *See also* **ring a bell.**

riot   **1** a person, incident or thing that is very amusing, as in *that girl's a riot!* From around 1931   **2** *see* **read the riot act.**

rip into   to defeat utterly in a fight; to reprimand or reprove severely or bitterly. Used in Australia since around 1910.

rip-off, n.   an overpriced article, service, etc.; a swindle, as in *ten pounds? It's a rip-off!*

rip off, v.   to overcharge; to swindle, as in *to rip off the tourists; we were ripped off something rotten in that restaurant.* Adopted from the USA around 1968.

rip-snorter   anything exceptionally good. Of US origin.

rise   an erection, esp. in *to get* (or *have*) *a rise, to give (sb) a rise,* to excite (sb) sexually. 19th–20th centuries.

rise to the occasion   to have an erection when desirable or appropriate. Since around 1920.

ritzy   rich; stylish, fashionable, as in *a ritzy apartment.* Adopted from the USA around 1935. From the *Ritz* hotels in various cities of the world.

riveting   very exciting; fascinating. Since around 1955.

roach   the butt of a marijuana cigarette. Drug users' slang. Adopted from the USA in the late 1960s.

roadie   the road manager of a touring pop or rock group; any of the people involved in looking after and setting up the group's equipment during a tour. Since the early 1950s.

rock, v.   to startle or astound, as in *the City was rocked by the news of the company's collapse.* Since late 1941.

rock, n.   *see* **rocks.**

Rock Cake   a Roman Catholic. Since the mid-20th century. From the initials *RC.*

rocker   **1** a member of a group of teenagers (esp. of the 1960s) chiefly interested in fast motorbikes, as opposed to a **mod.** From *rock-and-roll.*   **2** in *off (one's) rocker,* (temporarily) mad. Since the late 1890s. From *rocking-chair.*

rocket   a severe reprimand, as in *she got a rocket from the boss.* Since around 1934.

rocking-horse manure   applied to anything that is extremely scarce, as in the simile *as rare as rocking-horse manure.* Since the mid-20th century. *See also* **hens' teeth.**

rocks   **1** jewels, pearls, diamonds. From around 1920.   **2** in *on the rocks,* (of a strong drink) without water or soda, but simply poured over the rocks (lumps of ice). Of US origin; in general use in the UK by

1958. **3** testicles. **4** hence, *to get (one's) rocks off,* to copulate. Later 20th century. **5** heroin or small pure crystals of cocaine. Used in the USA since before 1969.

rocks in (one's) head, have   to be crazy, foolish or stupid, as in *you've got rocks in your head if you think you can do that.* Used in the USA and Canada since the 1940s or earlier. Probably from Yiddish.

rock the boat   to disturb the status quo, as in *don't rock the boat,* said to somebody who is about to disturb a comfortable situation. Since around 1920. The phrase is similar in meaning and usage to **make waves**.

rod   a revolver or automatic pistol. An Americanism used in the UK since around 1931.

roger, v.   (of a man) to copulate with. Since the mid-18th century or earlier. From *Roger,* a nickname for the penis since the mid-17th century (and also a name frequently given to bulls).

roger!   all right!; OK! Since the late 1930s. From the army signallers' alphabet where *Roger* = R, 'message received and understood'.

Roger the Lodger   a male lodger who has sexual intercourse with the mistress of the house. Since around 1925.

Rogues' Gallery   (jocularly disrespectful) any collection of photo-graphs of distinguished people.

roll, n.   **1** an act of sexual intercourse, esp. in *to have a roll,* to copulate. Perhaps since around 1920. Probably from **roll in the hay**. **2** in *on a roll,* on a winning streak. Used in the USA and Canada since the mid-1970s.

roll, v.   to steal from a person who is drunk, unconscious or engaged in sex. Since the early 19th century. Perhaps of nautical origin.

Roller   a Rolls-Royce car. Since around 1950.

rollicking   a telling-off, as in *to give (sb) a rollicking, to get a rollicking.* Since around 1920. From the verb *rollick,* to make a fuss, to become angry, to tell off; possibly considered as a euphemism for 'bollock-ing' (*see* **bollock,** v).

rolling in the aisles   (of an audience) helpless with laughter, over-come with laughter, as in *the comedian had them rolling in the aisles.* Since around 1920.

roll in the hay   an act of sexual intercourse, esp. a quick one. *See also* **roll,** n. 1.

Rolls-Royce   fancy; expecting too much, as in *he's a bit Rolls-Royce in his ideas.* Since around 1918.

roll-up   a handmade cigarette. Originally prison slang. Since before 1950.

Roman candle landing   a bad landing; the fall to earth of a parachutist whose parachute has failed to open. Since around 1938. From the flare of the parachute from its pack, like an unopened umbrella.

romp   a quick, casual and light-hearted act of sexual intercourse, as in *a romp in the hay*. Adopted from the USA around 1945.

root, n.   **1** the penis. 19th–20th centuries.   **2** hence, sexual intercourse. Chiefly Australian and New Zealand. Since the early 1900s.   **3** *see* **roots**.

root, v.   to have sexual intercourse (with). Chiefly Australian and New Zealand. Since the 1930s.

root about   to search, esp. by rummaging about. From pigs rooting in the earth.

root for   to support ardently (and often vocally). Of US origin.

roots   boots. Rhyming slang; an Australian shortening of **daisy roots**.

ropey or **ropy**   inferior, of poor quality, bad, as in *the food was pretty ropey; a ropey old car*. Since around 1930.

rort   something exceptionally good. Used in Australia since around 1920.

roses   a woman's menstrual period, as in *she has her roses*. Anglo-Irish slang. Possibly since the mid-19th century.

Rosie Lee   **1** tea, as in *a cup of Rosie Lee*. Rhyming slang.   **2** a flea. Rhyming slang.

rot-gut   alcoholic drink of inferior quality. Since the late 16th century. *See also* **gut-rot 1**.

rotten   very drunk indeed, as in *to get rotten*. Since before 1934.

rough   harsh, severe; unfair, unreasonable, as in *don't be too rough on her; that's a bit rough*. Since the mid-20th century.

rough as a badger's arse, as   (of skin) bristly; (of a young man's beard) coarse and straggly. Late 19th–20th centuries.

rough house, n.   disorder; a quarrel; a noisy disturbance or struggle. Used in the USA since 1887 and in the UK from around 1910.

rough-house, v.   to treat roughly. Used in the USA since around 1900 and in the UK from around 1914.

roughneck   a rough, ignorant person. Adopted from the USA around 1910.

rough row to hoe   a tough time of it, a difficult time, a hard time, as in *he's got a pretty rough row to hoe*. Used in the USA and Canada since the early 20th century.

rough trade, the   the underworld of homosexual practices, esp. homosexual prostitution. Since around 1950. *See also* **trade**.

rough up   to molest; to batter; to beat up, as in *they roughed him up and stole his wallet*. Since around 1925.

round file   a wastepaper basket. Later 20th century.

round heels, have   (of a girl or woman) to be sexually compliant. The implication is that the least push will topple her, i.e. put the girl or woman on her back.

round the bend crazy, mad. Since the mid-19th century. *See also* **round the twist.**

round the houses 1 trousers. Rhyming slang. Since the mid-19th century. 2 in *to go (all) round the houses*, to go by the most circuitous route; to give a very long-winded explanation of a simple point.

round the twist a variant of **round the bend.** Since around 1957.

round up to obtain; to gather together, as in *see if you can round up some more volunteers.* Since the mid-20th century or earlier. From cattle-farming or cattle-droving. *See also* **corral; rustle up.**

Royals, the members of a royal family, esp. the British royal family. Since around 1950.

rozzer a police officer, esp. in *the rozzers,* the police. Since the late 19th century.

rub-a-dub-dub a pub, a public house. Rhyming slang. Since the late 19th century.

rubber, n. a condom. Also called a *rubber Johnny.* Since the mid-20th century or earlier.

rubber, v. to gape or stare (at). Adopted from the USA around 1942. From **rubberneck,** v.

rubber cheque a worthless cheque, a cheque that bounces (like a rubber ball). Adopted from the USA around 1935.

rubber Johnny *see* **rubber,** n.

rubberneck, v. to be excessively curious or inquisitive. Of US origin. Hence the noun *rubbernecking. See also* **rubber,** v.

rubberneck, n. a very curious or inquisitive person. Of US origin. From the craning and stretching of the neck, as if it were made of rubber.

rubbish to criticize adversely, as in *she rubbishes everything he says and does.* Used in Australia since around 1925 and in the UK in the later 20th century.

rube 1 a country bumpkin. Used in the USA since the mid-1890s and in the UK by 1931 2 something exceptionally good or desirable. Used in Australia since around 1925. *See also* **ruby-dazzler.**

ruby-dazzler a synonym of **rube 2.** Since around 1930. A blend of **rube 2** and **bobby-dazzler.**

ruck a heated argument; a fight. Perhaps from *ruckus.*

rude, in the naked; in the nude. Since the mid-1930s.

rudery a rude remark; *risqué* conversation; an amorous gesture, amorous behaviour. Since the mid-1920s.

rug 1 a toupee or hairpiece. 2 *see* **pull the rug out (from under).**

rugged uncomfortable, characterized by hardship, tough. Since around 1935.

rug rats   young children. Later 20th century.

ruined   drunk. Young people's slang of the early 1980s.

rumble   a gang fight, often carefully planned. Of US origin. *See also* **clash**.

rumbustious (or **rambustious** or **rambunctious**)   raucous; unruly. Probably of Icelandic origin; since the 18th century.

run a mile   to avoid or be unable to face something frightening, intimidating, daunting, etc., as in *he's always chatting up the waitresses, but if one of them offered to go to bed with him, he'd run a mile.*

run-around, give (sb) the   to treat (sb) contemptuously, evasively or deceitfully. Also *to get the run-around*, to be treated in this way. Since around 1945 or earlier.

run a tight ship   to exercise firm command; to maintain one's control over a team, committee, department, etc.

run out (at)   to cost, to come to, as in *it runs out at about fifty pounds; at 10p a sheet, photocopying will run out pretty expensive.* Mostly Australian. Since around 1920.

run out of road   to have a motor accident that involves skidding into a ditch, ramming a telegraph pole, etc., rather than colliding with another vehicle.

runner   1 a clerk or collector for a street bookie, as in *a bookie's runner.* Used originally in Glasgow since before 1934.   2 a deserter from the armed forces. Since around 1940.   3 an absconder or a person who is likely to abscond. Later 20th century.   4 in *to do a runner*, to escape; to abscond; to leave without paying the bill. Since the 1980s.

rush, n.   a wave of drug-induced euphoria; hence, any sudden pleasant feeling.

rush, v.   to cheat, esp. to charge extortionately, as in *how much did they rush you for this?* Since 1885.

rush (one's) fences   to be impetuous.

Russki or **Russky**, n. and adj.   Russian, esp. (of) a Russian soldier. Since World War I. From *Russian* plus *-ski*, a frequent Russian name-ending.

rust-bucket   a very rusty car, a car that is in a dangerously rusty condition. Later 20th century.

rustle up   to obtain; to prepare, as in *she rustled up something to eat.* Since around 1950 or earlier. From cattle-stealing. *See also* **corral**; **round up**.

Rusty   a nickname for a red-haired person.

S

Sadie and Maisie   (the practice of) sadomasochism. Used in the USA since the 1970s.

sad sack   a spoilsport or wet blanket; a blundering, unlikeable or pitiable person. Adopted from US servicemen in 1943.

safe or **safety**   a condom. Mainly used in the USA, Canada and Australia. Since around 1925.

sag   **1** to be illicitly absent from work. Liverpool slang. Late 19th–20th centuries. **2** to play truant, as in *to sag off.* Merseyside slang. Since around 1930.

saga   a small job that develops into a major one. From the jocular use of the noun *saga* for any never-ending story, series of events, etc.

sags, have the   to lack energy. Used by racing cyclists since around 1930.

sail close to the wind   to take risks, esp. with the law; to conduct operations that are close to (or over) the line of illegality. Late 19th–20th centuries.

sailor's farewell   the attitude of love 'em and leave 'em. Since World War II.

sainted aunt!, my   a jocular expletive. Since around 1905. *See also* **giddy aunt!, my.**

salaams!   my compliments (to you, him, her, etc.)! Anglo-Indian slang. From the Arabic phrase *salām 'alaikum*, meaning 'peace be upon you'.

salad oil   hair oil. Since before 1923.

salami fraud   fraud that is so called because interest due to investors is sliced off a bit at a time and paid into the fraudulent operator's own false account. Later 20th century.

Sally or **Sally Ann**   **1** the Salvation Army. **2** a Salvation Army hostel or canteen.

salted   drunk. From before 1931.

samey   monotonous; much-of-a-muchness, as in *all his films are a bit samey.* From around 1920.

san   sanatorium. Originally public-school slang. From 1913 or earlier. *See also* **sanny 1.**

san fairy Ann   it doesn't matter; it's all the same. Since World War I. A perversion of the French phrase *ça ne fait rien*, it doesn't matter.

sanny **1** sanatorium. Public-school slang. *See also* **san**. **2** a sanitary towel or tampon. Mid-20th century.

Santa Claus a synonym of **sugar daddy**. Since around 1920.

sap a fool or simpleton. Since 1815 or earlier.

sarge sergeant. Mostly used as a term of address.

sarky sarcastic. Late 19th–20th centuries.

sarnie a sandwich. Since the early 20th century.

sashay to go; to stroll; to move smoothly or mincingly, as in *he sashayed over to the bar*. A perversion of chassé, a term used in dancing.

sauce in *on the sauce*, drinking (alcohol).

saus (pronounced, and often spelt, *soss*) a sausage. Mostly juvenile slang.

sausage, n. **1** money, cash, as in *I haven't got a sausage*, I'm penniless. Rhyming slang (short for *sausage and mash*). Since around 1870. **2** in *not a sausage*, nothing at all, as in *'Did you get anything?' 'Not a sausage.'* **3** a jocular or affectionate term of reproof, as in *you silly sausage!*

sausage, v. to cash, as in *to sausage a goose's*, to cash a cheque (from *goose's neck*, rhyming slang for 'cheque'). From around 1920. *See also* **sausage**, n. **1**.

sausage dog a dachshund. Since World War I or earlier.

sawn-off (of a person) short or small in stature. Since around 1920.

sax a saxophone. From around 1910.

say 'cheese'! a jocular command used by people taking photographs of friends and relations, in an effort to get at least a semblance of a smile for the picture. Possibly since the early 20th century.

say (one's) piece to say what one wants to say, or what one has planned or intended to say; to express one's opinion or point of view. Since around 1910.

say-so authority; the right, privilege or power to make decisions, as in *on whose say-so?* Since before 1885.

SBD silent but deadly (or dangerous); referring to a noiseless but pungent fart.

scads much, a lot, a great deal, as in *scads of money*. Adopted from the USA around 1935.

scag or **skag** heroin. Drug users' slang. Adopted from the USA around 1970.

scallie a scallywag; a street urchin; a young criminal or delinquent; any young person, esp. male. Liverpool slang.

scam a fraud or swindle; a risky or dubious scheme. Later 20th century.

scanties women's panties or briefs. From around 1930.

scared shitless very much afraid. Since the late 1930s. *See also* **scare the living daylights out of.**

scaredy or **scaredy-cat** a timorous or frightened person. Often used as a taunt for cowards, esp. by children. Since around 1910.

scare (or **frighten**) **the living daylights out of** to scare or frighten badly. 19th–20th centuries. Probably a euphemistic variant of the phrase to scare (or frighten) the shit out of (see also scared shitless).

scarper to run away; to decamp in a hurry. From the Italian *scappare*, to escape. Since before 1844.

scat! go away! Since the 19th century.

scatter-gun a shotgun. Used in the USA since around 1870 and in the UK from around 1920.

scatty crazy; slightly mad; feather-brained. Perhaps from *scatter-brained.*

scavenge to cadge money; to thieve in a petty way. Used in Australia since around 1925.

scene the favoured setting or activity of an individual or group of people, as in *ballroom dancing isn't my scene.* Adopted from the USA around 1966.

sceney up-to-the-minute in appearance, habits, practices, etc., as in *it was all very trendy and sceney at Theo's.* From the mid-1960s.

schimpf to complain, to grouse. Hence, *to be schimpfed*, to be peeved or irritated. Originally used by troops stationed in Germany. Probably since 1945. From the German *schimpfen*, to revile or abuse.

schizo, n. and adj. schizophrenic. Since around 1925.

schlep or **shlep**, v. to move or travel laboriously; to carry or transport laboriously. From the Yiddish *schlep* (or *schlepen*), to drag.

schlep or **shlep**, n. a clumsy or inept person.

schlock shoddy or overpriced goods. From Yiddish.

schlocky shoddy, inferior, trashy. From Yiddish.

schmaltz or **schmalz** excessive sentimentality; anything (such as music, a song, a performance, a story, etc.) that is sweetly or excessively sentimental. Since around 1955. From the Yiddish *schmaltz*, chicken fat used for cooking; hence, greasy or slick.

schmaltzy or **schmalzy** sweetly or excessively sentimental.

schmo a foolish or very naive person; an objectionable or contemptible person. Adopted from the USA around 1959. Perhaps from Yiddish or mock-Yiddish.

schmuck or **schmock** a fool. Since around 1910. From the Yiddish *schmuck*, penis, *Schmuck*, from the German *Schmuck*, ornament.

schmutter clothing, esp. a suit; rags or rubbish. From Yiddish.

schnozzle nose. Adopted from the USA around 1940. The term was popularized by the US comedian Jimmy 'Schnozzle' Durante, who had a very prominent nose. From the German *Schnauze,* snout, muzzle.

school   a regular gathering of the same drinkers.

schoolie   a schoolteacher of either sex. Used in Australia since 1907 or earlier.

school (or **university**) **of hard knocks**   experience, esp. as a form of education that is considered to be more effective than formal schooling and harder than academic life. Since around 1910.

schwartz or **schwarz**   a Black person; a Negro, Indian or Pakistani; a half-caste. Since around 1950. Via Yiddish from the German *schwarz,* black.

scoop the pool   to make a killing (in the financial sense of the word). From gambling.

score   **1** to buy or otherwise obtain drugs, esp. unexpectedly. Adopted from the USA around 1955.   **2** to succeed in seducing or having sexual intercourse (with), to find a sexual partner, as in *he's hoping to score at the party.* From around 1950.

scram!   clear out (or off)!; go away! Adopted from the USA by 1930. Perhaps from the verb *scramble.*

scrambled egg(s)   the gold braid on the peak of the cap of a senior officer in the armed forces. Since around 1925. *See also* **marmalade**.

scrape the (bottom of the) barrel   to have to make do with the least desirable, weakest, poorest or most inferior people or things, because there is nobody or nothing better. Since around 1945.

scream   an extremely funny or ridiculous person or thing, as in *read this: it's a scream!* Since 1915.

screamer   **1** a man who is very obviously homosexual. Since around 1950.   **2** *see* **two-pot screamer**.

screaming abdabs   *see* **abdabs**.

screw, v.   **1** to have sexual intercourse (with), as in *he's been screwing his best friend's wife, he accused her of screwing around,* i.e. sleeping around (*see* **sleep around**). Since before 1785.   **2** to ruin. *See also* **screw up**.   **3** to swindle, as in *you've been screwed!* Since around 1930.

screw, n.   **1** an act of sexual intercourse.   **2** a prison warder. Since before 1821.   **3** in *to take a screw at,* to glance or look at.

screwball, n. and adj.   eccentric. Mainly US and Canadian.

screw the arse off   to copulate with, vigorously and often. 20th century.

screw up   to do badly, to ruin, wreck or bungle, as in *this is your last chance: don't screw it up.* Adopted from the USA in the later 20th century.

screwy   crazy, mad. Since before 1935. Perhaps elliptical for the phrase *to have a screw loose,* to be mad.

script   a prescription for drugs. Used in the USA since before 1936.

scrote a term of abuse. Perhaps from *scrotum*.

scrounge, v. to cadge or beg, as in *he scrounged twenty pounds off his brother*. Since World War I. From the dialect verb *scrunge*, to steal.

scrounge, n. esp. in *on the scrounge*, cadging, begging, looking for what can be acquired illicitly or free of charge, as in *I'm on the scrounge again: have you got any spare floppy disks?* Since 1914 or 1915.

scrounger a person who scrounges. From 1915. *See* **scrounge,** v.

scrub to cancel, as in *scrub it!; scrub that, I've changed my mind; the plan has been scrubbed.* Since around 1910.

scrubber a vulgar or promiscuous girl or woman. Since around 1925. From the use of the term in the slang sense of 'prostitute'.

Scrubs, the the prison at Wormwood Scrubs. Since before 1916.

scruff or **scruff-bag** a scruffy-looking person. Since around 1950.

scrummy scrumptious, delicious. From around 1906.

sculling around wandering around, esp. aimlessly. From rowing.

scumbag an objectionable or despicable person. Adopted from the USA around 1985. From *scumbag*, condom.

scun to wander, aimlessly or purposefully. Since World War II. Perhaps a blend of *scull* (*see* **sculling around**) and **swan.**

scungy dirty, messy, sordid, miserable; a general pejorative.

scunnered physically exhausted. Later 20th century.

scupper to spoil or ruin, as in *he scuppered his chances at the interview by flirting with his prospective boss.* From the nautical term *scupper*, to sink one's ship or boat deliberately.

scuttlebutt rumour; gossip. Adopted from the USA in the late 1960s.

scuzzbag an unpleasant or disreputable person; a jerk. Used in the USA and Canada since around 1980. From **scuzzy.**

scuzzy dirty, filthy, unkempt, shabby; unpleasant, disgusting. Used in the USA and Canada since the early 1970s. *See also* **scuzzbag.**

seat of (one's) pants, by the relying on or proceeding by instinct rather than technology or theory, as in *to fly by the seat of one's pants*, using instinct rather than instruments. Since around 1930. From the feeling of centrifugal force against the pilot's seat.

see it coming a mile off an intensification of *to see it coming*, as in *you could see it coming a mile off*, it was obvious, bound to happen, not at all unexpected. 20th century or earlier.

see off to defeat, esp. in a race, as in *this car should be able to see off* most of its rivals.

seem to, can't (or **cannot**) to seem unable to, to be apparently unable to, as in *I can't seem to settle down to anything this morning.*

see red to become very angry, to fly into a rage, as in *that sort of remark really makes me see red!*

sell-out, n. a contest, entertainment, etc., for which all the seats are sold. From around 1930.

sell out, v.   to betray a cause, one's country, etc. Adopted from the USA around 1945.

sell the pass   to give away an advantage to one's opponent(s). From rugby.

semi 1 a semi-detached house. Since around 1930. **2** a semi-final. Sporting slang. Since around 1930.

send to excite or enrapture, as in *this music really sends me.* Adopted from the USA around 1960.

send down   (usu. passive) to expel from university. Since before 1891.

send up, v.   to mock or make fun of; to burlesque or parody, as in *he was sent up unmercifully by his classmates.* Since before 1931.

send-up, n.   a satire, burlesque or parody, as in *a brilliant send-up of the Eurovision Song Contest.* Since the late 1950s.

septic   an American, a Yank. Australian rhyming slang (short for *septic tank*).

seriously   an adverbial intensifier, as in *seriously rich.*

sesame   a password. Since around 1930. From the phrase *open sesame!,* used by Ali Baba in *The Arabian Nights.*

sesh   session, as in *a training sesh at the gym.* The term is also used in the slang sense of **session**.

session   a period of steady drinking in a group. Since the mid-20th century.

set   esp. in *all set,* ready and willing; thoroughly prepared.

set (sb) back   to cost (sb), as in *how much did that set you back?; those shoes must have set her back at least £100.* Adopted from the USA around 1932.

seven shades of shit   esp. in *to knock* (or *thump*) *seven shades of shit out of (sb),* to lay into (sb) with the intention of causing severe pain and injury. Since around 1950. The phrase is also used as a general intensifier in other contexts of violence or aggression.

sewn up   organized, arranged, settled; well in hand; satisfactorily completed, as in *everything's sewn up.* Since around 1936. *See also* **game sewn up, have the.**

sex-bomb or **sexpot**   a sexually attractive person, esp. female. Late 20th century.

sexiness   attractiveness, appeal; the state of being **sexy.**

sex-kitten   a sexually attractive girl or young woman, esp. one who makes the most of her sex appeal. Since the late 1950s.

sexpot   *see* **sex-bomb.**

Sexton Blake   a fake (antique, work of art, etc.). Rhyming slang of the later 20th century. Often shortened to *Sexton.*

sexy   attractive, appealing; popular; fashionable. A term of approbation used in commerce, marketing, finance, politics, etc. Since the 1960s.

shack up (of unmarried sexual partners) to cohabit, to live together, as in *they've been shacked up together for months; he shacked up with his ex-wife's best friend*. Adopted from the USA by around 1955.

shade to be superior to or better than. Australian.

shaded reduced in price. Used in trade and commerce since around 1920.

shades sunglasses, dark glasses. Since the 1930s. Perhaps from *eyeshade*.

shaft (of a man) to copulate with. Since the late 1940s.

shag, v. to have sexual intercourse (with). Late 18th–20th centuries.

shag, n. an act of sexual intercourse.

shagged (out) weary, exhausted, worn out. Since around 1930.

shambolic chaotic, completely disorganized; in a mess, in a shambles. Since the 1940s.

shaming shameful, as in *how shaming!* Around 1929–34.

shamus a private detective. Adopted from US servicemen around 1944. Perhaps from the Yiddish *shames*, a synagogue official.

sharp rather too smartly dressed. Of US or Canadian origin; used in the UK by around 1944.

sharp end, the 1 the bow of a boat or ship. A jocular term used by or for the benefit of ignorant landlubbers. 2 the place where there is most activity, danger, competition, decision-making, etc., esp. in *at the sharp end*, at the front, directly affected or involved. Since the late 1970s.

sharpish quickly, promptly, as in *they started shooting, so we moved out a bit sharpish; you'd better get over there pretty sharpish*.

shat a jocular form of the past tense or past participle of **shit**, v., as in *he nearly shat himself*. Since around 1920. *See also* **shat upon**.

shattered utterly exhausted, physically or mentally or both. Since the mid-20th century.

shat upon 1 humiliated, squashed, as in *I won't be shat upon!* Perhaps a punning blend of **shit** and *sat (upon)*. 2 in *shat upon from a great height*, reprimanded by somebody of much higher rank, as in *she deserves to be shat upon from a great height*. Since World War II. *See also* **drop on (sb) from a (very) great height**.

sheba an attractive girl or woman. Mostly US. Since 1926. From the reputed beauty of the *Queen of Sheba*.

sheeny a Jew. Since 1816. Perhaps from the Yiddish pronunciation of the German *schön*, beautiful, used by Jews to praise their wares; or from the *sheeny* (glossy) dark hair of the Jews; or from the Yiddish phrase *a miessa meshina*, an ugly fate or death, widely used by Jews.

she'll be apples (or **right**) *see* **apples 1**; **right**.

shell-like   ear, as in *may I have a word in your shell-like?* Since the mid-20th century. From the poetic phrase *shell-like ear.*

sherbet   a taxi, a cab. Rhyming slang (short for *sherbet dab*).

sherman   an act of masturbation. Later 20th century. From *Sherman tank*, rhyming slang for 'wank'.

shice   nothing, as in *to work for shice.* Since before 1859.

shicer   a worthless or idle person; a cheat or crook. Since before 1857. The term may be related to **shyster**.

shift   to move or travel speedily. Since around 1919.

shimmy   (esp. of the front wheels of a small car) to oscillate or vibrate.

shindig   a large and lively party. Used in the UK since the mid-20th century or earlier.

shiner   a black eye. Since around 1920.

ship   an aircraft. RAF slang of World War II, perhaps of US origin.

shirt-lifter   a male homosexual. Australian; since the 1960s.

shit, n.   **1** faeces; defecation, as in *dog shit*; *to have a shit.* Since the 16th century.   **2** a contemptible or objectionable person, as in *you little shit!*; *he's an awful shit.*   **3** anything bad, poor, inferior, unpleasant, etc., such as bad weather.   **4** short for **bullshit**, n., as in *don't give me that shit!* Since the mid-20th century.   **5** applied to various drugs, esp. marijuana (since around 1950) or heroin (since around 1960).   **6** abuse, unfair treatment, as in *she's taken a lot of shit from the authorities.*   **7** in the phrase *in the shit*, in trouble. Since the mid-19th century or earlier. *See also* **shite**.

shit, v.   to defecate. Since the 16th century. *See also* **shat**.

shit!   a strong expletive.

shit a brick!   an exclamation of annoyance or surprise. Since around 1960.

shit bricks   esp. in *to be shitting bricks*, to be really worried; to be thoroughly frightened. *See also* **brick it**.

shit creek   in *up shit creek (without a paddle)*, in very serious trouble. *See* **shit**, n. **7**.

shite   a dialectal variant of **shit**, n.

shit-faced   very drunk, esp. to the point of vomiting. Adopted from the USA in the later 20th century.

shit-for-brains   a dim-witted person, as in *you're a real shit-for-brains.* Mainly used in the USA, Canada and Australia. From the phrase *to have shit for brains.*

shithead   an objectionable person. Since the mid-20th century or earlier.

shit-hot   **1** very keen or enthusiastic, as in *they're shit-hot on safety procedures.* Since 1914.   **2** very knowledgeable or skilful, as in *a shit-hot performance.* Since around 1918.   **3** very topical or up-to-the minute, as in *a shit-hot story*. Since around 1950.

shit on (sb) from a (very) great height *see* **drop on (sb) from a (very) great height; shat upon 2**.

shits, the 1 diarrhoea. Since the mid-19th century. 2 terror. *See* **give (sb) the shits**.

shit-scared extremely scared, almost to the extent of nervous diarrhoea. Since around 1935.

shit to a blanket, like (or **as close as**) esp. in *to cling* (or *stick*) *like shit to a blanket*, to stay very close, usually in an unwanted way. Since around 1930.

shitty 1 of poor quality, as in *a shitty radio*. 2 (of behaviour or treatment) shabby and unfair, as in *what a shitty way to treat a bloke!*

shiv, n. and v. (to) knife. A variant spelling of the Romany *chiv*.

shlep *see* **schlep**.

shoestring, on a having or using only a small sum of money, esp. as working capital, as in *to operate on a shoestring*. Adopted from the USA in the 1950s or earlier. Hence the adjective *shoestring*, operating, produced, etc., on a very small capital, as in *a shoestring movie*.

shoo-in somebody or something that is favoured to win, esp. to win easily. Mainly US and Canadian.

shoot to inject (heroin, etc.). Adopted from the USA around 1965. *See also* **shoot up**.

shoot! 1 go ahead, speak! Adopted from the USA around 1925. Perhaps from the command *shoot!* given to camera operators in the cinema. 2 a euphemism for the expletive **shit!** Mainly US and Canadian.

shoot a line to boast or exaggerate, esp. in order to impress. Perhaps since around 1919.

shoot down (in flames) *see* **shot down; shot down in flames**.

shooting gallery a meeting place for drug users, where they inject drugs. Of US origin.

shooting-iron a rifle or pistol. Adopted from the USA around 1918.

shoot (oneself) in the foot to make a self-damaging blunder or counter-productive error of judgment. Since the 1980s. *See also* **own goal**.

shoot (one's) load (of a man) to have an orgasm, to ejaculate.

shoot (one's) mouth off to talk, esp. boastfully or indiscreetly. Adopted from the USA in 1930.

shoot the amber (or **the lights**) (of a motorist) to increase speed when an amber traffic light is showing, in order to pass before the red light comes on. From 1935. A motorist who does this is known as an *amber gambler*.

shoot the breeze to chatter idly; to gossip. Of US origin.

shoot the lights   *see* **shoot the amber**.

shoot through   to depart, as in *it's four o'clock – time we were shooting through*. Mainly Australian. Later 20th century.

shoot up   to inject drugs. Adopted from the USA in the mid-1960s. *See also* **shoot**.

shop (sb)   to inform on (sb), esp. to the police; to cause (sb) to be arrested or get into trouble, as in *he shopped his accomplice*. Since the early 19th century.

shop around   to have a number of different lovers before deciding to settle down with one of them, as in *I'm not ready for marriage yet: I'm still shopping around*. Since around 1960.

shoppie or **shoppy**   a shop assistant, esp. female. Since 1916 or earlier.

short, n.   a drink of spirits, esp. as opposed to beer, as in *they were drinking shorts*.

short and curlies, the   the short hairs, esp. the pubic hair. Chiefly used in the phrase *to get (sb) by the short and curlies*, to catch (sb) properly; to have or put (sb) in a difficult or helpless position; to have or get (sb) in one's power or at one's mercy. Since around 1935.

short of a bob or two, not   relatively wealthy, esp. in comparison with the speaker.

shot   exhausted. Since around 1920.

shot down   defeated in an argument. From around 1918.

shot down in flames   utterly defeated or routed, esp. in an argument. Since around 1939.

shotgun wedding   a wedding necessitated by the bride's pregnancy (i.e. originally at the insistence of her father, armed with a shotgun). Adopted from the USA, possibly in the early 20th century.

shout the odds   to talk loudly, boastfully or too much. Since around 1910. From the racecourse.

shove   to stop or forget; chiefly used in exclamations of dismissal, as in *you can shove that caper!* Since around 1910. From the phrase *shove it up your arse!* (or the British variant *shove it where the monkey shoves* (or *shoved*) *his nuts!*).

shove off   to depart, as in *shove off!*, go away!

shoving shit uphill   anal intercourse.

show, n.   in *bad* (or *poor*) *show*, *good show!*, expressions of disapprobation or approval. Since around 1925.

show, v.   *see* **show the flag; show up**.

showbiz   show business; the commercial and professional side of the world of entertainment. Possibly since the 1930s.

showboat, v.   to show off, as in *he was showboating around in his new uniform*.

show-down   a test of the real strength and backing of two people, parties, etc.; a final, conclusive or decisive confrontation, argument, fight, etc., as in *the government is seeking a show-down with the unions.* Adopted from the USA around 1930. From the game of poker.

shower   a group of worthless, contemptible, undesirable or unimpressive people, as in *what a shower!* Since around 1919. Short for *shower of shit* (or *bastards*).

show the flag   to put in an appearance. From around 1919.

show up   to appear or arrive, as in *she didn't show up.* Since before 1933.

shrimp, n.   a diminutive or puny person, esp. a child.

shrimp, v.   to suck the toe(s) of one's sexual partner; hence the noun *shrimping.* US slang, since the early 1990s. *See also* **toe-job**.

shrink, n.   psychiatrist, psychoanalyst. Adopted from the USA around 1965. A back-formation from **head-shrinker**. Hence the verb *shrink*, to psychoanalyse.

shtick   act, performance; behaviour. Adopted from the USA in the mid-1970s. Probably via Yiddish from the German *Stück*, bit, piece.

shtum   (pronounced *shtoom*) esp. in *to keep shtum*, to keep quiet, to keep one's mouth shut. Via Yiddish from the German *stumm*, dumb, silent.

shucks!   an exclamation of disappointment, frustration, annoyance, regret, indifference, etc. Of US origin.

shuffle-bottom   a fidgety child; often used as a term of address. Since the late 19th century.

shufty or **shufti**, v.   (usu. imperative) to look

shufty or **shufti**, n.   a look, glance or peep, as in *to have a shufty (at).* Since around 1925. Of Arabic origin.

shunt   a motor accident. Originally racing drivers' slang. Since the late 1950s or earlier.

shut-eye   sleep, as in *to get a bit of shut-eye.* Since the late 19th century.

shut-out   a game or match in which no goals, points, etc., are scored against the winner(s). Mainly US and Canadian. From the verb *shut out*, to prevent (one's opponent(s)) from scoring.

shy-making   *see* **-making**.

shyster   an unprofessional, dishonest or rapacious lawyer; any professional person who behaves in an unscrupulous or unethical manner. Since 1856. The term may be related to **shicer**.

sick   (of humour) morbid, esp. gruesomely morbid; callously or sadistically unkind, as in *a sick joke.* Adopted from the USA around 1959.

sick as a parrot, as   extremely annoyed, chagrined or upset, as in *he'll be as sick as a parrot if he loses this match.*

sickening   annoying; inconvenient; unfair; unpleasant; rude. From around 1920.

sickie   a day off, (allegedly) because of sickness; a day of one's sick leave, as in *to take a sickie.* Used in Australia since around 1930.

sick-making *see* -**making.**

side *see* **bit on the side.**

sidekick a close companion; an assistant, accomplice, partner or follower.

sign on 1 to enlist or re-enlist in the armed forces, as in *to sign on for seven years.* 2 (of an unemployed person) to register at an employment exchange.

sign on the dotted line to sign; to enter into a formal agreement, esp. by signing a document. From around 1925. From the instructions on official and legal documents.

sin-bin 1 the penalty box in ice-hockey. Since around 1946. 2 a special unit for disruptive schoolchildren. Later 20th century. 3 hence, any place where those who misbehave or break the rules may be sent for cooling off or correction, or as a punishment or penalty.

sing to confess or inform to the police, as in *do you think she'll sing?*; *he's been singing like a canary since his arrest.* Adopted from the USA around 1930.

sink, v. to drink; to knock back, as in *let's go out and sink a few beers.*

sink, n. in *down the sink,* lost, wasted, squandered, misspent.

sir one's (male) teacher, as in *she's got a crush on sir.* Used by schoolchildren. *See also* **miss.**

sister a term of address to any woman. Adopted from the USA around 1925.

sit pretty esp. in *to be sitting pretty,* to be in a very advantageous position. Since around 1920.

sit up and beg 1 in *(sb) can make it sit up and beg,* (sb) has become extremely proficient in working some material. Since around 1930. From the act of teaching a dog to sit up and beg. 2 a phrase used to describe (the position adopted by the rider of) an old-fashioned bicycle or motorcycle. The phrase is also applied to certain old-fashioned cars. Since around 1950.

skag *see* **scag.**

skates in *to get (one's) skates on,* to hurry. Since World War I or earlier.

sked a scheduled time to transmit/receive. Radio operators' slang. Possibly since around 1930. From the alternative (chiefly US) pronunciation of *scheduled.*

skedaddle to depart, esp. hastily; to flee; to escape. Since the 19th century.

skellington or **skelington** (jocular or dialectal) skeleton. 19th–20th centuries.

skiddoo *see* **skidoo.**

skid lid a motorcyclist's crash-helmet. Since the late 1950s.

skid marks smears of faeces on the inside of a person's underwear.

skidoo or **skiddoo** to depart, esp. hastily; to make off or run away. 20th century. From **skedaddle**.

skid row a depressed area of a town or city, where the hopeless down-and-outs live or congregate, as in *to end up on skid row*. Mainly US and Canadian. Late 19th–20th centuries. From *skid road*, a term used in logging.

skids esp. in *to put the skids under (sb)*, to dismiss (sb) from a job. Since around 1940.

skin 1 a skinhead, a member of a gang of young louts and hooligans characterized by closely cropped or shaven heads. Since around 1970. 2 in *under (one's) skin*, constantly irritated by or aware of, as in *that noise gets under my skin*, it irritates me; *I've got you under my skin* (a love song by Cole Porter). Since around 1925. 3 in *it's no skin off my nose*, it makes no difference to me, it doesn't affect me adversely or put me at a disadvantage. A declaration of disinterest or indifference, as in *it's no skin off my nose if you lose your driving licence*. The word *my* may be replaced by *your, his, her*, etc. 4 women, esp. young women, as in *a taut drop of skin*, a shapely young woman. 5 a cigarette paper. Mainly prisoners' and drug users' slang of the later 20th century.

skin and blister sister. Rhyming slang of the late 19th–20th centuries.

skinflick a pornographic film that includes scenes of nudity and sexual intercourse. Since around 1972.

skinful esp. in *to have had a skinful*, to be extremely drunk. Since the early 18th century.

skinny dip a swim in the nude. Of US origin. Hence the verb *skinny-dip* and the noun *skinny-dipping*.

skint almost or completely penniless.

skip it! it doesn't matter!; don't worry!; don't bother!; forget it! Adopted from the USA around 1939.

skipper a place where dossers can sleep for the night, esp. an empty house or derelict building. Later 20th century. The term originally referred to a barn (from the mid-16th century), then to a place where tramps and vagrants slept out of doors (from the late 19th century).

skirt esp. in the phrase *a bit of skirt*, a girl or young woman; girls or young women considered collectively.

skive, v. (often followed by *off*) to evade (work, responsibility, duty, parade, etc.). Originally military slang. From 1915.

skive, n. an evasion or dodge; a means or an instance of evading or skiving. Since around 1925.

skiver   a shirker, a person who skives. Since around 1915. *See* **skive**, v.

skivvy, n.   a menial servant, esp. female; a drudge. From around 1905.

skivvy, v.   to perform menial, boring or heavy household chores. Later 20th century.

skulduggery   underhand practices; villainy or trickery. Since the 19th century. From the Scottish *sculduddery*.

skull, out of (one's)   out of one's mind, crazy, mad; intoxicated by alcohol or drugs. Adopted from the USA around 1970.

sky   in *to have a sky*, to have a look, to glance around. Since around 1920.

sky-blue pink   an unknown, indeterminate, or non-existent colour. Since around 1885. Sometimes elaborated to *sky-blue pink with a finny-addy border* (finny-addy = finnan haddock).

sky pilot   a priest or clergyman, esp. a chaplain in the armed forces. Since the 19th century.

slag, n.   a promiscuous girl or woman; a prostitute. Since the late 1950s.

slag, v.   (often followed by *off*) to disparage, to run down, to malign. Since around 1945.

slam   to strike or punch. Since around 1910.

slammer   prison, as in *ten years in the slammer*. Adopted from the USA by the late 1970s.

slant   a Chinese, Japanese or other Oriental person. Of US origin. From *slant-eyed*. *See also* **slope**.

slap and tickle   esp. in *a bit of slap and tickle*, petting, fondling, caressing; sexual intercourse. Since around 1910.

slash, n.   an act of urination, as in *to have a slash; to go for a slash*. Since the mid-20th century.

slash, v.   to urinate. Later 20th century.

sleaze   sleaziness. Later 20th century.

sleazy   grimy, sordid, squalid or disreputable, as in *a sleazy nightclub*. Adopted from the USA in the late 1950s. Perhaps a blend of *slimy* and *greasy*.

sleep around   to have a number of sexual partners, to be promiscuous, as in *teenagers are warned of the dangers of sleeping around*. Since the late 1940s.

sleeper   a book, record, etc., that sells badly at first but eventually becomes a hit. Since around 1950.

sleep (one's) way   to gain advantage by dispensing sexual favours, as in *she slept her way to the top*. Later 20th century.

slicker   a person who dresses in very fancy, stylish or expensive clothing. Of US origin. *See also* **city slicker**.

sling (one's) hook   to depart, to leave, as in *sling your hook!*, go away!

slinky sneaky, mean, sly, furtive. Since the late 19th century.

slippery clever; very skilful or adroit (usually with an implication of shrewd cunning). Since around 1930.

slips (in a theatre or cinema) the sides of a gallery, as in *a seat in the slips*.

slip up, v. to make a mistake; to fail, as in *somebody must have slipped up*. Since the mid-19th century.

slip-up, n. an error, as in *you've made a bit of a slip-up there*. Possibly since the mid-20th century.

Sloane, n. and adj. (of) a **Sloane Ranger**. Since the mid-1980s. Also *Sloanie*.

Sloane Rangers a generic nickname for young people (esp. female) of the upper or upper-middle classes who live around Sloane Square, London, and go to their country homes at weekends. A punning blend of *Sloane Square* and the cartoon character the *Lone Ranger*, the term was coined by Peter York for an article in *Harpers & Queen*, October 1975.

slob a person (esp. male) who is slovenly, coarse, heavily-built, slow-moving, dull-witted and/or imperceptive. Since around 1920.

slope a Chinese, Japanese or other Oriental person. Of US origin; used in the UK and Australia since the early 1960s. From *slope-eyed*. *See also* **slant**.

slops beer. Used in Australia since around 1920.

slosh to hit, esp. resoundingly and often wildly, as in *I sloshed him one*.

sloshed drunk. Late 19th–20th centuries.

slot (sb) in to choose (sb) to fill a vacancy, as in *we're slotting you in as Tom's assistant for the time being*. Later 20th century.

slowpoke a dull or slow person; a slowcoach. Mainly used in the USA, Canada and Australia.

slurp to eat or drink noisily, messily, in an uncouth way, as in *to slurp (one's) soup*. Adopted from the USA around 1955. From the sound made when eating or drinking in this way.

slush fund a secret fund of money, usually raised from dubious sources, kept by a large political or commercial organization for bribery and other shady dealings. Of US origin.

slushy extremely sentimental.

smack heroin. Drug users' slang. Adopted from the USA in the mid-1960s. Perhaps via Yiddish from the German *schmecken*, to taste, reinforced by the sense of the violent effect of the drug that the word conveys.

smack-bang **1** suddenly and violently, as in *she drove smack-bang into the wall*. Probably since the mid-19th century. **2** right, exactly, as in *smack-bang in the middle*.

smacker **1** a loud or enthusiastic kiss. **2** a pound sterling or a dollar bill, as in *twenty smackers.*

smackeroonie an elaboration of **smacker**, as in *she gave him a real smackeroonie* (kiss); *five hundred smackeroonies* (pounds).

smack-head a heroin addict.

smack in the eye a rebuff, a refusal; a severe disappointment; a setback.

small fortune an extravagantly or excessively large sum of money, as in *that ring must have cost him a small fortune.* Since around 1890.

smalls underwear, as in *to wash (one's) smalls.*

small-time *see* **big time.**

smarm to behave with fulsome flattery or insincere politeness. Since 1915 or earlier. From *smarm,* to smooth down.

smarmy fulsomely flattering, insincerely polite, obsequious, toadying, Since around 1915. From *smarmy,* (of hair) sleek, plastered down.

smart Alec a know-all, an offensively smart (clever) person, as in *he's such a smart Alec.* Used in the USA since around 1870 and in the UK by 1930. *See also* **clever Dick, smartarse.**

smartarse an obnoxiously smart (clever) person, as in *OK, smartarse, what do you suggest?* Also used attributively, as in *a smartarse remark. See also* **clever Dick, smart Alec.**

smarty-pants a smart person (either clever or fashionably dressed), or one who thinks he/she is smart. Probably of US origin.

smashed 1 drunk, as in *we're getting smashed on airline champagne.* Since around 1960. 2 intoxicated by drugs, as in *he was smashed out of his skull.*

smasher any person or thing that is unusually excellent or outstandingly attractive, as in *she's a little smasher.* Since the mid-19th century.

smashing excellent. Since the mid-19th century.

smell like a whore's boudoir to be heavily scented (esp. of a man using highly scented hair oil, aftershave lotion, after-shave lotion, etc).

smell of the barman's apron, (sb) has had a applied to a person who easily gets drunk. Since around 1920.

smidgin, smidgen, smidgeon or **smidge** a very small amount; a bit. Used in the USA since the mid-19th century. Perhaps from the dialect noun *smitch,* a dirty mark.

smile bare flesh showing between the bottom of one's jumper, T-shirt, etc., and the top of one's jeans. Since around 1950. The term earlier (around 1910–50) referred to the gap between stocking and suspender belt.

smoke cannabis. Used in the USA since around 1946.

smoking gun directly incriminating evidence. Adopted from the USA by the mid-1980s.

smooch to kiss and cuddle amorously. Probably from the dialect verb *smudge* or *smouch*, to kiss.

smoothie a smooth-spoken person, esp. male. Since around 1925. In later 20th-century usage the term usually implies untrustworthy plausibility and deliberate charm.

smudge pornographic photographs, or magazines containing them.

snafu, n. and adj. acronym for Situation Normal: All Fucked Up. Referring to a perpetual or habitual state of chaos or confusion, usually caused by administrative or bureaucratic incompetence. 20th century.

snake bite lager and cider mixed.

snap a packed lunch or snack. Since around 1920.

snap! an exclamation called forth by any (usually minor) coincidence. From the card game of the same name.

snappy 1 short-tempered, irritable. Since the late 19th century. 2 in *make it snappy!*, be quick!; look lively! Adopted from the USA.

snatch the female genitalia. Late 19th–20th centuries.

snazzy fashionable, smart, as in *a snazzy little camera.* Adopted from the USA by 1954. Perhaps a blend of *snappy* and *jazzy.*

sneak a person who informs or tells tales on others. Used by schoolchildren since the late 19th century.

snip a bargain; a certainty; an easy win or acquisition, as in *it's a snip at twenty pounds.* Since 1894 or earlier.

snippy captious, fault-finding; snappy or brusque.

snitch 1 to purloin, as in *he's always snitching other people's ideas.* 2 to tell tales or inform (on). Since the early 19th century.

snog to kiss and cuddle, to indulge in (heavy) petting, as in *snogging on the back row of the cinema.* Perhaps from *snug* or *snuggle.* Mid-20th century.

snooks a term of endearment for a small child. Used in Australia since around 1925.

snookums a term of endearment, esp. for a small dog. Since 1928 or earlier.

snoop (often followed by *around*) to pry. Adopted from the USA around 1905. From the Dutch *snoepen*, to eat furtively.

snoot nose. A variant of *snout. See also* **droop snoot; snooty**.

snooty supercilious. Since around 1930. Perhaps from **snoot**, referring to the act of looking down one's nose (or turning up one's nose).

snort, n. a drink of spirits, as in *he pulled out his flask and took a snort.* Since the late 1920s.

snort, v. to take drugs through the nose, as in *to snort cocaine.* Adopted from the USA in the mid-1960s.

snout 1 tobacco, cigarette(s). Mainly prison slang. Since before 1896.

2 an informer. From around 1920.

snout baron in prison, a major trafficker in tobacco or cigarettes. Since around 1930.

snow, n. cocaine. Adopted from the USA around 1920.

snow, v. to deceive, to try to throw (sb) off the scent. Later 20th century.

snowball's, not a no chance whatsoever. Since around 1950. Elliptical for *not a snowball's chance in hell.*

snow-bunny a young female companion of male skiers or other winter sportsmen; a girl or young woman who goes skiing or frequents ski resorts but is more interested in sex than sport.

snowed under overburdened or overwhelmed, esp. with work. Adopted from the USA around 1930.

snow job deception, flannel, insincere charm. Of US origin.

snuck a jocular or non-standard form of the past tense of *sneak*, as in *I snuck in and took a look.* Adopted from the USA in the earlier 20th century.

snuff it to die, as in *if I snuff it, my wife gets £25,000.* Since before 1874. Probably from the snuffing (out) of a candle.

snuff movie a pornographic film in which a participant is actually murdered. Used in the USA since the mid-1970s and in the UK by the early 1980s.

soak a drunkard. Since around 1910.

so-and-so an objectionable person, as in *he's a right so-and-so.* 20th century.

soapy silly, stupid. Used in Australia since around 1920.

s.o.b. short for **son of a bitch**. Mainly US and Canadian.

sob sister a female journalist who writes sentimental or emotional articles for newspapers or magazines. Adopted from the USA around 1930. *See also* **agony aunt.**

sob story a hard-luck story.

sob stuff excessive sentimentality, intended to appeal to the emotions (and often to the pocket). Used in the USA since around 1919 and in the UK by 1921.

socked out out of commission. Later 20th century.

socko-boffo absolutely outstanding, as in *a socko-boffo hit.* Mainly used in the world of entertainment. Adopted from the USA in the later 20th century.

sod **1** a person, as in *you lucky sod!* Late 19th–20th centuries. **2** an objectionable, obnoxious or unpleasant person, as in *the rotten sod won't let me have the afternoon off.* Since the early 19th century. **3** a difficult or annoying thing, situation, etc., as in *this cooker is a sod to keep clean.* Later 20th century. **4** *see* **odds and sods.**

sod all nothing, as in *she's done sod all to help us.*

sodding a pejorative adjectival intensifier, as in *the sodding car won't start; you can keep your sodding job!*

sod it! an exclamation of annoyance.

sod off! go away!

Sod's law the rule or principle that if something can go wrong, it will, and even if it can't, it still might. Mostly applied to trivial inconveniences and mishaps. The term has been in general use since around 1970, but is probably of much earlier origin.

soft option the easier or easiest of a number of choices, as in *to take the soft option; teaching is regarded as a soft option.* Since the early 1970s.

soft-pedal to subdue or tone down; to proceed circumspectly in an affair, as in *we'd better soft-pedal it, do things by the book.* Later 20th century. From the pedal that lowers the volume of a piano, organ or other musical instrument.

soft roll a girl or woman who is easily persuaded to have sex. Since the late 1940s. From **roll**, n. **1**.

soft touch a person who is easy to impose on, persuade, borrow from, sponge on, etc., as in *you think I'm a soft touch, don't you?* Since around 1910.

soldier on to persevere, esp. in the face of peril and/or hardship. From 1916.

soldiers fingers of buttered bread, esp. for dipping into the yolk of a soft-boiled egg. Nursery slang.

sold on (sth), be (often negative) to be enthusiastic about (sth), to be very much attracted by (sth), as in *I'm not exactly sold on the idea myself.* Since the late 1940s.

something else applied to a person or thing that defies description; usually but not necessarily a term of approbation, as in *wow! that's something else!* (i.e. excellent, wonderful); *as a jazz trumpeter, he's something else* (i.e. outstanding); *her chocolate-chip cookies are something else* (i.e. delicious); *the prices in this restaurant are something else* (i.e. outrageously high). Since the 1960s.

son of . . . successor of . . ., as in *Son of Concorde; the new tax has been called 'son of poll tax'.* Since the 1970s. From sequel film titles, such as *Son of Dracula.*

song, on in good form, as in *any side on song would have given them the run-around.* Used in sport, esp. football, since around 1960.

song and dance **1** anybody's performance in the course of doing his or her job, such as a salesman reeling off his patter. **2** an unnecessary fuss, esp. in *to make a song and dance about (sth).*

son of a bitch or **sonofabitch** a disagreeable or despicable person, as in *that son of a bitch Martin has been sleeping with my wife!* The term is sometimes not derogatory, as in *the poor son of a bitch!*; *you lucky son of a bitch!* Mainly US and Canadian. Since the early 18th century. *See also* **s.o.b.**

sooper a phonetic spelling of **super**, adj., esp. when used as an emphatic exclamation. Since before 1909.

soppy foolishly sentimental, as in *a soppy love story*. Since the early 20th century.

soppy ha'p'orth a soft or silly person. Possibly since the 1930s. *See also* **ha'p'orth** 1.

soul-case the body; hence, a person. Late 18th–20th centuries.

sound as a pound, as right, correct, OK, esp. in *that's (as) sound as a pound!*

sound off to become very angry about a particular topic or on a particular occasion; to air one's opinions or grievances in a vociferous manner; to boast, as in *he started sounding off about the government*; *they're always sounding off about their daughter's achievements*. Adopted from the USA around 1955.

sounds music, esp. rock or pop music. Teenagers' slang of the early 1980s.

souped-up (of a car, motorcycle or engine) supercharged; modified to increase its power, as in *a souped-up Mini*.

sourpuss a morose person. Adopted from the USA in 1942. From the slang noun *puss*, face.

souse, v. to get drunk. From around 1920. Perhaps a back-formation from **soused**.

souse, n. a drunkard.

soused drunk. Since the mid-19th century.

southpaw a left-handed boxer; any left-handed person. Adopted from the USA in 1934. From US baseball slang: on a regulation baseball field the batter faces east (so that the afternoon sun will not be in his eyes) and the pitcher faces west; the pitcher's left hand (*paw*) is therefore on the south side of his body.

sov a pound sterling. Since the mid-19th century. Short for *sovereign*, a former gold coin worth one pound.

sow's ear a variant of **pig's ear**. From the proverb *you can't make a silk purse out of a sow's ear*.

s.p. information. Since around 1950. From bookmakers' jargon; short for *starting-price*.

space cadet originally used of a person who is or appears to be under the influence of drugs; it is now used more generally to mean a vague or weird person out of touch with reality. Of US origin, since the 1970s.

spaced out very high on a hallucinogenic or psychedelic drug; intoxicated or exhilarated by any drug, as in *she was spaced out on LSD*. Adopted from the USA in the late 1960s.

spacy   under the influence of a narcotic drug. Hence, weird; out of touch with reality. Probably adopted from the USA. Since the late 1970s. From **spaced out**.

spade   a Black person, esp. an Afro-Caribbean. Since around 1920. From the colour of the card suit and the simile **black as the ace of spades**.

spare   **1** very angry, esp. in *to go spare*. Since around 1940. **2** mad, crazy, as in *they send me spare*, they drive me mad. Since the late 1950s. **3** *see* **bit of spare**.

spare prick   a useless person. Since 1939. From the phrase *like a spare prick at a wedding*.

sparklers   sparkling gems, esp. diamonds. Since around 1820 (originally in Standard English).

sparks   an electrician. Since around 1945.

sparrow-fart   dawn, daybreak, esp. in the phrase *at sparrow-fart*. Since around 1910 (or earlier in dialectal usage).

spastic, n. and adj.   clumsy or incompetent (person). Since the mid-1950s.

spat   a minor quarrel, as in *it's just a spat*.

speak the same language   to have the same ideas, opinions, background, upbringing, etc. Since around 1930.

spear-carrier   a walk-on part in a play, a minor non-speaking role. Theatrical slang.

specs   **1** spectacles. **2** specifications. The term is also used in the singular, as in *job spec*, the details of a post. Since the mid-20th century.

speed   an amphetamine, esp. methamphetamine. Drug users' slang. Adopted from the USA around 1965. Hence *speed-freak*, amphetamine addict.

speed-cop   a police officer who observes and checks the speed of motorists. Used in the USA since around 1924 and in the UK by 1929.

speed-merchant   a person who drives at high speed. Adopted from the USA around 1920.

speedo   speedometer. Motorists' slang. Since around 1920.

spend a penny   to urinate, not necessarily in a public convenience. The first public convenience to charge one penny was opened outside the Royal Exchange, London, in 1855.

spew (one's) guts up   to vomit violently and comprehensively.

spic or **spick**, n. and adj.   Spanish; Latin American. Adopted from the USA, where the term has been in use since around 1915. Perhaps a contraction of *Hispanic*, or from a foreigner's mispronunciation of *speak*.

spiel, n. **1** a sales representative's (or con-artist's) patter. Late 19th–20th centuries. **2** a wordy explanation.

spiel, v. to talk glibly and plausibly. Since around 1870. Perhaps a back-formation from the noun *spieler*, gambler, cardsharper, professional swindler, from the German *Spieler*, player, gamester.

spike, n. a needle or syringe for injecting a drug. Drug users' slang. Adopted from the USA around 1960.

spike, v. to add alcohol (or some other potentially dangerous substance, such as a drug or poison) surreptitiously to a drink, as in *he spiked her orange juice with vodka*. Adopted from the USA in the mid-20th century or earlier.

spill the beans to divulge important and/or confidential information, intentionally or unintentionally. Adopted from the USA by 1928.

spin a drive in a car (or, occasionally, a ride on a motorcycle), as in *to go for a spin; she took me for a spin in her new Merc*. From around 1905.

spin-off a secondary or incidental result or by-product, as in *non-stick frying-pans were a useful spin-off from the US space programme*. Adopted from the USA in the late 1940s.

spit and sawdust (the public bar of) a public house, esp. one that is fairly basic or unrefined in decor or clientele. The term is also used as an adjective, as in *spit-and-sawdust bar; we'll go to the Nag's Head: it's a bit spit-and-sawdust, but the beer's good*. From the sawdust originally sprinkled on the floor of such a bar or pub and the spitting of the customers.

spit it out! speak!; confess! Usually addressed to somebody who seems unable to articulate or reluctant to say what has to be said.

spiv a man or boy, usually flashily dressed, who lives by his wits, either just within the law or on the fringes of criminality; a tout, racketeer or black-marketeer. Since around 1890. From the same origin as the dialectal *spif* or *spiff*, smart, dandified.

splash a small quantity of soda water (added to whisky, etc.). Since before 1927.

splash out to be actively extravagant with money, as in *he splashed out on a new set of golf clubs*. Later 20th century.

splat imitative of the sound of something soft being dashed against something hard, e.g. an insect against the windscreen of a moving car.

spliff a marijuana cigarette.

split to depart, to go away, to leave. Originally used by US hippies; in general usage by 1970.

split beaver   *see* **beaver**, n. 1.

spondulicks   money. Of US origin. From the later 19th century.

spoof   to hoax, to trick or deceive, to play a practical joke, as in *you're not spoofing, are you?* From around 1920.

spook   a spy or secret agent. Possibly since around 1950.

sport   1 a person who behaves in a fair, sporting, unselfish or generous manner, as in *be a sport!*   2 a term of address, often between men or boys. Used in Australia since before World War I.

spot   1 a small amount, as in *a spot of lunch.* 20th century.   2 in *(to be) in (a bit of) a spot,* (to be) in a very difficult or dangerous position. From around 1930.   3 an allotted space in a programme, agenda, etc., as in *they've given me a five-minute spot near the end.* Later 20th century.

spot-on   absolutely correct, accurate, precise, exact, etc. Since 1940.

spring   1 to get (sb) released from prison, esp. on a legal technicality. Adopted from the USA by 1950 or earlier.   2 hence, to get (sb) out of prison by assisting his or her escape. Since around 1960.

sprog   a child or baby, as in *his wife's just had another sprog; are you taking the sprogs on holiday with you?* Since the late 1930s.

spud-bashing   the duty or punishment of peeling potatoes. Mainly military slang. Hence *spud-basher,* a person who peels potatoes. Since around 1920.

squaddie   a private soldier. Since the 1930s. Probably from the earlier synonym *swaddy* (from the dialectal *swad,* country bumpkin), influenced by *squad.*

square, n.   an old-fashioned person, esp. concerning culture and customs. Young people's slang. Adopted from the USA around 1938, becoming particularly widespread in the 1950s.

square, adj.   old-fashioned; conservative, reactionary. Since the late 1950s.

square, v.   *see* **square off**.

square-bashing   drill, esp. by recruits on the parade ground. Military slang. From the *bashing* down of the recruits' feet on the *square,* the parade ground. Since World War II.

square-eyed   applied to a person who watches too much television, as in *to go square-eyed; square-eyed children.* Since the mid-20th century. From the reputed effect of staring for too long at the rectangular screen.

square-eyes   a person who watches too much television.

square off   to placate. Used in Australia from around 1905.

square peg in a round hole   a person who is badly suited to his or her job or post; a misfit.

squash a social gathering in which many people are crowded into a small room. Since around 1930.

squat a house or other premises in which squatters have settled. Since the late 1970s. A back-formation from *squatter* and the verb *squat*.

squawk, v. to complain, esp. loudly. Of US origin.

squawk-box an office intercommunication system; a public-address system; a walkie-talkie set.

squeaky-clean (of people or, occasionally, their activities) patently honest, above-board, innocent, good, etc. Since around 1975.

squeeze-box a concertina or accordion. Since World War I.

squeeze (sb) like a lemon to charge or tax (sb) very severely. An intensive form of the phrase, *to squeeze (sb) until the pips squeak*, was made famous by Sir Eric Geddes (in a speech concerning German reparations) in December 1918 and revived in the mid-1970s.

squib a plan that fails. Used in Australia since around 1910. From *damp squib*.

squiffy **1** slightly drunk. From around 1873. **2** crooked, askew. Perhaps a contraction of *skew-whiff*.

squire a jocular term of address between men.

squirrelled away hidden away; hoarded for future use.

squits or **squitters** (usually *the squits*) diarrhoea, as in *I can't drink cider: it gives me the squits*. Late 19th–20th centuries (the term *squitters* was in Standard English from the mid-17th century until the 19th century).

s.t. sanitary towel. Since around 1940.

stab an attempt, as in *to have a stab at (sth)*. Adopted from the USA around 1930.

stacked or **well-stacked** (of a girl or woman) having large breasts. Both forms have been common in the UK since the early 1960s.

stage to do or accomplish, esp. unexpectedly or very effectively, as in *to stage a comeback*. From around 1920.

stagger-through a preliminary and/or slapdash dress rehearsal. Show-business slang of the later 20th century.

stake-out, n. a surveillance operation, esp. by the police. Of US origin. Since the 1940s.

stake out, v. to place (a building, etc.) under surveillance, esp. in the hope of obtaining information. Of US origin. Since the 1940s.

stamping-ground territory, area of activity; habitual meeting place; favourite haunt, as in *how does it feel to be back in your old stamping-ground after all these years?*

stand for to endure or tolerate, as in *I won't stand for it!* Adopted from the USA in the early 1920s.

stand (sb) up to fail to keep a date with (sb, esp. a girlfriend or boyfriend). From around 1925.

stand up in to be wearing at the moment, as in *my luggage has gone missing: I've only got the things I stand up in.*

starbolic naked stark-naked. Since around 1870. A corruption of *stark-bollock naked. See also* **bollock-naked**.

stardust cocaine. Drug users' slang. Used in the USA since before 1954.

star in the East, a a fly-button showing. Public-school slang. Since around 1915.

starkers stark-naked. From around 1910.

stark staring bonkers utterly mad. Since the mid-20th century. A slang variant of the Standard English phrase *stark raving mad. See also* **bonkers**.

starters, for to begin with, in the first place, as in *for starters, I want to know why you didn't tell the police.* Since the mid-20th century. Probably from *starter*, hors d'oeuvre, first course.

start something to set afoot, deliberately or unwittingly, something that will have significant (desirable or undesirable) consequences, as in *now you've started something!* Adopted from the USA around 1938.

star turn the central or most important person; a person who is exceptionally good at his or her job and therefore much admired.

stash, v. (usually followed by *away*) to hide; to hoard, as in *she's got thousands stashed away in the bank.* From **stash**, n., or from an earlier meaning: to stop doing (sth); to set (sth) aside.

stash, n. a hidden supply, esp. of something illicit, such as drugs. Possibly a blend of *store* and *câche*. Of US origin. Early 20th century.

stats statistics. Since around 1945.

steal the show to gain most of the attention or applause; to outshine other performers or participants, esp. unexpectedly, as in *the young Japanese gymnast stole the show.*

steam, n. in *under (one's) own steam*, unaided.

steam, v. *see* **steaming**, n.

steamed-up angry; heated; excited, as in *there's no need to get steamed-up about it.* Since around 1925.

steaming, n. (of large gangs of muggers) the act of running through a crowd of people or a crowded place robbing everybody in their path. Originally used by Black people in the 1980s. Hence the noun *steamer*.

steaming, adj. an intensifier, as in *you great steaming idiot!* Mainly schoolchildren's slang. Since around 1955.

steam radio radio, esp. as outmoded by television (much as the steam engine was outmoded by the internal-combustion engine). In general use since around 1961.

steely heroic, indomitable, as in *a steely air-force pilot.* Later 20th century.

steepling the act of putting one's fingers together to form the shape of a church steeple (e.g. as an indication of confidence or smugness).

stengah *see* **stinger.**

steno stenographer; a shorthand typist. Adopted from the USA, where the term has been in use since around 1905.

step a step-brother or step-sister.

step on the gas to accelerate. Adopted from the USA around 1926. From *gas(oline)*, the US name for petrol. The phrase *to step on the juice* (*see* **juice** 1) is an earlier British variant (from around 1918).

stewed to the eyeballs (or **gills**) extremely drunk. An intensification of the slang term *stewed,* drunk, which dates from the early 18th century.

stick 1 a person, as in *she isn't such a bad old stick really.* Since the early 19th century. 2 punishment; physical violence or damage, esp. in *to give (sb) stick.* Later 20th century. 3 criticism; verbal abuse; nagging or teasing, as in *they gave him some stick about that; social workers get a lot of undeserved stick.* Later 20th century.

stickem adhesive cement or gum.

stick-in-the-mud a dull, staid, old-fashioned or conservative person; an old fogey; a spoilsport or wet blanket. Since the mid-19th century.

stick it on (sb) to strike (sb). Since around 1945. *See also* **stick one on (sb).**

stick (one's) neck out to ask for trouble; to risk failure, criticism, etc. Since the early 1930s. Perhaps from the act of exposing oneself to sniper fire or the executioner's axe.

stick one on (sb) to strike (sb), as in *he threatened to stick one on me.* Later 20th century. A more frequent variant of **stick it on (sb).**

sticks, the the countryside, the provinces, as in *to live in the sticks.* Adopted from the USA around 1950.

stick-up a hold-up, an armed robbery. Since the mid-20th century.

stick with it! a farewell exhortation of generalized encouragement. Later 20th century.

sticky (of a person, situation, etc.) unpleasant; difficult. From 1915.

sticky-beak, n. an inquisitive person. Used in Australia since before 1926. From a bird that gets its beak sticky in searching for food.

sticky-beak, v. to pry; to snoop. Used in Australia from around 1930.

sticky-fingered thievish. From around 1870.

stiffy or **stiffie** an erection of the penis.

sting to cheat, to overcharge. Often passive, as in *I was stung for six quid.*

stinger, stingah or **stengah** a small drink of spirit with soda, as in *a* *whisky stinger, a brandy stinger.* Since the late 19th century. From the Malay *sa tengah,* a half.

stinker anything that is very difficult or unpleasant, as in *the first question on the paper was a real stinker.* Since the later 19th century.

stinking disgusting; contemptible. The term was in Standard English until the 19th century, since when it has been considered a vulgarism.

stinko alcoholic liquor, esp. wine. Used in Australia since around 1925.

stir prison, esp. in the phrase *in stir.* Since the mid-19th century. From the Romany *stariben* or *steripen.*

stir-crazy (or **-happy**) adversely affected by prison life, either at the time or afterwards. Since around 1940.

stir the shit to stir up trouble. Since around 1950 or earlier. Hence *shit-stirrer,* sb who stirs up trouble.

stitches, in highly amused, laughing uncontrollably, as in *he had us in stitches.* Perhaps from the *stitch* (sharp pain) brought on by shortness of breath.

stitch up to defeat, outwit, swindle or frame; to deal with in an unscrupulous or underhand manner, esp. in *to be stitched up.* Since around 1950.

stockbroker belt the expensive residential area around London, esp. in Surrey, where wealthy commuters live. The term is also applied to similar areas outside other large cities.

stomp, v. 1 to dance. 2 to attack savagely, to beat up. Adopted from the USA in the late 1960s.

stomp, n. a dance.

stone me! a mild expletive or exclamation of surprise. Since around 1920. Perhaps from the exclamation *stone the crows!*

stoned 1 very drunk. Adopted from the USA around 1950. 2 very high on drugs. Adopted from the USA around 1960.

stones testicles. The term was in Standard English until around 1850, since when it has been considered a vulgarism.

stony broke *see* **broke.**

stook (usually pronounced *shtook*) in the phrase *in stook,* in trouble, in difficulties. Since the late 19th century. From Yiddish.

stoolie an informer; a person who spies on criminals. Since around 1920. From **stool-pigeon.**

stool-pigeon an informer. Adopted from the USA by 1916. From *stool-pigeon,* a pigeon tied to a wooden frame (*stool*) and used as a decoy.

stopped (or **stuck**) **for bobbins** unable to proceed with the job in hand because some essential item is not immediately available. The phrase originated in the Lancashire cotton mills.

stout fellow   a reliable, courageous and likeable fellow.

strafe   to reprimand severely. From 1916.

straight, n.   a heterosexual person. Adopted from the USA in the later 20th century.

straight, adj.   **1** heterosexual.   **2** not on drugs or alcohol any more.

straight and narrow, the   the path of virtue, morality, decency, honesty, legality, etc., as in *to keep (sb) on the straight and narrow*, to prevent (sb) from misbehaving or turning to crime. Since around 1925.

straight down the line   frankly, directly, without frills or prevarication, as in *I gave it to them straight down the line*. Later 20th century. An elaboration of *straight*, as in *to tell (sb) straight*.

straighten (sb) out   to stop (sb) taking liberties, being overbearing or bumptious, being a nuisance, etc., as in *he'll be all right when he's been straightened out: he just needs taking in hand*.

straight up!   honestly! Since around 1905.

strapped   penniless, broke, short of money. Late 19th–20th centuries. Short for the slang phrase *strapped for cash*.

strawbs   strawberries. A variant of the abbreviation *straws*.

streak   to run stark-naked through a public place or assembly, either as a form of protest or out of sheer exhibitionism. Since the early 1970s. Hence the nouns *streaking* and *streaker*.

streak of piss   a tall thin person, esp. one who is weak or wet by nature. Since the mid-20th century.

street credibility   the ability to communicate with and gain the approval of ordinary people, esp. the working classes and urban youth, e.g. by not flaunting one's wealth or being pretentious. The term is applied to pop and rock musicians, politicians, etc. Often shortened to *street cred*.

streetwise   imbued with the knowledge and cunning needed for survival on the inner-city streets, as in *a streetwise kid*. Adopted from the USA around 1980.

strides   trousers. Since the early 20th century.

string along   to deceive or mislead, to lead up the garden path, as in *she's been stringing us along*. Since around 1920.

stroll on!   an exclamation of surprise, disbelief, dismissal or indignation. Since around 1950.

strong   in *to go it strong*, to act recklessly or energetically. From around 1840.

strong-arm, v.   to bully; to knock about. Of US origin.

strong-arm, adj.   esp. in *strong-arm tactics*, the use of force, usually against people. Adopted from the USA in the later 20th century.

stroppy   obstreperous, awkward, angry, aggressive, as in *don't get stroppy* *with me!* From *obstropolous* and other slang variants of *obstreperous.* Mid-20th century.

strung-out suffering from the effects of drug addiction or withdrawal; weak, tense, distressed or demented. Adopted from the USA in the late 1960s.

stuck for bobbins *see* **stopped for bobbins**.

stud a virile man, esp. one who is sexually active. Since around 1925. From *stud*, stallion used for breeding.

stuff, n. drugs, esp. cocaine (in the earlier 20th century) or marijuana (since the mid-20th century).

stuff, v. 1 to copulate with. Possibly since the mid-19th century. *See also* **get stuffed!** 2 to dispose of; used in expressions of rejection, indifference or impatience, as in *I told them they could stuff their job, stuff it!* Since around 1930. From the phrase *stuff it up your arse!*

stuffed shirt a pompous fool. From around 1920.

stuffy strait-laced, prudish, staidly conventional. From around 1925.

stung for *see* **sting**.

stymied in an awkward position or situation; frustrated or non-plussed, as in *we're stymied: there's nothing we can do.* Since around 1920. From golf.

sub a submarine. From 1914.

sucker 1 a gullible person, a person who is easily taken in. Since before 1887. 2 hence, a person who is unable to resist the attractions of somebody or something, as in *I always was a sucker for funfairs.* Since the mid-20th century.

suckered, be to be fooled or cheated, as in *nobody wants to admit that they've been suckered.* Later 20th century.

sucks! an expression of derision or defiance, esp. in *sucks to you!* Mainly schoolchildren's slang. Since the late 19th century.

sudden death (in sports and games) a decision by a single game, throw, etc., usually to resolve a tie. Since 1834.

suds beer, ale. Early 20th century. Perhaps from the bubbles floating on a glass of beer, or from the 18th-century slang phrase *in the suds,* slightly drunk.

sudser a soap opera. Since the early 1970s. From soap *suds.*

sugar 1 a term of address to a girl or young woman. From around 1930. 2 the drug LSD, which was originally taken on sugar lumps. Drug users' slang. Adopted from the USA around 1965. Also *sugar lump.*

sugar! a euphemism for **shit!** Possibly also influenced by **bugger!**

sugar daddy a rich elderly man who spends lavishly on his young mistress. Adopted from the USA around 1931. *See also* **Santa Claus**.

sugar lump *see* **sugar 2**.

suit, n.   someone who wears a business suit at work; the term implies power or status and distance from the everyday routine, as in *it's the suits upstairs who make the real decisions*. Of US origin, since the 1980s.

sunny side up   an egg fried on one side only, not turned over.

sunshine   a cheerful term of address (esp. to a child), or an ironic one, e.g. to a gloomy person.

super, adj.   excellent, as in *we had a super time, super!* From around 1925.

super, n.   superintendent; supervisor. 20th century.

super-duper (pronounced *sooper-dooper*) an intensification of **super**, adj., esp. as an exclamation. From 1947.

supergrass   an informer who is instrumental in breaking up large and powerful criminal rings. Late 1970s. *See also* **grass**, n. **1**.

superintendent of the sidewalk   a pedestrian who stands (esp. habitually) on the sidewalk (or pavement) and gazes up at a new building in the course of construction. Of US origin.

sure-fire   certain (to succeed); infallible, as in *a sure-fire method*. Adopted from the USA around 1918.

surface   to wake, to get up and appear, as in *Pete doesn't usually surface till about noon*. Since around 1939.

surfie   a surfer, esp. a surfboard rider. Since the early 1960s.

sus   an arrest 'on suspicion'. Originally police and underworld slang. Since the 1930s. The term is also used as a slang shortening of *suspect, suspected, suspicion, suspicious* and *suspiciously*.

suss   (often followed by *out*) to work out, as in *it took her a while to suss it out; I think I've got it sussed*. Since the mid-1960s.

swan, v.   (often followed by *in, around*, etc.) to parade; to go or move in an ostentatious or purposeful manner; to wander aimlessly, as in *they began swanning into the bar in evening dress*.

Swanee   **1** in *down the Swanee*, ruined, headed for bankruptcy, as in *lots of the textile firms round here are going down the Swanee*. Later 20th century. **2** in *up the Swanee*, out of order, not working, as in *the switchboard's up the Swanee*.

swanky   showy, pretentious; conceited, boastful. Since around 1910. From the verb *swank*, to show off.

sweat blood   to work extremely hard; to make unsparing effort on behalf of oneself or another. Since World War II.

sweat cobs   to perspire heavily and freely. Since the mid-20th century or earlier. From *cob*, lump.

sweat on the top line   esp. in *to be sweating on the top line*, to be in eager anticipation. From bingo, referring to a player who needs only one more number on the top line to win.

sweat-room   the interrogation room at a police station. Since the mid-20th century.

swede-basher an agricultural labourer; a country bumpkin. Since around 1925.

Sweeney, the the Flying Squad (of London's Metropolitan Police). Rhyming slang (short for *Sweeney Todd*). Since around 1925. The shortened form was popularized by a UK television series of this name first broadcast 1974–8.

sweep under the carpet to conceal or hide (sth, such as a project or blunder), esp. in the hope that it will be overlooked or forgotten. Since around 1955. From the act of sweeping dust under the carpet rather than into a dustpan, to save time and effort.

sweet arranged, settled; all right; correct, in order, as in *it's* (or *she's*) *sweet*. Australian.

sweeten to increase (the collateral of a loan) by furnishing additional securities. Financial slang. Since before 1919.

sweetener a bribe.

sweet f.a. or **sweet Fanny Adams** an intensified euphemism for **fuck all**. *Fanny Adams* was an eight-year-old girl brutally murdered in 1867; her name subsequently entered nautical slang in the sense of 'tinned mutton'.

sweetie 1 sweetheart. Of US origin; used in the UK from around 1920. Also used as a term of endearment (*see also* **sweetie-pie**). 2 a kind, considerate, generous person, as in *he's been an absolute sweetie to me*. Since around 1945. 3 (ironic) a particularly unpleasant or disgusting person. Later 20th century.

sweetie-pie a term of endearment. Since around 1930.

swing to indulge in group sexual activities. Since around 1965. Hence the nouns *swinging* and *swinger*.

swing at (sb), take a to punch (sb). Used in the UK since the mid-20th century or earlier.

swinger 1 a person who is modern in outlook, behaviour, etc. Since the mid-1960s. 2 *see* **swing**.

swinging, adj. lively, progressive, as in *the swinging sixties*. Since around 1963.

swinging, n. *see* **swing**.

swing the lead to malinger; to loaf or evade duty. Perhaps from the synonymous nautical phrase *to swing the leg*, confused with the technical nautical phrase *to heave the lead*, to take soundings. Since World War I.

swish smart, stylish, fashionable.

switched on up to date, with-it. Since around 1960.

sync or **synch** synchronization, esp. in the phrase *out of sync*, not synchronized; uncoordinated; incompatible. Since around 1931.

syrup a wig. Rhyming slang (short for *syrup of figs*). Later 20th century.

T

tab **1** tablet. Used in medical and pharmaceutical circles since the early 20th century and by US drug users since before 1969. **2** *see* **pick up the tab**.

tache *see* **tash**.

tacky vulgar, unrefined. Adopted from the USA in the early 1970s.

Taff or **Taffy** a Welsh person esp. a man; often used as a nickname. *Taffy* (perhaps from *Dafydd*) has been used since the 16th century; *Taff* is a 20th-century abbreviation.

tag along to go (with another or others), as in *do you mind if I tag along?*

tagger a graffiti artist. Since the late 1980s.

Taig a Roman Catholic. Mainly used by Protestants in Northern Ireland. From the Irish surname *Teague*, used since the 17th century as a nickname for any Irishman and subsequently (by around 1900) for a Roman Catholic.

tail, n. **1** the penis. Since the 14th century or earlier. **2** the female genitalia. Since the 14th century or earlier. Women considered collectively as sex objects, as in *a bit of tail*. **3** a person who follows another, esp. a detective who follows a suspected criminal (*see* **tail**, v.), as in *to put a tail on (sb)*. Since the mid-20th century.

tail, v. to follow, esp. of a detective who follows a suspected criminal. Late 19th–20th centuries.

tail-end Charlie a person who brings up the rear, e.g. of a group of ramblers or on a sponsored walk. Since World War II.

tailgate, v. to follow very close behind. The term is chiefly applied to the act of driving very close behind the vehicle in front. Later 20th century.

tails a man's dress suit, esp. the coat, as in *white tie and tails*. From *tailcoat*. Since before 1888.

take, n. money received, esp. on one occasion; takings, as in *the day's take* (of a shop, stall, etc.).

take a dim view of to disapprove. Since around 1937.

take a dive to lose a boxing match deliberately, often for a (considerable) bribe.

take a figure out of the air *see* **figure out of the air**.

take a flier to fall heavily. Since before 1931.

take apart   to defeat utterly, esp. in physical combat; to criticize, reprimand or punish severely, as in *never tangle with the fuzz: they'll take you
apart!* Since the mid-20th century.
take a powder   to disappear, to run away, to depart (esp. hastily).
Mainly US and Canadian; also used in the UK (mid-20th century).
Probably an allusion to the effects of a laxative powder.
take a punt at   *see* **punt**.
take a screw at   *see* **screw**, n. **3**.
take care of   to eliminate by killing.
take five (or **ten**)!   take a break of five (or ten) minutes. Since around
1945.
take (sb) for (sth)   to impose on or deceive (sb) to the extent of
getting (sth); to sting (sb) for (sth), as in *she took me for a fiver.*
take (sb) for a ride   to dupe, con or swindle (sb). Since the mid-20th
century.
take (oneself) in hand   (of a man or boy) to masturbate. Since before
1953.
take off **1** to start, to get going, to depart, as in *he took off at a rate of
knots.* Since the late 1940s. **2** to become successful or popular, esp.
suddenly, as in *dinomania took off in a big way.*
take on board **1** to comprehend, as in *at last he took on board that I wasn't
joking.* Since around 1970. **2** to adopt an idea, as in *do you think they'll
take our proposal on board?* A vogue phrase of the 1980s.
take out   to kill. Of US military origin. Used in the armed forces and
by the police since around 1970.
take the can back   to be reprimanded. Late 19th–20th centuries. *See
also* **carry the can.**
take the heat off   *see* **heat 3.**
take the mickey   a synonym of **take the piss.** Since around 1950. From
Mickey Bliss, rhyming slang for 'piss'. *See also* **extract the Michael.**
take the piss   to mock, jeer, deride or tease, as in *are you taking the piss?;
they took the piss out of him.* From the idea of deflation. *See also*
piss-taking.
take the weight off (one's) feet   (usu. imperative)   to sit down; to put
one's feet up. Since around 1945.
take (sb) to the cleaners   *see* **cleaners.**
talent   a group of people of the same sex, seen and evaluated collectively as sexual prospects, as in *don't think much of the local talent.* Since
around 1930.
talk   to talk about, to discuss. Often used with reference to money, as in
we're talking megabucks. The term was Standard English until around
1850, since when it has been considered a colloquialism. It was revived
in the 1980s (possibly via the USA) after decades of disuse.

talk BBC   to speak in a clear, precise, polite and cultured manner.

talk funny   to speak oddly or strangely (i.e. with a different accent or in a foreign language). 20th century or earlier.

talking head   a person appearing on television who merely talks, either directly to the audience or in discussion with others in the studio, rather than presenting information in a more visually entertaining manner. Used in the world of the media since the late 1970s.

talk into (or **on**) **the big white telephone**   to vomit down a toilet, esp. as a result of drinking too much alcohol.

talk off the top of (one's) head   *see* **top of (one's) head, off the**.

talk through the back of (one's) neck   **1** to talk extravagantly. From 1904 or earlier.   **2** hence, to talk nonsense. From around 1920.

talk turkey   to talk business; to talk sense, as in *let's talk turkey*. Used in the USA since the mid-19th century. Adopted in the UK around 1930.

talk up   to advertise by word of mouth; to bring to notice by repetitious suggestion.

tall poppy   a wealthy or important person. Used in Australia since the early 1930s. From a threat (made by Jack Lang in the early 1930s) of taxation that would 'cut off the heads of the tall poppies'.

ta muchly!   thank you very much! An elaboration of *ta*, thank you, *muchly* being a deliberate and jocular solecism.

tangle with   to become involved in a fight with; to get into trouble with, as in *I wouldn't tangle with him, if I were you.* Since the mid-20th century.

tan (sb's) hide   to beat or thrash (sb). Since the mid-17th century.

tank, v.   **1** to travel at high speed, esp. in a motor vehicle, as in *tanking down the motorway.* Later 20th century.   **2** *see* **tank up**.

tanked   drunk. From around 1917. *See also* **tank up**.

tank up   (also *to get tanked up*) to drink a lot of alcohol. Adopted from the USA around 1916.

tap, on   available immediately or at a moment's notice. Probably from draught beer (or hot and cold water). Since World War II or earlier.

taped   esp. in *to have (sb or sth) taped*, to have sized up or seen through (sb or sth), as in *we can't fool him: he's got us taped.* Since around 1916. From the verb *tape*, to measure with a tape.

tap (sb) for   to ask (sb) for (money), as in *she tapped me for twenty quid.*

tapped   eccentric; slightly mad. Earlier 20th century. From the Hindustani *tap*, fever. *See also* **doolally**.

tart   a promiscuous girl or woman; a prostitute. Since the late-19th century.

tart up   (often passive)   **1** to dress up, put on make-up, etc., esp. in the manner of a **tart**, as in *to tart oneself up for a party; she went out half* *an hour ago, all tarted up.* Since the early 1920s. **2** hence, to make (sth) smart or flashy, often with reference to meretricious changes, improvements, decorations, etc., as in *the pub has been tarted up.* Since around 1960.

tash or **tache** moustache. Since around 1920.

tat mediocre art or craft; shoddy or tawdry articles. Since the 1920s.

taters *see* **potatoes in the mould.**

tattie-bye! or **tatty-bye!** goodbye! A form of farewell popularized by the Liverpool comedian Ken Dodd from the 1960s. Probably a conflation of *ta-ta* and *bye-bye.*

taxing the collecting of protection money with threats of violence.

tea marijuana. Drug users' slang. Adopted from the USA around 1945. From the resemblance between marijuana leaves and tea leaves.

tea-head a habitual user of marijuana. Later 20th century.

tea-leaf thief. Rhyming slang. Since the late 19th century.

tear-arse, v. (usually followed by *about*) to rush about; to behave violently or recklessly. Since World War II.

tearaway a person who tends to violence or recklessness, as in *her brother is a bit of a tearaway.* Since around 1960.

tearing up pound notes in a gale engaging in something that is very expensive, e.g. modern Grand Prix motor-racing. From the later 1970s.

tear into to attack vigorously, either physically or verbally.

tear-jerker a very sad or sentimental book, story, play, film, etc. Adopted from the USA around 1954. *See also* **weepie.**

tear (sb) off a strip to reprimand (sb) severely, as in *the boss tore him off a strip for being late.* Since around 1938.

teaser a preliminary advertisement, often specifying neither the article nor the advertiser, prior to an advertising campaign. From around 1920.

technicolour yawn an act of vomiting. Used in Australia since around 1965 and popularized in the UK by the 'Barry McKenzie' comic strip (*see* **beef bayonet**). *See also* **burp a rainbow; lose a meal.**

ted a teddy-boy. Since around 1954.

teeny-bopper a teenager, esp. a young teenage girl, who avidly follows the latest trends in pop music, clothes, etc. Adopted from the USA around 1966. A blend of *teenager* (influenced by *teeny,* tiny) and *bopper* (*see* **bop,** v. **2**).

teething troubles initial problems with any new invention, device, project, system, etc., as in *once we've got over the teething troubles, it'll be fine.*

telephone numbers very large amounts of money, as in *we're talking* *telephone numbers.* From telephone numbers with a long string of digits.

tell all to tell everything (esp. confidential or sensational information).

telling 1 in *I'm telling you!*, there is no argument necessary or possible. 2 in *you're telling me!*, I agree with you wholeheartedly.

telling-off *see* **tell off**.

tell off to scold or rebuke severely. Since the late 19th century. Hence the noun *telling-off*, reprimand, as in *to give sb a telling-off.*

tell (sb) where to get off *see* **get off**.

telly television, as in *on (the) telly; we haven't got a telly.* Since around 1947.

temp, n. 1 temperature. Late 19th–20th centuries. 2 a temporary employee, esp. a typist or secretary. Since around 1950.

temp, v. to work as a temp (*see* **temp**, n. 2).

ten, adj. first class, very good. Teenagers' slang. Around 1977. From *ten out of ten*, full marks.

tender loving care *see* **TLC**.

Terrier a member of the Territorial Army. From 1908 or earlier.

thanks a million thank you very much. Since around 1950.

thataway in that direction, as in *they went thataway.* Adopted from the USA around 1955. Originally a US dialect term, much used in Westerns.

thee and me you and me, (just) the two of us, as in *that only leaves thee and me; there's nobody here but thee and me.* Later 20th century. A deliberate and jocular use of the archaic or dialect term *thee* (instead of *you*), to rhyme with *me.*

thickening for something visibly pregnant. Since the late 1950s. A pun on the phrase *sickening for something.*

thickie a foolish person; a stupid, thick-headed, ignorant or unintelligent person. Since the early 20th century.

thick on the ground abundant. The natural, subsequent opposite of **thin on the ground**.

thing 1 referring to a person whose name is temporarily forgotten, as in *Mrs Thing from the post office.* 2 *see* **do (one's) own thing**.

think-tank a group of experts or specialists who, by pooling their ideas, may or may not come up with the best solution. Adopted from the USA in the mid-1970s.

thin on the ground sparse, as in *cars like this are thin on the ground.* Originally applied to troops during World War I. *See also* **thick on the ground**.

thou (pronounced with the unvoiced *th* of *thin*) 1 a thousandth of an inch, as in *accurate to within a couple of thou.* 2 a thousand pounds, as in *she's earning fifty thou.*

thrash a party, with drinks, food, dancing, etc. Since the late 1930s.

three in . . . *or three,* used for emphasis in place of '. . . or two', as in *it looks to me as if you're going to need another bookcase or three.* Probably since the early 1930s.

three whippets, the *see* **whip it in, whip it out and wipe it.**

throne (usually *the throne*) lavatory, esp. in *on the throne,* sitting on the lavatory, as in *he often spends half an hour on the throne, reading the paper.* Since around 1920.

throw, n. in . . . *a throw,* referring to the price or charge per item or time, as in *five quid a throw.* From fairground sideshows. Since the late 19th century.

throw, v. **1** (in tennis) to lose a game or set deliberately, in order to obtain service or conserve energy. From 1933. **2** to disconcert, upset, confuse or surprise, as in *her unexpected arrival threw me.* Perhaps elliptical for **throw for a loop.** Since around 1961.

throw a fit to become very angry or agitated. Sometimes intensified to *to throw forty fits.* Since around 1930.

throw a wobbly to become angry, agitated or mentally unbalanced; to behave irrationally or unpredictably. Later 20th century.

throw for a loop to startle or upset, as in *the announcement threw him for a loop. See also* **throw, v. 2.**

throw forty fits *see* **throw a fit.**

throw the baby out with the bath-water to carry an act of rejection or reform too far, so that the good is lost along with the bad. Since around 1946.

throw the book at to sentence or punish with the maximum penalty, as in *if they catch you speeding again, they'll throw the book at you.* Adopted from the USA around 1944.

throw (one's) weight about to exert one's authority unduly; to boast or swagger. Since around 1910.

thud and blunder a jocular spoonerism for 'blood and thunder' (describing a melodramatic film, play, novel, story, etc.). Since the mid-20th century.

thumbs down an indication of failure, rejection, refusal, disappointment, etc., or a sign that things are going badly, esp. in *to give* (or *get*) *the thumbs down.* From the gesture used in ancient Rome to indicate that a gladiator should be killed. *See also* **thumbs up.**

thumbs up an indication of approval, acceptance, agreement, encouragement, etc., or a sign that all is going well, esp. in *to give* (or *get*) *the thumbs up.* Since the mid-20th century or earlier. From the gesture used in ancient Rome to indicate that a gladiator's life should be spared. *See also* **thumbs down.**

thump seven shades of shit out of (sb)   *see* **seven shades of shit**.

thunder-box   lavatory. Originally used in India, or among those who had served in India, in the sense of 'commode'. Since the later 19th century.

thunder-thighs   a woman who is overweight or of a very heavy build. Probably of US origin.

thunk   a jocular or non-standard form of the past participle of *think*, as in *who'd have thunk it?* Since around 1935.

Tich or **Titch**   a nickname for a small person. From *Little Tich*, the stage-name of the comedian Harry Relph (1867–1928).

tichy or **titchy**   very small. From **Tich**.

tick   1 in *what makes (sb) tick*, (sb's) driving force, motivation, etc.; the way (sb's) mind works, as in *see* if you can find out what makes him tick. Since around 1930.   2 *see* **tick off**; **tick over**.

ticket   1 a certificate, as in *to get (one's) captain's* (or *pilot's*) *ticket*. Since the late 1890s.   2 *see* **ticketty-boo**; **work one's ticket**.

ticketty-boo or **tickety-boo**   correct; satisfactory; arranged, as in *everything's ticketty-boo*. Since the early 1920s. Possibly of Hindi or Hindustani origin; perhaps influenced by the word *ticket* in such phrases as *just the ticket*, absolutely correct or appropriate.

ticking-off   *see* **tick off**.

tickled   amused, as in *she'll be tickled when I tell her what happened.*

tickled pink   extremely pleased, as in *he was tickled pink to be chosen for the team.* Perhaps from the act of blushing with pleasure. Since the early 20th century.

tick off   to reproach, upbraid or reprimand, as in *she ticked him off good and proper.* From around 1916. Hence the noun *ticking-off*, reprimand, as in *to give sb a ticking-off.*

tick over   esp. in *to be ticking over (nicely)*, to be moving, progressing, etc., satisfactorily. Since around 1939.

tiddle   to urinate. Mainly children's slang.

tiddled   drunk. From around 1920. *See also* **tiddly 1**.

tiddler   anything small, such as a child or small animal. From *tiddler*, a colloquial name for a stickleback, minnow or other small fish; ultimately from *tittlebat* or *tiddlebat*, dialectal variants of *stickleback*.

tiddly   1 (slightly) drunk. Since the late 19th century.   2 little, as in *a tiddly piece of cheese*. 19th–20th centuries.

tiddly push!   goodbye! Around 1920–40.

tie one on   to get (very) drunk. Adopted from the USA in the later 20th century.

tight-arsed   stingy, mean with money. Since the 1960s.

tight as a tick   extremely drunk. Probably from the appearance of a tick gorged with blood.

tight-wad   a person who is mean with money. Adopted from the USA around 1934.

tiller   the steering wheel of a car. Used in Australia since around 1930.

timber!   (pronounced with the second syllable stressed and prolonged) an exclamation uttered when something is about to fall. Used in the UK since the mid-20th century or earlier. From the use of the term by US and Canadian lumberjacks when felling trees.

time   in *(it's) time I wasn't here*, I ought to have departed already. Since the mid-20th century or earlier. Other personal pronouns may be used in place of I.

time out   time set aside for a specific (usually enjoyable) purpose, outside one's normal routine; a break, time off, as in *we took time out to visit the castle*. Adopted from the USA in the early 1970s by advertising copywriters; in general usage in the UK by the late 1970s.

tincture   a drink of alcoholic liquor. Since the late 1970s (possibly a revival of earlier usage).

tin ear   in *to have a tin ear* (or *tin ears*), to be unmusical or tone-deaf. Hence the adjective *tin-eared*. The term is also used in non-musical contexts, such as literature. Since around 1945.

tinies   very small children. Since around 1920. From the phrase *tiny tots*.

tinker   a child, esp. a mischievous one, as in *you little tinker!* Since the late 19th century or earlier.

tinkle, n.   **1** a telephone call, esp. in *to give (sb) a tinkle*, to telephone (sb). Since around 1910.   **2** an act of urination. Since around 1930.

tinkle, v.   to urinate. Mainly children's slang. Since 1920 or earlier. From the sound of urine falling into a metal chamber-pot.

tinnie   a can of beer. Used in Australia since the mid-1960s and in the UK in the 1980s.

tip   a very untidy place, esp. a room, as in *your bedroom is an absolute tip!* Later 20th century. From *tip*, rubbish dump.

tiswas or **tizwas**   a state of excitement and confusion, as in *I'm all of a tiswas; she's in a bit of a tiswas*. From the early 1940s. *See also* **tizzy**.

tit   a woman's breast. Late 19th–20th centuries. From *tit*, teat or nipple. *See also* **get on (sb's) tits**.

Titch   *see* **Tich**.

titchy   *see* **tichy**.

tit-man   a man who is more interested in a woman's breasts than her legs, buttocks, etc. Since around 1910.

tit-show   an act or show featuring topless female performers. Since around 1930.

tittle-tat   a person who tattles or tells tales. Used in Australia since around 1930. From **tittle-tattle**.

tittle-tattle gossip, scandal, idle chatter. Since the 16th century.

titty 1 a synonym of **tit**. **2** *see* **tough titty!**

tizwas *see* **tiswas**.

tizzy a state of anxiety, excitement or confusion, as in *to get into a tizzy*, to get all worked up. *See also* **tiswas**.

TLC tender loving care, as in *all she needs is a bit of TLC.* Used by the caring professions (and others) since around 1965.

tod, on (one's) alone. Rhyming slang (from *Tod Sloan*, the name of a famous jockey). Since the late 19th century.

toddle to go; to walk, as in *let's toddle over to Nigel's?* 20th century.

toe-job, n. in the expression *to give (sb) a toe-job*, to suck the toe(s) of one's sexual partner. Since the early 1990s. *See also* **shrimp**, v.

toe-rag a contemptible or despicable person. Since World War I or earlier. The term was originally applied to beggars or tramps, from the pieces of old cloth they wrapped around their feet in place of socks.

toe the line to conform, as in *to toe the party line.* In general use since the mid-20th century.

toffee in *(sb) can't . . . for toffee*, (sb) is utterly incompetent at the specified activity, as in *she can't dance for toffee.* Late 19th–20th centuries.

toffee-nosed supercilious; snobbish. Perhaps a pun on *toffy*, rich, stylish, well-dressed, upper-class (from the noun *toff*). Since around 1925.

together having one's life, career, emotions, etc., under control; well-organized and self-possessed, as in *a really together guy.* Adopted from the USA in the mid-1960s. *See also* **get it together**.

to'ing and fro'ing constant or frequent movement, esp. back and forth, as in *there's been a lot of to'ing and fro'ing in the flat upstairs this morning.* Since around 1945.

toke, n. a puff of a marijuana cigarette. The slang term originally referred to a drag on any cigarette.

toke, v. to inhale the smoke of a marijuana cigarette.

tom a prostitute. Police and underworld slang. Since the 1940s.

tom-tit defecation. Rhyming slang for 'shit'. Since the late 19th century.

ton 1 a hundred pounds, as in *half a ton*, fifty pounds. Since around 1940. **2** a hundred miles an hour, as in *to do a ton.* Since around 1948. *See also* **ton-up**.

tongue wrestling kissing, esp. French kissing.

ton of bricks, come (or be) down on (sb) like a to be very angry with (sb); to reprimand or punish (sb) severely, as in *if she catches you, she'll be down on you like a ton of bricks.*

ton-up esp. in *ton-up boys* (or *kids*), young motorcyclists who (habitually) travel at a hundred miles an hour or more (*see* **ton 2**). Since around 1955.

toodle-oo! or **toodle-pip!**   *see* **tootle-oo!**

tool   1 weapon. Prison slang. Probably since the mid-19th century. 2 penis. Since the 16th century.

tooled up   equipped with weapons, esp. in *to be* (or *get*) *tooled up*. Since around 1946.

too much   (always predicative) excellent, outstanding, as in *isn't she too much?* Used in the UK by 1960.

too much on (one's) plate, have   *see* **plate**.

toot, n.   1 money. Earlier 20th century.   2 a line of cocaine for snorting. Since the mid-1970s.

toot, v.   1 to drink heavily (at one session, e.g. a pub-crawl or drinking party). Since around 1939.   2 to snort cocaine. Since the mid-1970s.

tootle   to go, esp. in *to tootle off*, to depart. Since the 19th century. Probably from **toddle**.

tootle-oo!, toodle-oo!, or **toodle-pip!**   goodbye. Since around 1905. Perhaps from the sound of a car horn, or from the French phrase *à tout à l'heure*, see you later!

tootsie   1 foot. Mainly children's slang. Since the late 19th century. 2 a girl or young woman; a girlfriend or sweetheart. Often used as a term of address. Adopted from the USA in the 1920s.

top, v.   to kill, as in *the rebels topped the president*; *to top oneself,* to commit suicide. Since the 18th century. The term originally referred to execution by hanging or beheading.

top and tail   to wash the face and genitals of a baby, patient, etc. Later 20th century. From the phrase *to top and tail* (gooseberries, etc.) before cooking or preserving.

top brass   (usually *the top brass*) high-ranking officers or officials. *See also* **brass 2**.

top drawer   esp. in *out of the top drawer*, well-bred, gentlemanly, ladylike.

top of (one's) head, off the   extempore, without preparation and with facts unchecked, as in *to talk off the top of (one's) head*. Later 20th century.

top of the bill   first-rate; the best of all. From theatrical and music-hall advertisements.

top of the world, on   very happy, confident or prosperous, as in *to feel on top of the world*; *to be sitting on top of the world*. Adopted from the USA around 1930.

tops, n.   in *the tops*, the best, the most likeable, admirable, etc., as in *he's the tops*. Adopted from the USA around 1943.

tops, adj.   first-class, excellent. From 1944.

tosh   1 a term of address to a friend or stranger (esp. male), as in *wotcher, tosh!* From the late 1930s. **2** nonsense, as in *a load of tosh.*

toss to throw away, esp. as useless or worthless, as in *I don't need it any more – you can toss it.* Used in Australia since around 1930.

toss (one's) cookies to vomit. Mainly US and Canadian. Around 1920–55.

tosser a stupid or irritating person. *See also* **tosspot.**

toss off to masturbate. Since the 18th century.

tosspot a stupid or irritating person (*see also* **tosser**). Also used in Australia as a jocular term of address, esp. between men. Late 19th–20th centuries. From the Standard English *tosspot,* heavy and habitual drinker.

total, v. to destroy totally; to kill outright; to wreck beyond repair, as in *to be totalled in an accident; to total a car.* Of US origin.

totty or **tottie** a girl or young woman, esp. considered sexually. The term originally referred to a high-class prostitute.

touch of the . . . (always followed by a plural noun) characteristic of . . ., as in *a touch of the Harvey Smiths,* referring to the V-sign used as an offensive gesture.

toughie **1** a tough; a rough or vicious person. Since around 1945. **2** a very difficult thing, situation, problem, question, etc., as in *the maths exam was a toughie.* Later 20th century.

tough it out to endure to the finish. Adopted from the USA in the mid-1980s or earlier.

tough titty! bad luck!, hard luck! The phrase is often used ironically or unsympathetically.

touristy full of tourists; catering (excessively) to the needs and de- mands of tourists, as in *one of the less touristy areas of Switzerland.* Later 20th century.

town **1** *see* **go to town.** **2** in *on the town,* applied to anybody who goes into town in search of social, sexual or other entertainment, as in *he's out on the town every night.* Since around 1920.

toy-boy an older woman's young lover. Since around 1981.

tracking injecting intravenously along a vein. Drug users' slang.

track record the record of past performance, achievements, etc., of an individual or group, as in *the candidate must have a proven track record in manufacturing management; the government's track record.* Mainly used in business, commerce and politics. Adopted from the USA around 1970.

tracks needle marks. Drug users' slang. Adopted from the USA around 1955–65.

trad traditional. Since around 1960.

trade **1** homosexual activity or commerce, as in *did you have any trade last night? See also* **rough trade.** **2** homosexual partner(s), esp. the client(s) of a homosexual prostitute, as in *he's been bringing trade back to his digs.*

trade-in a car (or other article) given in part exchange when a new one is purchased. In general use, esp. in the motor trade, by the mid-20th century. The term is also used adjectivally, as in *a trade-in price.*

tragic no good. Teenagers' slang. From around 1979. The opposite of **magic**.

tramp a promiscuous girl or woman. Adopted from the USA around 1955.

tranks tranquillizing drugs, as in *she's been on tranks for years.* Later 20th century.

trannie or **tranny** 1 a transistor radio. Since around 1965. 2 a transparent slide film; a transparency. Photographers' slang.

trash, v. 1 to destroy, to smash up, as in *the heavies came round and trashed the place.* 2 to attack sb or sth verbally, as in *she trashed his reputation.*

tray three (either as a number or set). Since the mid-1890s. From *trey,* the three at dice or cards.

tree, out of (one's) 1 crazy; stupid, as in *are you out of your tree?* Since the 1960s. 2 intoxicated by alcohol or drugs.

trendy, adj. following the sartorial, social, intellectual or artistic fashion, as in *trendy clothes; trendy ideas.* Since 1966. Hence the noun *trendy,* a trendy person. Since 1967.

trick a prostitute's client. Adopted from the USA around 1944.

trick cyclist a psychiatrist. Since 1938 or earlier.

tricksy sly, cunning, wily, craft, tricky.

triff excellent. Used by teenagers since the early 1980s. An abbreviation of *triffic,* in use since the 1960s, itself a contraction of *terrific.*

trigger-happy likely to use a firearm at the slightest provocation, or without any provocation at all. Adopted from the USA in the early 1940s.

trip a hallucinogenic experience produced by LSD or a similar drug, as in *to take a trip; to have a bad trip; she was on an acid trip.* Since around 1966.

trog to walk, esp. heavily; to go, to depart, as in *to trog off; well, I'll be trogging along then.* Since around 1950. Perhaps a blend of *trudge* and *slog* (or *jog*).

troll 1 to saunter or wander aimlessly, as in *we were just trolling around looking in shop windows.* Since the mid-1970s. 2 to stroll around in search of sexual partners. Homosexuals' slang.

trolley, off (one's) mad, crazy. Since the late 19th century.

trolleys underpants, panties, knickers. Since around 1950.

trombone telephone. Defective rhyming slang. Since around 1930.

trot, on the   in succession, as in *for six days on the trot*. Since the 1940s or earlier.

trots, the   diarrhoea. Early 20th century.

trough, v.   to eat.

trouser-ferret   penis. Later 20th century.

trouser-snake   penis. Since the mid-20th century. Also *one-eyed trouser-snake*.

true   in *it just isn't true*, an intensifier, as in *he's so mean it just isn't true*. Later 20th century.

trumpet   telephone. Later 20th century.

trumps   in *to turn* (or *come*) *up trumps*, to turn out well, to be successful, to do well, esp. unexpectedly. Since 1862 or earlier. From card games.

trust you!   an ironic response to an act or action that is considered typical of the person concerned, as in *'I've spilt the coffee.' 'Trust you!'* The personal pronoun *you* may be replaced by others, as in *'He got away with it.' 'Trust him!'* Since the late 19th century.

tube   a can of beer; hence, the drink itself, as in *he's never been known to say no to a tube*. Mainly Australian.

tubes, down the   ruined; lost. Since the 1960s.

Tudorbethan   (of a house) built in a mixture of architectural styles or in no particular style. Since around 1950.

tuft   a woman's pubic hair, as in *brothel scenes showing plenty of tuft*. Since the 17th century.

tug, have a   (of men or boys) to masturbate. Mainly Australian.

tummy banana   penis. Mainly nursery slang.

turd   1 a lump of excrement. The term was in Standard English until the mid-18th century, since when it has been considered a vulgarism. From the Old English *tord*. 2 an objectionable or contemptible person. Since around 1925 or earlier.

turd-burglar   a male homosexual. Since the mid-20th century or earlier.

turf   one's home territory, as in *what are you doing so far from your turf at this hour of the morning?* Later 20th century.

turf off   to remove, esp. forcibly, as in *he turfed me off the stage*.

turf out   to expel or eject, to kick or throw out, as in *she was turfed out of the club, I've turfed out all those old photos*. From around 1912.

turkey   1 a disaster or resounding failure, as in *the show was a turkey*. Originally US theatrical slang; adopted in the UK in the later 20th century. 2 *see* **cold turkey**; **talk turkey**.

turn off, v.   to disgust or repel, as in *that sort of behaviour turns me off*. Adopted from the USA around 1960.

turn-off, n.   something that turns somebody off, as in *nylon shirts and string vests are the biggest turn-offs*. Adopted from the USA in 1970.

turn on, v.   to exhilarate, excite or inspire; to arouse sexually, as in *this* *music turns me on.* From around 1956.

turn-on, n.   something that turns somebody on, as in *leather boots are a real turn-on.* Adopted from the USA around 1970.

turn on a sixpence   (of a car or other vehicle) to have a small turning-circle.

turn-out   clothing or general appearance, as in *a smart turn-out.* Since the late 19th century.

turn over 1 to set upon and beat up. Since around 1950. 2 (of the police) to stop and search, as in *he was turned over by the police, they turned over the van.* From around 1850.

tush   buttocks. From the Yiddish *toches.* Since the 1960s.

tux   a tuxedo or dinner-jacket. Of US origin.

twat 1 the female genitalia. Since the mid-17th century. 2 a foolish or contemptible person. Since the late 19th century.

twee   over-dainty; sentimentally pretty or sweet. The term has been used with derogatory or contemptuous overtones since the 1940s. From *tweet,* an affected or childish pronunciation of *sweet.*

twerp   a foolish or contemptible person. From around 1910.

twist (sb's) arm   to persuade (sb), esp. with difficulty. Also used jocularly, as in *'Another drink?' 'Well, if you twist my arm, . . .'* Since the late 1950s.

twister 1 a swindler; a crook; a trickster. Since the early 1830s. 2 a whirlwind or tornado.

twit   a foolish or contemptible person. Since around 1925. Possibly from the verb *twit,* to tease or taunt.

twitch   a bout of nerves, a highly emotional state, as in *she had a bit of a twitch on,* she was nervous or het up. Since the late 1930s. Hence the adjectives *twitched-up* and *twitchy.*

two-and-eight   a state; a synonym of **Harry Tate**. Rhyming slang. Since World War I.

two-bit   insignificant; inferior; cheap. Mainly US and Canadian; used in the UK since around 1945. From *two bits,* 25 cents.

two ha'pennies to rub together, not have   to be very poor or penniless.

two-pot screamer   a person who very easily becomes drunk. Used in Australia since around 1950.

two-time   to double-cross, esp. by carrying on a relationship with two different lovers at the same time. Adopted from the USA in 1939. Hence the noun *two-timer* and the adjective *two-timing.*

two-tone   referring to a combination of Black musicians and White musicians, esp. in a rock or pop group or band.

two-year-old, like a   in a very lively, energetic or vigorous manner. From two-year-old racehorses.

U

uey *see* **u-ie**.

ugsome thoroughly unpleasant. Later 20th century.

u-ie U-turn (in its literal or figurative sense), esp. in *to do a u-ie*. Variant spellings include *uie, uey* and *youee*.

umpteen an unspecified large number, as in *I've told him umpteen times not to park his car across the end of our drive.* Since 1916 or earlier. Hence the adjective *umpteenth*.

umpty or **umpty iddy** indisposed, off colour, ill, esp. in *to feel umpty*. From 1915.

Uncle Tom a Black person who is deferential towards White people; a synonym of **coconut**. Adopted from the USA around 1965. From the novel *Uncle Tom's Cabin* by Harriet Beecher Stowe.

uncool the opposite of **cool** in both of its adjectival senses. Adopted from the USA in the mid-1960s.

undergraduette a female undergraduate.

under the influence (slightly) drunk. From the phrase *under the influence of alcohol*, which is sometimes jocularly spoonerized to *under the affluence of incohol.*

undies underwear, esp. women's underwear. Since around 1918.

unflappable imperturbable. Since around 1944.

uni university. Later 20th century.

university of hard knocks *see* **school of hard knocks**.

unlucky for some the number 13. Used in bingo and generally.

unstuck, come *see* **come unstuck**.

untogether the opposite of **together**. From around 1970.

up exhilarated by drugs. Since the early 1960s.

up against confronted by, esp. in *up against it*, in serious difficulties. Used in the USA since 1896 and in the UK by 1914. *See also* **wall 1**.

up and up, on the genuine; honest, trustworthy, dependable. Of US origin. From around 1919.

upper an amphetamine. Drug users' slang. Adopted from the USA around 1960. *See also* **downer 1**.

uppity above oneself; snobbishly or conceitedly arrogant; recalcitrant. Adopted from the USA.

up the duff *see* **duff, n. 1**.

up the wall *see* **drive (sb) up the wall; wall 2**.

uptight tense, nervous, anxious; embarrassed; angry, as in *there's no need to get uptight about it*. Adopted from the USA around 1967. Probably from the phrase *wound* (or *screwed*) *up tight*.

up to here to an unspecified but considerable degree (often accompanied by a gesture indicating one's throat or the top of one's head), as in *I've had it up to here, I'm thoroughly fed up*. Later 20th century.

up your jumper! an exclamation of defiance or derision. Perhaps elliptical for *oompah, oompah, stick it up your jumper!* or a euphemism for 'up your arse!'

up yours! an exclamation of refusal or defiance. An abbreviation of *up your arse!* (or a similar phrase). Late 19th–20th centuries.

use esp. in *(sb) could use (sth)*, (sb) needs or would like (sth), as in *you look as if you could use a cool shower; I could use a stiff drink*. Since around 1935 or earlier.

used to was used to be, as in *I'm not so young as I used to was*. Since around 1910.

useful very good, capable, effective or effectual, as in *he's a pretty useful boxer*. From around 1929.

use (one's) loaf to use (one's) common sense; to think hard; to exercise ingenuity. Often imperative. Since the 1940s or earlier. *See also* **loaf**.

use nor ornament, neither a contemptuous description of an utterly useless person or thing.

U-turn a sudden reversal of policy, esp. in *to do a U-turn*. From the mid-1970s. *See also* **u-ie**.

V

vac 1 vacuum cleaner. From around 1950. Also used as a verb, as in *to vac the carpet.* 2 vacation (esp. at a university or other institute of higher education), as in *the long vac,* the summer vacation. Since the late 19th century.

vallie the tranquillizing drug Valium. Mainly Australian.

vamp a woman who seeks to seduce or exploit men by unscrupulous use of her sexual charms. From 1918 or earlier.

vanilla ordinary. Mainly used by computer technologists and enthusiasts. Later 20th century.

Vatican roulette the rhythm method of contraception (as used by Roman Catholics). Since 1960. By analogy with the riskiness of *Russian roulette.*

veg vegetable(s), as in *meat and two veg.* Since the mid-19th century.

veggie, n. and adj. vegetarian. Since the 1970s.

vent ventriloquist, ventriloquism, as in *a vent act.* Mainly used in the world of entertainment. Since the late 19th century.

verbals oral confessions (allegedly) made by suspected criminals at the time of arrest and often subsequently denied in court. Police slang of the later 20th century.

vet to make enquiries about a person's character and suitability for employment, esp. in a sensitive post, as in *she was vetted by the security services.* Mid-20th century.

vibes atmosphere, ambience, general mood or feeling; the aura or 'vibrations' emanating from people, places or things, as in *good vibes; I was getting bad vibes from him.* Mainly used in the jazz world and by beatniks and hippies. Adopted from the USA around 1960.

vicky verky vice versa. Late 19th–20th centuries.

vidiot a person who watches television constantly and mindlessly. Used in Australia since around 1960. A blend of *video* and *idiot.*

villain a criminal; anybody with a criminal record. Since around 1935.

-ville a suffix attached to adjectives or nouns to denote or describe a place or thing with the specified characteristic, as in *the lecture was really dragsville.* Adopted from the USA around 1960. *See also* **dullsville**.

vino wine, esp. Italian or Spanish wine. Since 1942. From the Italian or Spanish *vino*, wine.

vital statistics a woman's bust, waist and hip measurements. Since around 1945. From the term used in Standard English for statistics relating to births, deaths, etc.

W

wack, wacker or **whacker** a term of address, esp. between men, as in *hey, wacker!* Chiefly used in and around Liverpool. Perhaps from the dialect verb *wack*, to share out; hence, one who does this, a friend.

wacko or **whacko** crazy, eccentric, a synonym of **wacky**. Adopted from the USA in the late 1970s.

wacky unusual, out of the ordinary; eccentric, crazy, as in *a wacky method; some of his relatives are pretty wacky*. Adopted from the USA around 1942.

wake (one's) ideas up (often imperative) to pull oneself together. Since around 1930.

walk to disappear, often implying theft or unauthorized borrowing, as in *expensive books like these tend to walk; my pen seems to have walked again*. Since around 1910.

walkabout an informal tour on foot by an important person (such as a visiting member of the royal family, politician or celebrity) to meet the general public, as in *the Queen went walkabout in the city centre; the Prime Minister's walkabout was cut short by a heavy shower of rain*. Since the late 1970s. From the Western Pacific pidgin word for journey.

walkies a walk with a dog. The exclamation *walkies!* was popularized around 1980 by Barbara Woodhouse's dog-training classes broadcast on TV.

walkie-talkie a small portable radio with both receiving and transmitting equipment. Since 1940.

walking disaster area a person who is particularly inept and accident-prone. Since the late 1960s.

walk it (of a racehorse, dog or person) to win easily. Since the 1930s.

wall 1 in *up against the wall*, in serious difficulties. Since around 1916. Perhaps from being put up against a wall to be shot. *See also* **up against**. 2 in *up the wall*, mad, crazy; angry, furious, as in *she went up the wall when she found out*. Since around 1944. *See also* **drive (sb) up the wall**. 3 esp. in *to go over the wall*, to escape. Prison slang. 4 *see* **hit the wall**.

wallop 1 a resounding or severe blow. Since before 1823. 2 hence, the strength to deliver such a blow, as in *he has a prodigious wallop,* *but no great skill.* Mainly boxing slang. From around 1910. **3** beer. Since around 1930. Perhaps from its potency.

wall-to-wall abundant, thick on the ground, widespread, all over, as in *wall-to-wall bears,* police everywhere (*see* **bear**). Adopted from the USA in the late 1970s. From *wall-to-wall* carpeting.

wally a fool. Since the late 1970s.

wang penis. Possibly from *whang,* a heavy blow, or short for *wanger* or *whanger,* anything very large.

wangle to contrive or obtain cunningly, deviously or illicitly; to manipulate or fake, as in *I managed to wangle myself an extra day off.*

wangler a person who wangles. From around 1910.

wank, v. to masturbate. Since the late 19th century.

wank, n. an act of masturbation. Since the mid-20th century.

wanker **1** a masturbator. Since the late 19th century. **2** a foolish or contemptible person, as in *you stupid wanker!; the directors are a bunch of wankers.* Since the early 1970s.

wank-pit bed. Since around 1920.

wank-stain an idiot, a stupid person. Used mainly by youths since the mid-1970s.

wannabee or **wannabe** a person who wants to be like somebody else (esp. a show-business or sporting idol); a person who has unfulfilled ambitions, aspirations, dreams or desires. Since the mid-1980s. From the phrase 'I want to be . . .'.

want in to wish to enter, be included, etc., as in *we're planning a raid: do you want in?* From around 1840.

want jam on it *see* **jam on it.**

want out to wish to leave, be excluded, etc., as in *I'm sick of this job: I want out.* From around 1840.

warm and runny excited or aroused, esp. by a rock or pop musician's improvisation, as in *to get all warm and runny.* Early 1970s. Possibly an allusion to wetting oneself or having an orgasm.

waser a girl or young woman. Cockney slang of the early 20th century. From the French *oiseau,* bird.

wash out to cancel. Since the 19th century.

wash your mouth out! addressed to a person who uses a swear-word or bad language. Since around 1910. Often jocular in modern usage.

Wasp or **WASP** a person descended from north European, usually Protestant stock, who is considered to be socially powerful, dominant or influential. Adopted from the USA around 1975. An acronym of White Anglo-Saxon Protestant.

waste to kill, esp. in crime or warfare, as in *he knows too much – waste him!; hundreds of innocent civilians were wasted.* Adopted from the USA in the late 1960s.

wasted 1 under the influence of drugs. Used in the USA since before 1967. **2** drunk. From the early 1980s.

watch it! be careful! Often more of a threat than a warning. Since the 1920s.

watering-hole a pub or other drinking-place, as in *this is one of his favourite watering-holes.* Later 20th century.

waterworks 1 weeping, crying, tears, esp. in *to turn on the waterworks,* to start crying, usually in order to gain attention or sympathy. Since before 1857. **2** the urinary system, as in *she had a problem with her waterworks after the operation.* Since the 19th century.

wavelength a way of looking at, thinking about or tackling things, as in *we're on the same wavelength; he's not on my wavelength; they're on different wavelengths.* Since the late 1960s.

way-out extremely eccentric; unconventional or avant-garde; excellent. Used by jazz-lovers and beatniks since the 1950s and by hippies in the 1960s.

wazzock a fool, as in *you stupid wazzock!* A term of mild abuse that was briefly popular in the early 1980s.

wazzocked drunk.

wear to accept, tolerate or put up with, as in *do you think they'll wear it?; the old man'll never wear that!*

weasel and stoat coat. Rhyming slang. Often shortened to *weasel.*

wedding tackle a man's genitalia. Since around 1918.

wee or **wee-wee**, v. to urinate. Mainly nursery slang.

wee or **wee-wee**, n. urine; an act of urination, as in *to have a wee.* Mainly nursery slang. Since the late 19th century.

weed 1 (usually *the weed*) tobacco, as in *I went back on the weed when my marriage broke up.* Since the 17th century. **2** marijuana. Adopted from the USA in the late 19th century.

weed head a habitual user of marijuana. Adopted from the USA in the later 20th century.

weekend habit a pattern of occasional drug use. Mid-20th century. Hence *weekender,* someone with such a habit.

weeny-bopper a child, esp. a girl aged 8–12, who is an avid fan of pop music and pop musicians. Since the early 1970s. A blend of *weeny,* very small, and **teeny-bopper**.

weepie a sentimental film, play, story or novel. Since around 1930. *See also* **tear-jerker**.

wee small hours, the the period immediately after midnight, the early hours of the morning. An intensification of the Standard English phrase *the small hours.*

wee-wee *see* **wee**.

weigh into to attack, to punch vigorously, as in *he weighed into his* *opponent.* Since around 1910. Possibly from a boxer *weighing in before a fight.*

weigh in with to produce or introduce (something additional, extra or unexpected), as in *she weighed in with a higher bid.* Since 1885. Possibly from a jockey *weighing in after a race.*

weight one pound (or half a kilogram) of cannabis. Since the early 1970s.

weirdo an eccentric; a very odd or unconventional person, as in *his sister's a bit of a weirdo; long-haired weirdos.* A later 20th-century variant of the synonymous term *weirdie.*

well very, as in *well bad,* very good. Since the mid-1980s.

well away drunk, as in *after a couple of these cocktails you'll be well away.* Later 20th century.

well-endowed **1** (of a woman) having well-developed breasts. Since around 1925. **2** (of a man) having large genitals. Since the late 1920s.

well-heeled rich, either temporarily or permanently. Adopted from the USA by the mid-20th century at the latest.

well-hung (of a man) having large genitals.

wellie or **welly** **1** (usu. pl.) wellington boot. *See also* **green wellie brigade; yellow wellie**. **2** force, power, esp. in *to give it some welly,* to put all one's effort into (sth), e.g. to accelerate hard in a car or on a motorcycle. Since the 1970s.

well-oiled *see* **oiled**.

well-stacked *see* **stacked**.

welly *see* **wellie**.

wet, n. **1** a drink, esp. an alcoholic drink, as in *fancy coming round for a couple of wets?* Since before 1879. **2** a dull, stupid, feeble or ineffectual person. Since the later 19th century. **3** hence, a politician (esp. a Conservative) who has moderate views or liberal tendencies; a politician who is not a radical or hard-liner, as in *Tory wets.* Since around 1980.

wet, adj. **1** excessively sentimental. Since around 1930. **2** dull, stupid, feeble or ineffectual (*see* **wet**, n. 2). **3** (of a politician) having moderate views or liberal tendencies (*see* **wet**, n. 3).

wet behind the ears inexperienced, ignorant, naïve, immature, youthful.

wet dream an erotic dream accompanied by an involuntary emission of semen. Since the 19th century or earlier.

wet week, like a miserable or wretched, esp. in *to look* (or *feel*) *like a wet week.*

whacker *see* **wack**.

whacko **1** good, excellent, as in *whacko!,* splendid!; *a whacko time.* Since 1945 or earlier. The term was popularized in the 1950s by the BBC television series *Whacko!* starring Jimmy Edwards.   **2** *see* **wacko**.

whack off   to masturbate. Adopted from the USA in the late 1960s.

whack the illy   *see* **illywhacker**.

whale of a . . ., a   a very good, large, etc., . . ., as in *we had a whale of a time*, we thoroughly enjoyed ourselves; *it was a whale of a party*. Adopted from the USA around 1918.

wham-bam-thank-you-ma'am   a quick act of sexual intercourse, usually with a selfish lack of concern for the woman's satisfaction. Since the early 1970s. *See also* **whip it in, whip it out and wipe it**.

what for   *see* **give (sb) what for**.

what makes (sb) tick   *see* **tick 1**.

what's with . . .?   **1** in *what's with (sb)?*, what's the matter with (sb)?, as in *what's with Sarah? – she hasn't said a word all evening*.   **2** in *what's with (sth)?*, what's the reason for or purpose of (sth)?, as in *what's with the dinner jacket?*, why are you wearing a dinner jacket? Adopted from the USA; since before the 1970s. Possibly via Yiddish from the German: *Was ist mit . . .?*

what the fuck   an intensification of *what*, as in *nobody knows what the fuck's going on*. Since the mid-20th century at the latest.

what the hell   **1** an intensification of *what*, as in *what the hell do you think you're doing?*   **2** what does it matter?; who cares? An expression of resignation, indifference or defiance, as in *what the hell, let's give it a try!*

wheeler-dealer   an adroit, quick-witted or scheming person, esp. a person with many business interests. Adopted from the USA in the later 20th century. Also the noun *wheeling-and-dealing* and the verb *to wheel and deal*.

wheelie   esp. in *to do a wheelie*, to raise the front wheel of a bicycle or motorcycle off the ground while riding at speed.

wheels   a car, as in *hey, I like your wheels!* Since the late 1960s.

wheeze   a good idea. Since the early 20th century.

whinge or **winge**, v.   to complain frequently or habitually, as in *what's she whingeing about now?* The term originated in the UK but is largely associated with Australian and New Zealand usage, esp. in the phrase *whingeing pom* (*see* **pommie**). Possibly from (a blend of) *whine, wince* and/or *cringe*.

whinge or **winge**, n.   the act of whingeing; a complaint, as in *to have a whinge; what's his whinge? what's he complaining about? See* **whinge**, v.

whingey or **wingey**   querulous; cantankerous; peevish; fretful. Used in Australia since around 1930.

whiny   given to whining or complaining; querulous. Late 19th–20th centuries.

whip it in, whip it out and wipe it a quick act of sexual intercourse. Sometimes called *the three whippets. See also* **wham-bam-thank-you-ma'am**.

whirlybird helicopter. Since the 1950s; largely superseded by chopper (*see* **chopper 2**) during the 1960s.

whisper to urinate. Schoolchildren's slang. From around 1920. Imitative of the sound of urinating.

whistle and flute suit (of clothes). Rhyming slang of the early 20th century. Often shortened to *whistle*.

whistle-blower *see* **blow the whistle on**.

whistle-stop tour a tour in which only a short time is spent at each stopping-place, esp. such a tour made by a politician during an election campaign. Adopted from the USA in the later 20th century. From *whistle-stop*, a very small town where the train stops only if signalled by a whistle.

whistle up to send for; to rustle up, as in *he whistled up another round of drinks*. Since aroud 1925.

whitey a White person. Chiefly used by Black people, often as a term of address. Adopted from the USA around 1955.

whiz or **whizz** a lively or energetic person; a person who is particularly good at something, as in *she's a whiz at making meringues*. Since the late 1950s. Perhaps from **whizz-kid** or **wizard**, n.

whizz-kid a bright, go-ahead or pushy young person who is precociously successful, rising rapidly in his or her career. Adopted from the USA around 1960.

whizzo! splendid! Mostly used by children. Since around 1944. From **wizard**.

whodunit or **whodunnit** a detective novel, a murder story. Adopted from the USA in 1942. From the (non-standard) phrase *who done it?*, who did it?, who committed the crime?

who he? an editorial interpolation after the name of a little-known individual, as in *there is a statue of Richard Bosworth (who he?) in the centre of the square*. This use of the phrase is attributed to Harold Ross (1892–1951), editor of the *New Yorker. Also who she?, who they?*

whole kit and caboodle, the the whole collection, the lot, everything. Adopted from the USA by 1950 at the latest.

whole shebang, the the whole matter or affair, everything. Adopted from the USA in the later 20th century. Perhaps from *shebang*, a hut, shack, cabin or tent; hence, the contents thereof.

whole shooting-match, the the whole thing, everything. Since around 1915. From the earlier phrase *the whole shoot*, perhaps influenced by World War I.

whoopee, make 1 to enjoy oneself, to make merry, to whoop it up.

Adopted from the USA by 1933 at the latest. **2** to have sexual intercourse, to make love.

whoop it up   to live it up, to have a riotously good time, to celebrate noisily, to go on a spree. Since the late 1940s.

whoopsie   **1** a mistake, usually a minor but embarrassing one. Later 20th century. From the exclamation *whoops!* **2** defecation; faeces, esp. in *to do a whoopsie*, as in *the cat's done a whoopsie under the bed.* Since the early 1970s.

wick   *see* **dip (one's) wick; get on (sb's) wick; Hampton Wick.**

wicked   excellent. Used by youths as a vogue term of approval since the 1980s.

widdle   to urinate. A blend of **wee** and **piddle**.

wide boy   a boy or young man who lives by his wits, with a combination of shrewdness and unscrupulousness. Perhaps from *wide-awake,* alert. Since the 1930s.

widget   a mechanical contraption, device or gadget. Since the 1970s.

wiggle   *see* **get a wiggle on**.

wilco!   from an amalgam of the initial letters of 'will' and 'comply' in *I will comply* (with the message or instruction just received). Since World War II. From telecommunications jargon.

will do!   I will obey your order, follow your advice, etc. Since the 1970s. Probably influenced by **wilco!**

willie   *see* **willy.**

willies, the   a feeling of nervousness, discomfort, vague fear, etc., esp. in *to give (sb) the willies,* as in *this place gives me the willies.* Adopted from the USA around 1925.

willy or **willie**   penis. Mainly children's slang; also used jocularly among adults. Since before 1905.

wimp   a weak, cowardly, timid or ineffectual person; a drip. Used in the USA since around 1920. Gained popularity in the UK in the late 1970s.

wincey   very small. Used in Australia since around 1930. Perhaps from the German *winzig,* tiny, or from the children's finger-game 'Incey-wincey spider'.

winco   wing commander. Used in the RAF since before 1930.

window, out (of) the   ridiculous, out of the question. The phrase is usually applied to a rejected idea or proposition.

wind up, n.   **1** in *to have* (or *get*) *the wind up,* to be or become frightened or alarmed; *to put the wind up (sb),* to frighten or scare (sb). Since around 1915. **2** *see* **wind up**, v.

wind up, v.   to tease, provoke, mock or deceive; to make nervous, excited or angry, as in *of course it's not true: he was just winding you up!; the kids enjoy winding up their teachers.* Since the late 1970s. Perhaps from the Standard English sense of winding up a watch, clock, clockwork toy, etc., by tightening the spring. Hence the noun *wind-up*.

windy afraid or very nervous. From the phrase *to get the wind up* (*see* **wind up**, n. 1).

winge *see* **whinge**.

wingey *see* **whingey**.

wings a pilot's badge, worn on the left breast. Hence, *to have (one's) wings*, to be qualified to fly; *to get (one's) wings*, to complete (one's) flying training and qualify as an operational pilot. Since 1916. The pilot's badge is a double spread of wings.

winkers (on a car or other motor vehicle) directional indicators in the form of flashing lights, as in *put your winker on before you overtake*. Since the late 1950s.

winkle penis. Mainly children's slang; also used jocularly among adults. Mid-20th century.

winner anything that seems certain to succeed, as in *I think we're onto a winner here*. From around 1920.

wino an alcoholic, esp. one who drinks cheap wine. Adopted from the USA around 1945.

wiped-out very high on drugs; hence incapable, unaware of one's surroundings, bewildered. Adopted from the USA in the late 1960s.

wipe out to kill. Probably since around 1850.

wipe the floor with to defeat utterly. Since the mid-20th century or earlier.

wired tense, nervous, anxious. Late 1970s.

wires crossed, get (or **have**) **(one's)** to talk at cross-purposes; to be under a misapprehension; to misunderstand, as in *I thought she was coming next weekend: we must have got our wires crossed*. Since around 1935. From telephone wires.

wise (to) aware (of), informed or warned (about), esp. in *to be* (or *get*) *wise* (*to*); *to put (sb) wise (to)*. Adopted from the USA around 1910.

wisecrack a smart, pithy saying. Hence the adjective *wisecracking*. Adopted from the USA around 1932.

wise up to become aware or informed; to inform or warn, as in *you'd better wise up!* Adopted from the USA around 1918.

with it alert; well-informed; up to date; fashionable. Since around 1959.

witter (often followed by *on*) to talk or prattle, esp. at great length, pointlessly and/or irritatingly, as in *she went wittering on about her children; what are you wittering on about?* Since before 1940.

wizard, n. an expert; a genius, as in *she's a bit of a computer wizard*.

wizard, adj. excellent, first-rate. From around 1924.

wobbly   *see* **throw a wobbly.**

wolf   a philanderer or womanizer. Adopted from US servicemen around 1944. From the predatory nature of the animal.

wonky   damaged, injured, weak; unsteady, shaky, unreliable, as in *a chair with a wonky leg*. Early 20th century, from 19th-century printers' slang term *wanky*.

woodwork   esp. in such phrases as *to crawl* (or *creep*) *out of the woodwork*, referring to the appearance of an undesirable character or the reappearance of somebody who has been in hiding. A jocular or derogatory comparison between such people and woodworm, deathwatch beetle, etc.

woof   to eat fast, hungrily or greedily. Since around 1925. Perhaps from the synonymous verb *wolf (down)*.

woofter   a male homosexual. Since the mid-1970s. A variant of **poofter.**

woollies   woollen clothing, esp. knitted garments (such as jumpers and cardigans) made from wool or similar yarn. Often used in the phrase *winter woollies*, as in *I've packed my winter woollies, in case the weather turns cold*. Late 19th–20th centuries.

woozy   fuddled, dazed, dizzy, as in *the injection made her feel woozy*. Used in the USA since the late 19th century and in the UK from 1917 or earlier. Perhaps a blend of *woolly* and *muzzy* (or *dizzy*).

words   esp. in *to have words*, to quarrel, to speak angrily, to complain, as in *he and I had words, and now he's not speaking to me; you'll have to have words with her about this*. Late 19th–20th centuries.

workaholic   a person who is addicted to work. Adopted from the USA in the early 1970s.

work over   to beat up. Since around 1930.

works   1 esp. in *to give (sb) the works*, to give (sb) the complete treatment, which may be pleasant or unpleasant, desirable or undesirable. Adopted from the USA around 1930.   2 in the phrase *in the works*, in preparation. Since the mid-1940s. 3 (usually *the works*), the paraphernalia used for injecting drugs. Drug users' slang. Adopted from the USA in the later 20th century.

work (one's) ticket   to obtain a certificate of discharge from the armed forces by having oneself adjudged physically unfit. From the late 1890s.

worry wart   a chronic worrier. Mainly used in the USA and Canada. Since the 1920s.

worse for wear, the   drunk.

worth a bob or two   (of a person) wealthy; (of a thing) valuable.

worthy   honest and good-natured, but rather dull. Since around 1944.

wotcher!   a term of greeting, of Cockney origin, as in *wotcher, cock!* 20th century. From the phrase *what cheer!*

wow, be a to be a great success; to be excellent, most admirable, extremely attractive, etc. Adopted from the USA by 1929.

woz a deliberate misspelling of *was*, as in the graffiti *Gary woz ere.* Since the 1970s or earlier.

wrapped enthralled. Used in Australia since around 1955.

wrapped up carefully arranged or prepared; entirely in order, as in *don't worry: it's all wrapped up!* Since around 1935.

wrap up (usu. imperative) to stop talking, to stop making a noise, as in *wrap up! I'm trying to listen to the radio; I wish she'd wrap up.* Since around 1930.

wrath of God, like the terrible, awful; ill, hungover.

wrinkly an old or middle-aged person.Since the 1970s.

wrist *see* **one off the wrist**.

write-off anything that is completely wrecked or damaged beyond economic repair, esp. an insured vehicle.

written all over it, have . . . referring to the obvious involvement of the specified person, organization, etc., as in *the job has Small-time Sid written all over it,* the crime was obviously committed by him.

X

x-factor an indefinable quality or characteristic, esp. of personality, as in *there's no accounting for the x-factor; he has that x-factor, don't you think?*

x-rated originally indicated a film that was not suitable for anyone under the age of eighteen, but since 1982 this has been indicated by '18'. The term is now used more generally to indicate films and other forms of entertainment (esp. pornography) that are suitable only for adults, as in *live x-rated show; triple x-rated Danish porn for sale.*

Y

Y, the the YMCA (Young Men's Christian Association). The term usually refers to the accommodation provided by this organization, as in *I stayed at the Y*. Since around 1919.

yack, yak, yackety-yack or **yackety-yak** to talk or chatter volubly and idly. Adopted from the USA in the late 1950s. The term is also used as a noun.

Yank, n. and adj. American. Short for *Yankee*.

yarn in *to have (a bit of) a yarn with*, to chat with (e.g. over a drink at a bar).

yassoo! a term of greeting. Since around 1950. From the Greek *giasou!*, hello!, goodbye!

year dot, the a long time ago, esp. in *since the year dot*, for as long as can be remembered. Since the late 19th century.

yellow cowardly. Of US origin. From around 1910.

yellow wellie an amateur yachting enthusiast, a Sunday sailor. From the yellow wellington boots worn by such a person. *See also* **green wellie brigade**.

yer actual true, real, genuine, as in *one of yer actual royals*. Since around 1955 or earlier.

yes-man a sycophant; a servile assistant or subordinate. The term has been used in this sense (of US origin) since the mid-20th century.

yikes! an exclamation of surprise, shock, excitement or pain. Adopted from the USA in the later 20th century. Perhaps from the hunting cry *yoicks!*, influenced by *crikey!* (a euphemism for 'Christ!').

yippee! an exclamation of delight. Adopted from the USA around 1930.

yob a lout, an uncouth, aggressive, surly or arrogant youth. Originally 19th-century back slang for 'boy', the term has been used in this derogatory sense since the early 20th century, but did not become widespread until around 1960.

yobbo a variant of **yob**. Since around 1948.

yomp (of troops) to march with weapons and equipment over rough terrain. A vogue word of the Falklands War (1982). Perhaps from a term used by rally-drivers (or skiers) for driving (or skiing) over rough ground, obstacles, etc.; of Scandinavian origin.

yonks ages, an indefinitely long time, as in *I've been waiting yonks; it'll take yonks to do this; we haven't seen them for yonks; yonks ago.* Probably from *years*, perhaps influenced by **donkey's years**. Since the 1960s.

youee *see* **u-ie**.

young fogey a person (esp. male) below the age of about forty who deliberately acts, dresses and appears to think like a member of the older generation. Since the 1980s. From the phrase *old fogey.*

yuck! an exclamation of disgust. Since the early 1960s.

yucky or **yukky** disgusting, revolting; nauseating, excessively sentimental. Since the late 1960s.

yummy (of food) delicious; (of people or things) very attractive. Later 20th century. From the exclamation *yum-yum!*, delicious, excellent.

yuppie an ambitious or high-flying young person with a lucrative job and a lifestyle to match. A vogue word of the economic boom of the 1980s. An extended acronym of Young Urban (or Upwardly mobile) Professional.

Z

zap, n. impact; effectiveness. Adopted from the USA in the early 1970s.

zap, v. **1** to defeat heavily. Adopted from the USA around 1966. **2** to kill. Adopted from the USA around 1968. **3** to change television channels using a remote control device. The term usually refers to rapid switching from one channel to another, e.g. during a commercial break. Since the mid-1980s.

zilch nothing. Since around 1948.

zing vigour, energy, as in *put a bit more zing into it* Since 1940 or earlier.

zippo nothing.

zippy lively, bright; energetic, vigorous; fast, speedy. Since 1923 or earlier.

zit a pimple or spot. Of US origin; used in the UK since the early 1980s.

zizz a nap or snooze, as in *to have a zizz.* Since around 1925. Probably from the string issuing from the mouth of a sleeping cartoon character that is composed of the letter 'z'.

zonked (often followed by *out*) extremely intoxicated by drugs or alcohol. Adopted from the USA in the late 1960s.

zoot suit a flashy suit of clothes. Adopted from the USA around 1945. The original *zoot suit* consisted of a long jacket with padded shoulders and baggy trousers that tapered at the ankle.